When There Was No Money

Heather A. Clark

When There Was No Money

Building ACLEDA Bank in Cambodia's
Evolving Financial Sector

Heather A. Clark
1301 Lopez Rd. SW
Albuquerque, NM 87105
USA
heather_clark@comcast.net

ISBN-10   3-540-28876-7 Springer Berlin Heidelberg New York
ISBN-13   978-3-540-28876-3 Springer Berlin Heidelberg New York

Cataloging-in-Publication Data
Library of Congress Control Number: 2005932110

Springer is a part of Springer Science+Business Media

springeronline.com

© Springer Berlin · Heidelberg 2006
Printed in Germany

Hardcover-Design: Erich Kirchner, Heidelberg

SPIN 11553793   43/3153-5 4 3 2 1 0 – Printed on acid-free paper

"The stark reality is that most poor people in the world still lack access to sustainable financial services, whether it is savings, credit or insurance. The great challenge before us is to address the constraints that exclude people from full participation in the financial sector ... Together, we can and must build inclusive financial sectors that help people improve their lives."

UN Secretary-General, Kofi Annan, 2003

Map of Cambodia and ACLEDA Bank Operations

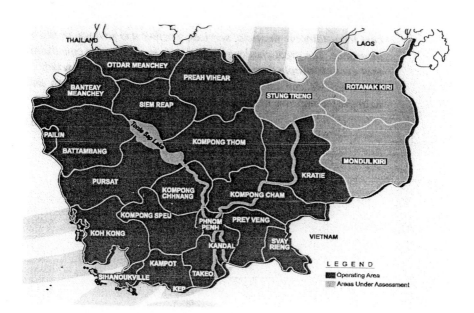

Source: ACLEDA Bank

Foreword

The challenges in development often seem insurmountable. They overwhelm nations and the builders of their most basic institutions. I am often asked how development finance agencies can work together to meet this challenge. In reply I invite you to read a story about cooperation in re-building one of the most basic institutions of any society — the banking system.

KfW Bankengruppe places great emphasis on financial sector development. Our experience in our own country, and beyond our borders, shows that one of the first steps is building a banking system that fuels growth through investment in enterprises. Micro, small and medium enterprises are the backbone of many economies; they are also the wealth of the people and generate their hope in the future. We believe that the depth of the financial sector is related to economic growth; the growth and safety of deposits, the facility of payments, and the innovation to develop new products and services that strengthen markets and promote investment. A strong banking system supports economic growth by attracting unproductive capital and injecting it into the economy, increasing the productivity of the country's capital base and leveraging it by attracting outside capital.

Our dedication to building financial sectors that include the people – poor people and rich people alike – rests on the principle that access to reliable financing is the cohesive source of support and stability that joins the people's ideas and their innovations together with their assets to generate sustainable growth. Pushing the boundaries of the financial sector to make it inclusive rests on a platform of policy dialogue and exchange of ideas, supporting innovation at the organizational level and commitment to technically sound practices. In pursuing the vision of an inclusive financial sector, we are guided by our commitment to sustainability, a focus on pro-poor growth, the promotion of micro, small and medium-sized enterprises as the backbone of the economy, and our dedication to technically sound and efficient business practice.

Yet tremendous courage and skill are required of those who opt to push the outer bounds of finance. The twentieth-century German playwright and poet, Bertolt Brecht, wrote, "Those in the dark see those in the light, but those in the light do not see those in the dark." In the transition from the dark to the light we encounter what is hidden and frightening; we make our way slowly, tentatively, but with a clear purpose. We find these sentiments, and the challenges they pose for development, running throughout this story.

This book traces the history of building ACLEDA Bank in Cambodia, from a time when there was no money. The book takes us on a journey through time, from the unique perspectives of the customers, the thinkers and innovators, the organizational architects, and the policy makers who influenced the development of ACLEDA Bank. The centerpiece is a rich amalgamation of theory and practices punctuated by vivid stories of builders of ACLEDA Bank as they challenged their ideas of organizational development, market-based strategies, business practices and product design in a dynamic environment.

Just as the development of microfinance globally influenced the growth of microfinance in Cambodia, so did the evolution of Cambodia's formal financial sector. The microfinance pioneers in Cambodia – practitioners and policy makers alike – had choices about how to position their innovations within the broader financial sector; they could wait for the financial sector to develop, or become a part of it as it developed. The ideas were often closely guarded and vigorously defended. We glimpse those debates of the past and see, with the benefit of hindsight, how changing views led to bold experiments and new advancements.

At the core, this book is about how a small group of people made a great difference in the way financial services reach the Cambodian people. We see the creation of new institutions, and the laws and the regulations that allowed them to emerge. We examine the thinking of the risk-taking donors and investors, and gain insight into those strategies and the precise mechanisms that mitigated risk in the transition from a donor supported organization to a commercial bank. We see ACLEDA Bank attracting Cambodian capital into the system and leveraging international capital, expanding Cambodia's existing capital base to work for its own development – supporting the people's ideas with a source of finance to work for their own development.

As national policy makers and their international counterparts strengthen their commitment to building inclusive financial sectors across the globe, we tempt our imaginations to envisage what that shared commitment might mean in practice. This is a story about that practice and how it unfolded in Cambodia. It is a story that is relevant to all of us who have pledged together to build inclusive financial sectors that help people improve their lives.

Acting on behalf of the German federal government, we at KfW Bankengruppe appreciated the opportunity to support and accompany ACLEDA in its development. We are pleased and honored to support the publication of this book.

Wolfgang Kroh   August 2005
Member of the Board of Managing Directors, KfW

Acknowledgments

This book was made possible only through the significant contributions of many people. ACLEDA Bank staff, management, board members and former technical advisors revealed their stories one by one. I thank Mr. Chea Sok for reaching back into his memories of Cambodia's first banking system and how it dissolved overnight. In Channy's openness about the challenges of growth, his insights as a skilled manager and leader who values innovation, and his commitment to the people of Cambodia are central to this book. I am grateful to Chhay Soeun for his expert guidance in helping me understand the intricacies of ACLEDA's financial evolution, including reviving records that stretched back over a decade and his clarity in interpreting them. The stories of building an organization in a tenuous environment are told by Chan Serey, Cheam Teang, In Siphann, Kim Sotheavy, Keo Chamroeun, Terry Mach, Mak Sokha, Men Sophal, Nheng Yong, Nay Sok-samnang, Prom Visoth, Rath Yumeng, Sar Roth, Sim Sopheak, So Phonnary, So Sovannareth, Som Sambo, Vann Saroeun, Yann Reangsey, Yee Sok Kim and the customers and staff of the Siem Reap, Phnom Penh-Kandal, Kampong Cham, Kampong Siem District and Prey Veng branches. Each unique perspective, from internal auditor to branch manager, from credit officer to long time and new customers, helped put a piece of history in place. I also thank Peuo Tit Mithona, who served as able translator during the field research. She, along with E Thanra, Piv Thary, Prum Nary, Son Sai, and Tiv Dynare, impressed me with the importance the new generation attributes to belonging to an organization that represents a different way of doing business in Cambodia.

The story recalls ACLEDA's transition from a donor project to a commercial institution. In the telling of that tale, views from deep in the past to the present were essential. ACLEDA's technical advisors, Roel Hakemulder, Peter Kooi and John Brinsden, inspired me to wish that every fledgling organization can be accompanied by such talent, commitment and flexibility as it grows to reach its own potential. I am grateful to Dennis Cengel, Antoinette Ferrara, Morgan Landy, Scott Leiper, Sven Svensson, Joachim Trede and Marilou van Golstein Brouwers for their views of the past and their willingness to share them with the benefit of hindsight. ACLEDA Bank's board members, Femke Bos, John Brinsden, Emile Groot, Deepak Khanna, Peter Kooi, Lonh Tol, Sok Vanny and Jutta Wagenseil provided the fiber of the story from an investor's perspective. Bretton Sciaroni and Tip Jahnvibol discussed the legal environment and the challenges found there, from the lawyer's perspective.

I extend my sincere appreciation to Tal Nay Im and Phan Ho of the National Bank of Cambodia, Dr. Ngy Tayi of the Ministry of Economy and Finance, Son

Koun Thor of the Rural Development Bank, and Mr. Seang Nam, Member of Parliament, for their perspectives on the developments of Cambodia's financial system. Betsy Abrera, Bun Mony, Robert Cater, Chea Phalarin, Hout Ieng Tong, Ing Varony, Paul Luchtenberg, Southeary Luchtenberg, Klaus Mueller, Mark Pierce, Phal Pisay, Johann-Friedrich Ramm, and Olga Torres have helped over the years to interpret microfinance in Cambodia and its evolution from a time when there was no money. Kimanthi Mutua, Chuluun Ganhuyag, Maria Otero, Rich Rosenberg, Elisabeth Rhyne, Stuart Rutherford, John Tucker, J. D. von Pischke and Graham Wright helped interpret ACLEDA's experience from a broader international perspective.

I am particularly grateful to Nimal Fernando, John Brinsden, Patrick Honohan, In Channy, Peter Kooi, Ann Norman and Joachim Trede for their careful reading, substantive comments and helpful advice on many aspects of this book. Their balanced and critical reviews helped improve interpretation of historical issues and their meaning.

My special thanks go to Marshall Bear who provided encouragement, as well as expert editorial advice, making the book more friendly to the reader. I am grateful to him for helping me articulate the many voices of ACLEDA as a contribution to nation building.

Linda Golding and Markus Richter showed exquisite care and attention to detail in the preparation of the manuscript.

Finally, I am grateful to Haje Schütte and Joachim Trede of KfW and Martina Bihn of Springer ·for their professional dedication to seeing microfinance as an important part of financial sector development and their enthusiasm for including this book in the KfW series on this topic.

Heather A. Clark   28 July 2005

Table of Contents

PART III: VELOCITY

PART IV: ODYSSEY

PART V: MOMENTUM

List of Illustrations

Abbreviations

ACLEDA	Association of Local Economic Development Agencies
ADB	Asian Development Bank
AFD	Agence Française de Développement
ASA	ACLEDA Staff Association, Inc.
BRI	Bank Rakyat Indonesia
BMZ	German Federal Ministry for Economic Cooperation and Development
CARERE	Cambodian Resettlement and Rehabilitation Programme
CCRD	Coordinating Committee on Rural Development
CFD	Caisse Française de Développement
CGAP	Consultative Group to Assist the Poor
CMEA	Council for Mutual Economic Assistance
CPP	Cambodia People's Party
CRS	Catholic Relief Services
DEG	Deutsche Investitions- und Entwicklungsgesellschaft
EU	European Union
ESOP	Employee Stock Ownership Plan
FMO	Netherlands Development Finance Company
FUNCINPEC	National United Front for an Independent, Neutral, Peaceful and Cooperative Cambodia
GDP	Gross Domestic Product
GRET	Groupe de recherche et d'échanges technologiques
IFC	International Finance Corporation
ILO	International Labour Organization
IMF	International Monetary Fund
KfW	Kreditanstalt für Wiederaufbau
LEDA	Local Economic Development Agencies
MFI	Microfinance Institution
MIS	Management Information System
MPDF	Mekong Project Development Facility
NBC	National Bank of Cambodia

NGO	Non-Governmental Organization
PAR	Portfolio at Risk
PRASAC	Programme de Réhabilitation et d'Appui au Secteur Agricole du Cambodge
PRK	People's Republic of Kampuchea
Prodem	Foundation for the Promotion and Development of Micro-enterprise
RDB	Rural Development Bank
SEISP	Small Enterprise and Informal Sector Promotion Project
Sida	Swedish International Development Cooperation Agency
SNC	Supreme National Council
UNAMIC	United Nations Advance Mission in Cambodia
UNDP	United Nations Development Programme
UNFPA	United Nations Population Fund
UNHCR	United Nations High Commissioner for Refugees
UNICEF	United Nations Children's Fund
UNTAC	United Nations Transitional Authority in Cambodia
USAID	United States Agency for International Development

Introduction

In 1991 a large unquiet peace swept the land, quelling a silent little war in a mostly forgotten corner of the world. For more than one million Cambodians that piece of inconsequential land, wedged between a burgeoning Thailand and an industrious Vietnam, had been forcibly abandoned twelve years before; for more than nine million others, it was the only piece of land they had ever known. For both groups it was neither irrelevant nor forgotten. It was home.

In 1991 Grameen Bank in Bangladesh was well established as the grandfather of microfinance institutions. That same year Prodem in Bolivia wrestled with the revolutionary angst of transforming an NGO into a bank. Both organizations dominated discussions in the evolving field of microfinance. At the time they represented two starkly different approaches to serving their country's poor borrowers with credit. The first approach, called the "poverty lending" approach in the early 1990s, focused on the power of a small loan to support families in their climb out of poverty. It aimed to build an alternative banking system exclusively for poor people. Its realm outside the existing formal financial system, a system that rejected poor people by design, policy or indifference, caught the attention of international aid agencies. The initial and rapid success of loan repayment in microcredit programs targeted at poor women who owned tiny enterprises seemed to be the spark of hope for alleviating poverty. It was a bright light on the otherwise dismal development finance record of the 1980s. Increased donor allocations to fund microcredit programs for poor women followed in a trickle and then in a torrent.

The second approach, the financial systems approach, owned the same goal, but chose a different means to achieve it.[1] The center of the financial systems approach coveted independence from donors and international aid transfers, at first by connecting to the financial system and later by becoming an intrinsic part of it. The radical idea of a commercial operation serving poor people as worthy customers carried with it the winds of change for the formal financial system. The pioneers of the financial systems approach aimed to change the fundamental way the existing financial system worked by pushing it to become inclusive and cater to vast numbers of poor and low-income people. The banking sector was not alone in a long list of society's institutions that excluded poor people, nor was it the most obvious culprit. Poor and low-income people are excluded roundly from most economic systems, political processes and social services. Yet this quiet system,

---

[1] The first exploration of the financial systems approach to microfinance was articulated in Maria Otero and Elisabeth Rhyne, eds. *The New World of Microenterprise Finance: Building Healthy Financial Institutions for the Poor* (West Hartford, Conn.: Kumarian Press, 1994), Chapter 1.

the banking system with its aura of mystery, marbled halls and whispering men in suits, occupied much of the revolutionary energy of the early pioneers of the financial systems approach to microfinance.

Neither approach to microfinance sounds particularly ideological, nor does one approach sound like a trigger for a passionate debate. At the time though, the sustainability of credit operations was regarded as the enemy of poverty reduction. Even the term sustainability was introduced as a euphemism for profitability, a word that was rarely spoken aloud for fear of alienating one powerful group or another. At the center of the debate was an unspoken premise: the poverty alleviation approach assumed continued access to donor funding. The financial systems approach challenged that assumption. With that challenge, questions about future roles for traditional players spun out along a logical path. What role would the original development partners play in this young field as it eventually matured and took on new commercial partners? Regulated financial institutions would replace NGO and government credit programs; investors would replace donors; professional bankers would replace social activists and development professionals. Technical assistance networks and those organizations that monitored performance standards and transparency would seem redundant. Eventually, they too would be replaced by national government supervisory and regulatory authorities, bankers' institutes and associations, and commercial rating services. The end point of the financial systems approach had many more radical changes in store for microcredit operations; some of them were easily anticipated, others came as a surprise.

In 1992 the currents of the time ran fast and furious; they were less focused on the maturation of microfinance as a part of the formal financial system. The debates centered on the poverty impact and empowerment properties of microfinance. They centered on questions about the extent to which women were beneficiaries of the new approach, or dupes of traditional household power structures. Minimalist credit programs and credit programs integrated into larger development services vied for equal attention among donors. Many doubted microfinance as a viable business model. Few imagined that an NGO could survive without a large cache of donor money, or a long list of new potential contributors. When financial projections were offered to justify higher interest rates for poor people, an equal number of moral arguments were offered to counter these usurious mathematical proofs. The great subsidy and sustainability debate was just entering the radar screen as something that might gain notice.

These were some of the issues that gained momentum in the field of microfinance in 1992.

1992 was an unforgettable year. The Soviet Union had disintegrated only weeks before the New Year approached. The Gulf War dominated global headlines. Buoyant prospects for economic growth in Asia quietly fueled a financial crisis five years away, and 370,000 Cambodians prepared to return to their Kingdom. At the Site II refugee camp on the border between Cambodia and Thailand it was a time when ILO recruitment staff met ACLEDA's future leadership as they prepared to go home with a fifty dollar repatriation allowance in their pockets, or a dubious claim on two hectares of land in the heavily mined Cambodian countryside.[2] On the dusty and dilapidated streets of Phnom Penh, in the Provincial capital of Kampot, in the jungles of Strung Treng, it was a time when ACLEDA's future leadership was recruited by the ILO and CARE International to staff a business development project for demobilized soldiers. The rumbling of ox carts making their way across the border and the rounds of distant explosions that punctuated the journey deafened debates about microcredit and which approach could better serve poor people or produce the greatest amount of impact for the least amount of donor funding. At the time, the envisaged future of microfinance in Cambodia was not centered on building an inclusive financial sector; it was centered on getting something on the ground as quickly as possible.

*   *   *

This is a story about the unlikely success of microfinance in a war-torn country. It is a story about building small legends and big dreams. This is not a romantic tale; it is a story about poverty produced by war and neglect. The story makes us doubt idealistic notions of microfinance and poverty; yet it confirms some of our most profound beliefs in why microfinance makes a difference to poor people and the societies in which they live. This is the story of ACLEDA Bank that is working on becoming a legend in Cambodia; not because it makes tiny loans, but because the bank can make Cambodia a better place to live.

The ACLEDA story traces the trials and triumphs of a group of people as they built an employment generation project for demobilized soldiers in 1992 into the largest commercial retail bank network in Cambodia by 2003. It is a story about the two approaches to microfinance that emerged as early as 1992 and continue to this day. The ACLEDA story is the story of an organization that pursued both approaches to microfinance, one after the other. The changes they witnessed in their customers and their operation encouraged further experiments as they gained experience in the marketplace and overcame challenges in a formidable environment. What they discovered was a variation on the financial systems approach to microfinance; one that goes beyond the creation of strong retail microfinance organizations and a favorable policy environment for commercial and financial institutions. Their approach is rooted in their beliefs about how they should behave in society and how they should treat others. The approach is one that attempts to influence the way business is done in Cambodia at a fundamental level. It centers on the way transparent operations and no tolerance for corruption offer poor and low-income people a fair stake in a system that has long denied them one. This is a story of corporate values and the people who have them; it is a story of perseverance and professionalism. By example, they attempt to change the way banking and business work in Cambodia.

*   *   *

---

[2] Repatriation allowances included cash grants of USD 50 for each adult and USD 25 per child or two hectares of land. The promise of land quickly faded as few areas could be found that were not saturated with mines. Janet Heininger, *Peacekeeping in Transition: The United Nations in Cambodia* (New York: The Twentieth Century Fund Press, 1994), 51

Microfinance as it developed in Cambodia is not as well known as it is in other countries, such as Bangladesh, Bolivia and Indonesia. Yet the experience offers rich lessons to microfinance professionals. A broader audience interested in the reconstruction of society after years of conflict that ravaged basic institutions and left a population scarred by war will draw lessons from this story. Those who are engaged in rebuilding their own countries will find a heartening example, if not helpful advice for consideration in their own endeavors. The voices of ACLEDA staff, their technical advisors, donors, investors, policy makers and banking authorities each add a unique perspective to the story. These views are likely to be of interest to their counterparts across national borders and organizational boundaries.

The ACLEDA Story has fascinated me since 1996, the first time I met In Channy, who later became the General Manager of ACLEDA Bank. At that time, ACLEDA was struggling with its future as a microfinance organization; it experienced such rapid growth in the demand for credit that it ran head on into a liquidity crisis that clouded its future with uncertainty. What continued to attract me was how quickly ACLEDA evolved, breathing life into emerging theories about commercial microfinance in such a tenuous environment. With every step, ACLEDA brought something new to Cambodia, risky endeavors no doubt, but ones that have lasting influence in the developing financial sector. Today ACLEDA Bank, Plc., is the first commercial bank in Cambodia to be rated by Moody's Investors Service.

This small step towards increasing transparency in the banking system paves the way for others to be as bold.

My interest in ACLEDA's history grows from my professional commitment to understand and support the wider field of microfinance. How do microfinance organizations emerge, how are they built, and ultimately what difference do they make to the societies that allow them to develop and nurture them along the way? Why do so few succeed, and so many fail? What role does risk-taking and innovation play? And how do leaders emerge and embrace innovation in a field overwhelmed by models and perfecting recipes? I have long been intrigued by the amount of passion in a field that counts adjusted return on average assets and argues about who is the poorest based on a poverty line below USD 1 a day per capita adjusted for purchasing power parity (in 1993 prices). To what extent does this passion fuel or deter leadership and innovation? And above all, why is there still such a yawning gap between the supply and the demand for financial services by poor and low-income people in most countries?

As I learned about ACLEDA and Cambodia's financial sector through the writing of this book, I discovered much more than I intended to at the outset. Those discoveries are grouped into the main thesis and themes of this book. The main thesis of this book is that sustainable microfinance is about more than the number of tiny loans borrowed by poor people and creating strong banking organizations that can deliver them. Sustainable microfinance is about changing the way the financial system works at its very core. It is about beliefs and values and making fundamental changes in entrenched social and financial systems. Those changes come about by degrees. They are resistant to quick fix policies and large amounts of donor funding. The change is a gradual one since the financial system is a reflection of the society in which it operates, its social values, cultural traditions and the accepted way of doing business. As is often the case in post-conflict societies, where the breakdown of traditional institutions is severe and broad, re-building waits for new values to emerge and a new generation to hold them dear. In a case where all institutions flounder, priorities become easily scattered as basic human needs cry out for urgent attention. Yet, it is in just such a situation that the greatest amount of change is often possible; it is matched only by the difficulty of implementation in an often chaotic environment energized by the absence of war.

This story begins well before the founding of ACLEDA. It aims to introduce the reader to the special characteristics of a microfinance operation in the context of conflict, one that does not go away with the outbreak of peace. This first theme continues throughout the ACLEDA story and yields important operational lessons about the development of microfinance in areas in conflict. What makes microfinance different in times of conflict and in post-conflict societies? Do these special circumstances call for lessened expectations? What additional investments are required? Are timeframes lengthened to achieve results? Lessons from ACLEDA's experience defy some common myths about microfinance in post-conflict areas; they also confirm principles and practices that are broadly applicable in war and peace.

Organizational development is the second broad theme of the ACLEDA story. The field of microfinance recognizes that the lack of capable retail institutions is one of the main reasons why there is still such a huge gap between the supply of microfinance services and the demand for them by poor and low-income people. But why are these capable retail institutions absent from the financial sector? What are the elements of the business model, the perceptions about the customers and the dynamics of the policy environment that create significant barriers for emerging retail institutions? How does a microfinance organization start? What makes it succeed, what holds it together and what tears it apart? The ACLEDA story shows that aiming for and reaching financial self-sufficiency is an attainable goal for a microfinance organization. What held ACLEDA together and enabled it to grow were its shared organizational values, true ownership, accountability and trust. Solid financial performance over time rests on this organizational glue. Organizational development as presented in this book is the drive to learn, adapt and innovate. This drive is what distinguishes a mediocre microfinance organization from a good one, and what distinguishes a good one from one that brings with it lasting value to society.

The third theme centers on commercial microfinance and poor people, the heart of the debate from the early 1990s. Questions about the compatibility of profit motivation and social goals still invite substantial philosophical argument in 2005. In the transition from donor subsidy to the marketplace, does the organization leave poor people behind? The concept of mission drift, the idea that a commercial operation abandons its poorer borrowers in pursuit of higher profits, receives the attention it deserves. Contrary to common belief, ACLEDA's experience shows that as revenues grew it moved closer to poor and low-income customers, not further away from them.

On a more practical level, this theme explores the legacy of donor money in a newly founded commercial enterprise. The often dissonant relationship between donor funding and commercial operations leads to several pointed questions of unique interest to donors. What happens to the accumulated donor funding? What mechanisms limit the subsidy in a new commercial operation and preserve donor capital for its originally intended purposes? ACLEDA's transformation from an NGO to a commercial bank is explored in light of other transformations that have taken place internationally. This theme examines the reasons NGOs transform into regulated financial institutions and the precision of financial mechanisms that limit subsidy. Considerable attention is given to the legal and regulatory framework and the organizational infrastructure that enable a new commercial ownership structure to emerge.

Lastly, this theme explores how one institution contributes to financial sector development. The shape of the financial sector depends on many aspects of the economic and political environment, including the range of financial institutions and their inter-action with one another and with their customers, the mind-set of banking authorities and the regulatory frameworks they choose, and the dialogue between national policy makers and their international counterparts. These affinities shape an inclusive financial sector as it develops, turning it from a nebulous concept into one that serves a concrete purpose.

During the course of the research and writing of this book, my admiration has only grown for ACLEDA staff, their technical advisors, their risk-taking donors, their risk-adverse investors, and the microfinance champions in the National Bank of Cambodia. It will be obvious as you read the story that I make no attempt to conceal my biases in interpreting ACLEDA's experience as a sound example of the financial systems approach to microfinance. The ACLEDA story is a compelling tale of what a group of persons can do for their country and their people. The example would not be as inspiring if the frailties of development and organizational blunders were not told as well. I have attempted to be fair in relating the successes and the failures that are recounted in this story; there are ample examples of each. The aim is not to congratulate ACLEDA on a job well done; rather it is to show a microfinance success story in one of the most difficult contexts of a post-conflict country. With this example, the hope is that the microfinance field that has built up over the past twenty-five years will be effective in producing many more ACLEDA stories.

Too frequently the history of microfinance organizations ends up in an analysis of progressive balance sheets. We see them represented in global tallies of outreach to poor clients. The important lessons lie hidden in the memories of the organizational architects and those who quietly build a financial sector. The five parts of this book – from heritage to momentum – capture those important lessons of the emergence, rise and significance of one bank and one financial sector that is relevant to many others.

Part 1: Heritage

Part 1 sets the context of a society in turmoil in the mid-1970s, uprooted by a regime that is widely recognized as the most vicious in modern times. The first chapter provides a brief historical overview of Cambodia and the banking system from its destruction in 1975 to its re-emergence in the 1980s. The historical context of Cambodia relies on the substantial documentation written by historians on Cambodia's tragic past and refers the reader to those sources, not repeating the judgments, debates or many of the events and analysis that accompany them. The focus of this chapter is to provide an overview of the development of the banking system in Cambodia, which features throughout the story. The second chapter visits ACLEDA's origins as a development project. It provides small vignettes on the first accomplishments and challenges of building a local organization out of a donor project. It introduces the first ACLEDA staff, their vision for the future and how the first organizational values took root; they would later become the driving force of ACLEDA's evolution.

Part 2: Discovery

Part 2 centers on ACLEDA's transition from the vestiges of a development project into an organization specialized in the delivery of micro and small enterprise credit. Chapter 3 relates early discoveries about the "marketspace" – and the position of potential customers and existing products within it. The budding market approach to microfinance underscores the difference between products that are perceived as valuable by the organization and its sponsors, and products that are valued by customers. Chapter 4 shows ACLEDA at a crossroads as it makes the choice to respond to customers or respond to donors. The chapter offers a profile of ACLEDA's sophisticated consumers who led the organization's growth. It pauses briefly to draw a comparison between ACLEDA's early performance as a development project in a post-conflict environment and another microfinance institution, Prodem in Bolivia that specialized in the delivery of microenterprise finance from the start. Chapter 5 links the changes in attitudes that prompted the organization to grow, unveiling the mystery of ACLEDA's growth formula. It addresses the question of what drives a young organization to commit to the challenges of organizational change and offers insights based on ACLEDA's experience that are relevant to any environment.

Part 3: Velocity

Part 3 explores two distinct stages of growth, stages common to many microfinance institutions. The first stage of growth is rooted in a customer orientation that allows the organization to expand, often at a pace that quickly overwhelms systems designed to support an operation of a different era. The second stage begins as the organization learns how to combine customer orientation with risk management techniques that produce sustainable growth. Chapter 6 explores ACLEDA's expansive growth period, telling the stories of branches in crisis and the radical overhaul of organization-wide systems that clamored for attention. It discusses the fund raising strategies, the adequacy of systems and difficult decisions that were made by the people who managed the organization. Chapter 7 places ACLEDA in the dynamic Cambodian context. It examines the policies and preferences of leaders in national government and donors that supported microfinance. The chronicle centers on what they were thinking at the time about microfinance and its place in the financial system, how that thinking evolved, and why the evolution was important for building an inclusive financial sector in Cambodia. The chapter concludes with an analysis of the underlying factors that enabled sustainable growth.

Part 4: Odyssey

Part 4 follows ACLEDA management and staff on their journey into the world of commercial microfinance. The story begins with a brief foray into the formal financial sector in Cambodia as it looked in the late 1990s. Chapter 8 examines the rules of the game, and why a non-profit organization would opt to play by them. The story continues with ACLEDA's visit to Bolivia and the lessons it gathered to apply to its own model of transition into the commercial world. Chapter 10 centers on the invitation to investors. It develops around an investor risk-return framework, and shows how ACLEDA's plan to mitigate investor risk led to innovative structures and mechanisms that mimicked many elements of a well-functioning financial system absent in Cambodia at that time. From the investor perspective, it was this plan that allowed the strong institution to prevail in an environment fraught with risk.

Part 5: Momentum

Part 5 examines the significant changes commercial microfinance has brought to Cambodia's financial sector, ACLEDA Bank, Plc., and its customers. The chapters in this section re-visit several misconceptions about microfinance and the commercial approach. Chapter 11 examines how ACLEDA Bank and its customers dealt with new opportunities and risks associated with commercial banking. The following chapter moves on to explore the topical notion of "mission drift", a concept that causes considerable consternation in the donor world as it meets the commercial world. The thesis of this chapter is that a commercial approach to microfinance can enhance an organization's outreach and depth of outreach to poor and low-income customers, rather than limit it. The concluding chapter pulls experience from ACLEDA Bank's history, microfinance as it has developed in Cambodia, and how both contribute to building an inclusive financial sector. The experience offers lessons to the rest of the world.

PART I:

Heritage

"Not everything that can be counted counts;
and not everything that counts can be counted."

Albert Einstein

Prologue

Siem Reap, July 1997

On a back street in the town of Siem Reap a radio was tuned to static. Further, along Highway 6, the volume was high. Troops moved in pairs and groups of four or five. Each soldier pinned a red ribbon to the shoulder of his uniform. It would serve to distinguish him from the enemy; it would prevent mistakes.

After four years of sporadic peace, AK-47s and rocket launchers again shocked the capital of Phnom Penh. The battle, temporary in the capital, would become embedded in Siem Reap Province. A stalemate between CPP troops and FUN-CINPEC would continue for 18 months until the town of O'Smach and many others along the Thai border were deserted by civilians. Over time, abandoned houses would be disassembled by soldiers to construct their own protection; the scavenged remains would be sold in exchange for food and supplies.

Kang Laing sat pillion on a small motorbike traveling the dusty road from her village. She was on her way to the ACLEDA branch to pay the balance of her loan. Hundreds of others were to travel the same journey over the following several months for the same reason. Something significant was happening. People were searching for a safe place to guard the little cash they owned. They were paying their loans in advance before any excess income fell into the hands of troops of many factions who wore ribbons and scarves of different colors.

As early as the first shot in July, In Channy, ACLEDA's General Manager, worried about the 5,000 customers and 27 staff at the Siem Reap branch and district offices who were caught in the worst of the fighting. Branches had closed before. In 1993 and 1994 branches in Batambang, Banteay Mencheay and Kampot had closed for months as soldiers fought along the main roads and occupied district towns. This was different; the fight was expected to be long and protracted, with no sign of peace. And, for ACLEDA, there was much more at stake. While other credit operations closed, In Channy and the ACLEDA staff felt responsible for keeping the branches open to serve Kang Laing and thousands of others who depended on ACLEDA in this critical time. Despite the roadblocks and bridges blown away to delay advancing troops, every ACLEDA branch in Siem Reap Province remained open during that year, until the cease-fire in August 1998 and beyond.

Channy's thinking centered on the safety of the customers, the staff and the branch. When he decided to pay salaries three months in advance, it was not a decision made lightly. It was a decision based on trust – trust of the borrowers, trust of the staff – even though there was so little to trust in the environment.

Overall repayment remained strong, despite an increase in late payments, and surprisingly, loan disbursement continued. Managing a credit operation cut off from any institutional banking service poses risks in times of peace. In times of war, the peril accelerates for the borrowers and the credit operation. ACLEDA branches ensured that borrowers could pre-pay loans, offering safety for any ac- cumulated cash. Loan installment payments, once collected, were recycled into the hands of other borrowers. These two features lowered the risk of households and the branch becoming targets. Risk was spread among thousands of borrowers, coming and going at no particular time, with no particular sign that would iden- tify them as an easy mark. In these circumstances, ACLEDA's methodology of having the borrower come to the branch, coupled with a strict confidentiality pol- icy, allowed the lending operation to continue. Many village banking operations and their clients were not so fortunate; the convenient village location, one of the most appealing features of village banks in times of peace, turned into a magnet for armed robbery in times of war.

Channy recalls borrowers in Siem Reap asking, "Why is it that you continue here when so many others have gone?"

He responded, "Because we are just like you. We are always here. We will al- ways be here." At this most critical time, the belief in the permanence of the op- eration was backed by credible action.

Today, ACLEDA Bank is the largest retail bank branch network in Cambo- dia. By mid-2005, ACLEDA Bank was operating 136 of the 165 commercial bank offices in the country. Service outlets are located in city centers, small towns, and deep in the rural areas. A staff of 2,341 manages over 130,000 loan accounts and 74,300 deposit accounts. The number of domestic transfers ex- ceeded 42,000 in 2004. Products range from international and domestic wire transfers to an array of cash management services – payroll services and over- drafts for companies of all sizes. Loans for small and micro enterprises, the mainline of the bank's business, continue to grow. The bank has a deposit to loan ratio of 65% and intermediates deposits to support Cambodia's micro, small and medium enterprises.

International institutions of grand stature, conducting transactions in multiple foreign currencies, avail themselves of ACLEDA Bank services, as do rice grow- ers in distant and isolated Banteay Meanchey Province, who scrape together de- posits in small notes, badly worn by passing through many hands.

* * *

ACLEDA's heritage, the Cambodian banking system and international aid to build peace in a war-torn country, introduces the ACLEDA story. The lineage of both ancestors fostered more than either could claim alone; they molded ACLEDA's path and the pace of the journey. The first chapter provides a brief overview of Cambodia, the banking system and its interrupted evolution during the last three decades. Against the backdrop of a shell-shocked nation and the flood of foreign assistance our story looks at ACLEDA's inheritance, one that continues to shape its growth.

Chapter two tells the stories of ACLEDA's founding as a development aid project. The stories of the first ACLEDA staff illustrate the most tenuous beginnings of the organization. It is here that the "firsts" of any organization are found. They are never as neatly organized as development literature would claim; they are not systems, they are individual values that merge as a group of people together forge the future organization. The first stories are often relegated to a forgotten past as more tangible organizational structures replace them, but arguably they form the foundations of a corporate culture. This chapter introduces ACLEDA's corporate culture and some of the people who framed it. Each chapter in this book follows the advancement of the organization's culture as the dominant factor leading the organization's growth, strength and vitality.

CHAPTER 1:

Cambodia and the Banking System

Timeline	
1963	Banque Nationale de Paris nationalized. Banque Khmer du Commerce established.
1970	US-backed Lon Nol overthrows Sihanouk government.
1970-1975	1.5 million rural Cambodians flee to Phnom Penh for safety and sustenance.
April 1975	Khmer Rouge capture Phnom Penh and begin forced evacuation of cities.
1976	**Grameen Bank begins in Bangladesh.**
January 1979	Vietnamese army invades Cambodia, ousts Khmer Rouge and installs the People's Republic of Kampuchea (PRK).

The Khmer Rouge: 1975-1979

When the Khmer Rouge came to power in April 1975, they destroyed Cambodia's institutions together with their guardians. The National Library, archives of ministries and educational institutions, banks, and money all disappeared overnight. So did many of their countrymen who had a stake in preserving these systems. These were the "new" people, class enemies – city people – students, doctors, lawyers, politicians, bankers, businessmen and women, teachers, government civil servants, and their families. They were all targeted for execution in the early years. Later, as the enemies grew in the minds of the leadership and its followers, the distinction about just who the enemy was became blurred.

The Party of Democratic Kampuchea, as the Khmer Rouge was officially known, blew up the Central Bank, one of the few buildings in Phnom Penh they completely destroyed at the time. A forced march of two million Phnom Penh citizens to rural areas began. In two weeks, Phnom Penh, a city of over two million in April 1975, was reduced to less than 10,000 inhabitants – a situation which was to last for the next three years.[3] Cities in the Provinces were emptied. Currency became worthless; later it was outlawed altogether, along with ownership of private property. Literacy, the arts and trade became capital crimes. Markets were shuttered tight; even the smallest business transaction was punishable by death. These vestiges of civilization would have no place in reaching Year Zero or in the new agrarian society beyond.

> *Mr. Chea Sok, the Chairman of ACLEDA Bank and former Deputy Governor of the Central Bank, is a sprightly man with a charming smile and the weight of the world in the brief case he carefully puts behind him on his chair. He speaks of that time with disarming clarity. "In 1975 I worked for the Banque Khmer du Commerce and I didn't think I would be able to live." As he walked from the city to a distant village in Battambang Province along with millions of Cambodians, shaken from their professional lives and separated from their families, Mr. Chea Sok owned a new sense of terror. He represented the highest form of the "new people", educated, fluent in Khmer, English and French, a young banker with a passion for Khmer classical music and basketball.*
>
> *"When I arrived at the village, the old people were sent to investigate me.[4] 'Is this your paper?' they asked. I could see the words there in English and French and Khmer. It was an inter-office shipping memo of a private company." Such a simple piece of paper that would, he was sure, determine his fate.*
>
> *"I told them it was not my paper. They insisted, 'You must know what it says.' I told them I did not. I pretended not to read; only a little bit of the Khmer and badly. Something told me, I couldn't pretend not to read at all."*

For the next three years and eight months, Mr. Chea Sok spent his time planting rice, something he truly knew very little about. He worked far from the village where he was first received. His isolation from the village saved his life.

---

[3] Catharine Dalpino offers the following description and analysis: "After capturing Phnom Penh the Khmer Rouge blew up the Central Bank, converted the National Library into a pig abattoir, and systematically destroyed the archives of ministries and educational institutions. The extent of this devastation has made reconstruction all the more difficult." *From Paris to Bonn: Lessons for Afghanistan from the Cambodian Transition.* Working Paper No. 14. (Washington, D.C.: The Brookings Institution, June 2002), 6.

[4] "Old People" were rural people, trusted by the Khmer Rouge and organized into local authorities. Old people were tasked with interviewing newcomers to the community, as well as determining those who would leave, most often in the middle of the night.

The People's Republic of Kampuchea: 1979-1990

Timeline	
1979 – 1990	12 years of civil war hasten the exodus of 500,000 people; 370,000 settle in refugee camps on the Thai border
1979	National Bank of Cambodia established
1980	Currency introduced for the first time in five years
1980	International embargo extends to Vietnamese-occupied Cambodia
1985	**Prodem, forerunner of Banco Sol, begins in Bolivia**
1986	Private sector formally recognized as part of the Cambodian economy
1989	Vietnamese forces withdraw
1989 – 1991	Council for Mutual Economic Assistance (CMEA) crumbles and ends with the impending dissolution of the Soviet Union

By the time the Khmer Rouge were driven from power by the Vietnamese invasion in January 1979 almost two million Cambodians, or 21% of the country's population, had been executed or died due to starvation or illness and exhaustion.[5] Hundreds of thousands had fled the country. Of the 400 to 600 legal professionals active in early 1975, no more than twelve were alive and still in Cambodia by January 1979.[6] Of the 1600 agricultural planners, technicians and policy makers, only 200 remained; ten were graduates of technical schools. There was only one licensed veterinarian in the country.[7]

Mr. Chea Sok remembers that at that time there were three people in Cambodia who knew about banking. Recruited for his prior experience and proficiency in languages, he was selected to go to Vietnam to study the banking structure. He, along with others, accepted the task of laying the foundations for a new National

---

[5] See the Yale University Cambodian Genocide Program, a project of the Genocide Studies Program at the Yale Center for International and Area Studies. Accessed December 2004. Information can be found at http://www.yale.edu.cgp.

[6] Dolores Donovan, "Cambodia: The Justice System and Violations of Human Rights", Lawyers Committee for Human Rights, May 1992, cited in Kathryn E. Nelson, "They Killed All the Lawyers Rebuilding the Judicial System in Cambodia". Occasional Paper No. 13. (Vancouver, B.C.: Centre for Asia-Pacific Initiatives, October 1996), 1.

[7] Patrick Heenan and Monique Lamontagne, eds. *Southeast Asian Handbook* (London: Fitzroy Dearborn Publishers, 2001).

Bank in Cambodia. A mono-banking system, structured loosely on the Vietnamese model, was built. In theory, the banking system had three main functions – to issue currency, to transfer payments for government salaries, and to finance state-owned companies. In practice, the theory floundered.

In March 1980, a new currency – the Cambodian Riel – was issued by the National Bank, which was still under construction. The problem with the re-issue of a currency in society where there had been none for more than five years is that "it works only if everyone agrees simultaneously."[8] What is a significant task in any economy was a colossal one in Cambodia. People were immune to convincing arguments put forward by any government. Farmers doubted that one kilogram of rice equaled the value of one riel.[9] Skeptical traders and their customers preferred to rely on Thai baht, Vietnamese dong, gold and barter. Savvy government civil servants were reluctant to accept salaries paid in riel that had no purchasing power. The National Bank encountered significant obstacles in financing state-owned enterprises – first they had to be set up and staffed. The human infrastructure devastated in the plunge to reach Year Zero plagued the attempts of Cambodia's liberators to build even the most basic blocks of an economic system.

Cambodia's experiment with a classic command economy under the patient if somewhat ideologically strict advice of Vietnamese experts inevitably required more pragmatic adjustments to fit the shattered state of society. The people of Cambodia, exhausted by the rigors of agrarian extremism, never embraced the new collective agricultural production units, or Solidarity Groups – Krom Samaki.[10] Nor did they have a particularly high regard for prices set by government authorities well below the emerging market rate. The communal distribution system that again appealed in theory, in practice led to increased resentments and massive migration to the urban areas. Land, confiscated under the Khmer Rouge, was now re-distributed unevenly by the state. The people's expectations were otherwise.

From 1979 through 1990, Mr. Chea Sok was the Branch Manager of the National Bank in Battambang. He recalls the Bank's experiment with agricultural credit:

---

[8] Evan Gottesman's Cambodia: *After the Khmer Rouge Inside the Politics of Nation Building* (New Haven & London: Yale University Press, 2003), 98. Gottesman presents a vivid account of the challenges of re-introducing currency into a moneyless economy in this chronicle of Cambodian politics throughout 1979-1991, after the Khmer Rouge and prior to UNTAC.

[9] The new currency issued by the Heng Samrin government, the riel, reintroduced the country to currency. In March 1980, the value of one riel equaled the value of one kilogram of rice.

[10] The translation of "Krom Samaki" is solidarity group. The term was also used by the Khmer Rouge to form forced labor groups for agricultural production.

"As part of the government's food production strategy, the Bank provided loans to state owned enterprises to buy rice from farmers and finance agricultural industry. We provided loans to people's cooperatives to purchase buffalo, seed, boats, and nets for fishing.

The Bank was charged with organizing solidarity groups. We could issue only group loans, not loans to individuals. Groups of 40 people were organized and the loan was guaranteed by the group. The groups required official recognition by the District governments and a license from the Ministry of Agriculture. We tried to select people with experience in each agricultural activity."

It was not a particularly successful experiment. Mr. Chea Sok recalls, "The loans were generally repaid, but the technology suffered."

People were not enthusiastic about the solidarity groups.

*   *   *

At the Fifth Party Congress in 1985, the PRK leadership recognized the limited success of the collectivized economy. It fell short of producing the dramatic results needed for economic recovery. The private economy, considered as part of the recovery strategy as early as 1980, was now formally recognized as one of the four official sectors in the economy. The others comprised the state, the collective, and the family economy.[11] The "family economy" legitimized the concept of small and micro businesses for the People's Republic of Kampuchea, although these enterprises had quickly emerged and had been multiplying unnoticed since 1979. Private property was re-introduced, and small businesses were sanctioned by an amendment to the constitution in February 1986. By late 1986, the Cambodian economy had opened up to foreign direct investment through joint ventures. As Cambodian leaders began to look outside their borders for assistance, the collective system was officially abandoned, although it had quietly disappeared by the mid-80s.[12]

Throughout the 1980s Cambodia's broken economy remained heavily dependent on the Council for Mutual Economic Assistance (CMEA) for foreign aid and imports of rice. In the late 1980s with the break-up of the Soviet Union and the CMEA, Cambodia, like other CMEA countries, saw its economic lifeline

---

[11] The "private economy" was added to the economic system and legitimized with a constitutional amendment in February 1986. For an overview of the Cambodian economy and political changes through 1989 see Russell R. Ross, ed. *Cambodia: A Country Study* (Washington, D.C.: Federal Research Division, Library of Congress, December, 1987).

[12] For a view of villagers' attitudes towards the agricultural collective system see Judy Ledgerwood, "Rural Development in Cambodia: The View from the Village", in *Cambodia and the International Community: The Quest for Peace, Development and Democracy*, eds. Frederick Brown and David Timberman (New York: Asia Society, 1998).

snapped. The leadership resorted to the printing press, or monetary finance, to cover government expenditures. By 1990, the country was in a deep fiscal crisis with monetary financing covering close to two thirds of the fiscal deficit.[13]

*   *   *

Historically Cambodia has been buffeted by external events. The country's misfortunes fluctuated between volatile and violent international events and a unique set of responses by the Cambodian leadership. The dissolving CMEA was only the next in the series of international entanglements that led to successively deeper isolation and economic crisis. In an atmosphere of rising inflation – the rate exceeded 150 % in 1990– major economic reforms were introduced. The reforms aimed to initiate privatization, increase autonomy for remaining state-owned enterprises, privatize agriculture and decontrol prices. A new foreign investment law was passed. In 1990, the multiple official exchange rates were unified into a single official rate that was linked to the parallel market price.[14]

The reforms extended to the banking system. Throughout the 1980s the National Bank of Cambodia (NBC) performed both central and commercial banking functions. With the structural reforms of 1989, the NBC began to implement the changes required for a two-tiered banking system. In the transition, the National Bank established joint ventures with foreign owned banks.[15] After a sixteen-year hiatus, in 1991, the first private commercial bank to foray into Cambodia was established as a joint venture between Siam Commercial Bank in Thailand and the National Bank of Cambodia. A year later the NBC developed a regulatory and supervisory framework for commercial banks. The NBC gradually moved out of the retail credit business during the late 1980s, but held its joint partnership status with foreign banks until 1998.

Those few farmers and rural businesses that had access to credit through government-organized cooperatives suddenly found themselves without the backing of state finance through the National Bank. The task of providing credit to the rural areas shifted to the line Ministries. The Ministry of Women's Affairs with initial support from UNICEF in 1989 became the first to act. Later, in 1991, the French NGO, Groupe de recherche et d'échanges technologiques (GRET), started a pilot rural credit project with the Ministry of Agriculture. However, it was the informal moneylenders who filled the great vacuum for financial services in the rural and urban "family economy".

---

[13] The World Bank, "Kingdom of Cambodia, Technical Assistance Project, Technical Annex", Report no. T-6424-KH (Washington, D.C.: World Bank, 1994), 9.

[14] The World Bank, "Cambodia From Recovery to Sustained Development". Report No. 15593-KH (Washington, D.C.: World Bank, 1996).

[15] Decree No. 58 dated 26 July 1989, allowed the formation of private commercial banks as limited liability companies.

Despite significant advances from Year Zero, the ultimate low base, poverty accelerated in the highly mobile and disenfranchised population. The decade of the 1980s produced another ten years of internal civil war and external incursions. Nearly 370,000 people relocated across the Thai boarder in search of peace and to avoid famine. Another 250,000 fled to distant parts of the globe. Basic institutions were rebuilt on a wing and a prayer and with considerable patronage and corruption – perhaps the only two social and economic institutions that were not completely eradicated by years of war. But war continued. And with it, desperate efforts to keep the population fed and the economy afloat led to a failed attempt at socialism, and an increasingly impoverished country abandoned by the entire international community.

Cambodia, the "sideshow" of the US-Vietnam war, the "killing fields" of the 1970s, the "pariah state" of the 1980s, the destitute satellite of a defunct Council for Mutual Economic Assistance, becomes a full-blown tragedy requiring the urgent attention of the international community.[16]

UNTAC – United Nations Transitional Authority in Cambodia

The arrival of UNTAC abruptly changed the Cambodian landscape ... forever perhaps. UNTAC was the largest and most comprehensive peacekeeping mission in the United Nations history up to that time. It was charged with ensuring an environment conducive to free and fair elections among the four recognized political parties that until 1990 had waged a 20-year war against each other. The four parties made up the Supreme National Council, Cambodia's legitimate, but temporary and politically fragile, national administrative authority. UNTAC held complete authority over existing government administrative structures. It was charged with administering the country to provide for human rights guarantees and a peaceful atmosphere for drafting the new constitution. The UNTAC mandate included demobilization of approximately 150,000 soldiers, repatriation of 370,000 refugees,

---

[16] For historical analysis of the distinct periods, see Ben Kiernan, *The Pol Pot Regime: Race, Power and Genocide Under the Khmer Rouge* (New Haven: Yale University Press, 1996); William Shawcross, *Sideshow: Kissinger, Nixon and the Destruction of Cambodia* (New York: Simon and Schuster, 1979) and his *The Quality of Mercy – Cambodia, Holocaust and Modern Conscience* (New York: Simon and Schuster, 1984). David Chandler's *A History of Cambodia*, 3d ed. (Boulder, Colo.: Westview Press, 2000) covers 2000 years of Cambodian history and provides a brief section on Cambodia after 1979. Evan Gottesman's *Cambodia: After the Khmer Rouge* (New Haven: Yale University Press, 2003) is a fascinating and detailed account of events, ideologies and policies of the Cambodian leadership from 1979 to 1990.

Timeline	
1990	Formation of the Supreme National Council (SNC) composed of six PRK, State of Cambodia members and two from each of the three opposition factions, – the Khmer Rouge, FUNCINPEC Sihanouk's royalist party, and the KNFPL, led by former Prime Minister Son San.
1991	Paris Peace Accords signed October 23 bring an end to a period of more than 20 years of war and civil war.
1992	UNAMIC – the advance mission to UNTAC – arrives in Cambodia.
1992	**BancoSol in Bolivia established.**
1992	Khmer Rouge withdraw from the electoral process.
May 1993	Elections held under UNTAC administration. With a turnout of more than 90 per cent, and few irregularities, elections are considered successful. FUNCINPEC wins a 45% majority; CCP 38%. With failure to reach the two-thirds majority required to promulgate the new constitution, a coalition government is formed.
September 1993	The UNTAC mandate ends with the ratification of the Constitution for the Kingdom of Cambodia and the formation of the new Government.
November 1993	The last UNTAC peacekeepers leave Cambodia.

and the resettlement of 170,000 internally displaced persons. UNTAC was supported by a budget of USD 1.7 billion.[17]

Few people believed there was a banking system in Cambodia before the arrival of UNTAC in 1993. In fact, there was. Perhaps not the most effective or efficient by today's standards, or even those of 1993, but there was an institution, a network with thirty branches throughout the country, a rudimentary payments system, and a national currency where there had been none before. A shift from a

---

[17] *United Nations. Cambodia – United Nations Transitional Authority in Cambodia.* (New York: United Nations, 1996). For an overview of the UNTAC period and the role of international development organizations, see Grant Curtis, *Cambodia Reborn? The Transition to Democracy and Development* (Washington, D.C.: Brookings Institution Press, 1998). Janet E. Heininger's *Peacekeeping in Transition: The United Nations in Cambodia* (New York: Twentieth Century Fund Press, 1994) provides a detailed chronology of events leading up to and during the UNTAC period. *Cambodia and the International Community: The Quest for Peace, Development and Democracy*, eds. Frederick Brown and David Timberman. (New York: Asia Society, 1998) provides short essays on peace-keeping, politics and the economy during the post-UNTAC period.

mono-banking system to a two-tiered banking system was gradually taking place. Foreign commercial banks began a tepid re-entry into Phnom Penh. There were early, technically challenged experiments to provide agricultural credit to solidarity groups. Expectations aside, the main banking system for the people of Cambodia depended on the amity of moneylenders and the depth of their pockets.

As Cambodia gains the attention of the international community, peacekeeping, reconciliation and rehabilitation begin. The formal banking system slips into the background, and the age of the quick impact project arrives.

CHAPTER 2

The Accidental Organization

The Small Enterprise and Informal Sector Promotion Project (SEISP)

Every organization begins somewhere. Some begin with a great fanfare and initial public offerings. Some begin in the garage of a genius, or as a hamburger stand on the beach. Few organizations of lasting merit begin in the chaos of post conflict reconstruction.[18]

ACLEDA was briskly midwifed in the expectant atmosphere of peace. The chaotic arrival of 22,000 peace-keepers, foreign advisors, donors and NGOs matched a whirlwind of political activity, the excitement of national elections and the fear of Khmer Rouge insurgency. This was the world ACLEDA joined in February 1992 as a project of the International Labour Organization (ILO) and the United Nations Development Programme (UNDP).

In the barrage of donor relief and rehabilitation efforts most donors saw their task as short-term reconstruction. They followed strict mandates not to create organizations, but to manage their own projects or to finance the initiatives of international non-governmental organizations (NGOs). The urgent need to provide relief and services as quickly as possible translated into one goal, "to have a great and immediate impact on the ground." In a very real sense, the lack of infrastructure made strong arguments for parachuting in foreign aid and its managers. Most organizations, including several of the most prominent foreign banks established in Phnom Penh, carried large suitcases stuffed with great amounts of cash into and out of the country. But sustainable development it was not, nor was it considered such at the time; and while there may have been legitimate justification for this model in 1993, now it seems distant and colonial.

The Small Enterprise and Informal Sector Promotion Project (SEISP), ACLEDA's parent project, was a roughly drawn small business development, vocational education and employment generation project for demobilized soldiers. At the heart of SEISP were the Local Economic Development Agencies (LEDAs) that would enable poor Cambodians to take advantage of economic opportunities through an integrated package of business development, training and credit. The LEDAs in Cambodia were conceived as independent professional service providers from the start,

---

[18] BRAC, the Bangladesh Rural Advancement Committee is an example of one that did, following the Liberation War of 1972. CARE is another, older example of a post-conflict relief effort following World War II. Both organizations continue to this day.

unlike many local economic development efforts that depend on communications between government and its local constituents. The uncertainty about what kind of government would emerge, and how, urged a stand-alone operation.

The First Project Strategy

The project included a credit component to complement the vocational and business training for small enterprises in fifteen of Cambodia's provinces. From May to October 1992, after the initial assessment, the project design lay on the conference room tables in New York and Geneva. When the project was approved in October 1992 for USD 4.3 million, it looked very different. The geographic focus was limited to five Provinces instead of fifteen. The target groups were expanded to include returned refugees, widows, internally displaced persons and other victims of war. A dual focus emerged; the project would include self-employed people in the informal sector – microenterprises — as well as small businesses.

The initial project assessment conducted extensive interviews with 1,000 soldiers to build potential employment profiles. There was no assessment of the new, much broader target groups and their barriers to economic security. An early project review notes, "No research was done on local economies. Project design was instead based mostly on secondary information, most of which was inadequate, and the ILO experience elsewhere in the region. There were no mechanisms for consultation with the local population: none of the local authorities were part of a recognized government. There was little trust between authorities and the local population and no local organizations that represented them."[19] If project design suffered from a lack of adequate research and distance from the local population, efforts to get it off the ground were equally plagued by armed robbery, warring political factions and the proximity to exploding mines. Sporadic violence, uneven compromises and the sudden emergence of 22 political parties with electoral aspirations threatened a return to war.

Something had to get going as soon as possible; this was clear. And this was the first project strategy.

The project's integrity was not a matter of the preciseness of design or the list of outputs; it consisted of the practical ideas and beliefs of those who were to implement it. They understood that any success in the fluid environment of half-war half-peace would require flexibility. A project to support demobilized soldiers, a distant strategy to support institutional development in the most dangerous of times, a contract to put something on the ground where no foundation existed, evolved bit by bit into an organization of abiding substance. Despite the sense of urgency, what mattered most about the SEISP project was not its immediate impact, but the small band of people who would make it happen. And that is the first lesson of the ACLEDA Story.

---

[19] Roel Hakemulder, "Promoting Local Economic Development in a War-Affected Country: The ILO Experience in Cambodia" (Geneva: International Labor Organization, 1997), 13.

The First LEDA Staff

Today, fourteen of the original 28 LEDA staff still work for ACLEDA Bank. In 1992 they came from all walks of life. They were teachers, government planners, accountants, and mechanics. Most had spent years in the Site II refugee camp on the Thai border; some came from existing government agencies in Cambodia. They were schooled in Cambodia, Vietnam, Thailand, Eastern Europe and the United States. Selection was not based on the depth of their small enterprise skills or their abundant knowledge about informal sector credit. They were recruited because of their potential to contribute, their values, and their business insight.

Microfinance literature often emphasizes the importance of the human capital that an organization is fortunate enough to hire and retain. Perhaps there is a tendency to underestimate how individual ethos is molded by the experience of working with others. Team inter-action was and continues to be the strength of ACLEDA's development and growth. There were many people who formed the early operations of the LEDAs, and later their national association, ACLEDA. They each brought something unique to the organization, and left their imprint on the way it runs today. At the outset we meet In Channy, the General Manager of ACLEDA Bank, Chhay Soeun, ACLEDA Bank's Finance Department Manager, and Mak Sokha, Chief Credit Officer in the Siem Reap branch. Later, as the story advances, we have the opportunity to meet many others who were formed by the genesis of the ACLEDA Bank and, in turn, formed its success

In Channy spent his twenties in the Site II refugee camp, a vast, treeless plot of land that stretched four miles along the Thai-Cambodian border. At its peak 180,000 people called Site II their home. Channy was 18 years old and alone when he made his way from Battambang to the border camp of Rithysen. He settled there until Vietnamese shelling in 1985 destroyed the camp. Homeless once again, he traveled to Site II with others caught in the midst of war.

Channy was a conscientious student who was determined to finish an education that was interrupted by Pol Pot. After completing pedagogy training courses organized by the Camp Education Center in Banteay Ampil (the Headquarters of Khmer People National Liberation Front along the Cambodian-Thai Border), he was assigned to teach first grade, then third grade, and then sixth. By the end of his teaching career he taught 12th grade pupils, and high school teachers. He studied Mathematics and English and held four jobs simultaneously. As the Chief Secretary to the Camp's Director of Education, he served as a translator and an administrator, and managed a network of correspondence courses sponsored by the Australian Sisters of Mercy. When he returned from his studies in the United States, after successfully competing for a scholarship to Mercy College in Pennsylvania, he taught the first accounting courses at the Management Training Center and English at the Faculty of Advanced Education at Site II.

Seventeen years after his high school education in Cambodia was suddenly terminated, Channy earned a Bachelor's degree from the Faculty of Advanced

in the camp in Thailand. Later in 2003, he completed an MBA from
University in Phnom Penh.

.nanny did not intend to become a banker. His career choice was largely influenced by the way ACLEDA developed. Three principles guided him through his
long journey to pursue an education and a professional career that had been denied:

> *"I once told my Mother I wanted to be a* conseiller, *even though at
> the time, I didn't know what a* conseiller *was," Channy remembers.*
>
> *"What I did know was that to be that person you had to commit
> yourself to do the job; you had to work hard, trying your best to
> complete it ... and you had to be honest to gain support. This is the
> way I understood it."*

The first LEDA staff was recruited from inside Cambodia as well.

> *Sokha, the Chief Credit Officer in Siem Reap branch, once paid 490
> riel, 10 riel for each kilogram he weighed, as the penalty for the
> crime of studying English. Penalties for the teachers of English
> were much harsher in 1985. Sokha, a small boy with a curiosity to
> learn, felt fortunate to escape imprisonment.*
>
> *In 1992 CARE International in Cambodia, ILO's partner, inter-
> viewed Sokha in the language of his transgression. He recalls Gra-
> ham Storer asking him many questions that must have been impor-
> tant for the job:*
>
> *"Did you study Socrates and Aristotle?" Mr. Storer asked.*
>
> *Sokha replied, "I studied Socrates and Aristotle, a little; and Marx
> and Lenin a lot."*
>
> *He was asked whether he had ever been a soldier or worked with
> soldiers. The much younger Sokha thought about his experience as
> a student. He was assigned by the government to assist Commune
> Chiefs along the border to plan production quotas for their villages.
> "I wore a uniform and carried a gun, but I was not a soldier", he
> replied.*
>
> *Later he wondered what Socrates would say about that.*

*   *   *

> *Chhay Soeun, ACLEDA's Finance Department Manager, is an ath-
> lete who played football on the Provincial championship team in the
> early 1980s. He uses his mathematical skills to calculate the diffi-
> cult angles of snooker and "petan", a popular game inherited from
> Cambodia's French colonial past. Soeun aspired to be a teacher.*

*The respect accorded to teachers and their role in contributing to
the social good and discipline of the nation's youth appealed. In
1982 Soeun landed in his true calling – accounting. For the next ten
years, Soeun was employed as the Deputy Chief of Accounting at
the Kampot Provincial Trade Department, under the Ministry of
Commerce.*

*Soeun recalls, as only an accountant would, the ILO interviews
for "Project CMB-92/010". Working for the ILO attracted him; the
ILO would stay in Cambodia longer than UNTAC and would promote fair labor practices, something he thought were sorely needed.
While some people returning from the border expected to face dis-
crimination from those who stayed, Soeun remembers, "I was very
happy when people came back from the border. I respected their
knowledge of the world outside. I thought their return was good for
Cambodia. People could finally be together again."*

*Soeun cannot abide corruption, and he recognizes corruption is
endemic in Cambodia's business environment. "Corruption is the
core problem in Cambodia; if this can be solved, everything can be
solved," he states. ACLEDA Bank's reputation for transparency
and taking a hard-nosed attitude against corruption makes Soeun
proud of what Cambodians can achieve. "We like to advance anti-
corruption in Cambodia through our work; every institution in
Cambodia can do the same. ACLEDA is successful in this; others
outside of ACLEDA can be successful as well."*

*"My beliefs about corruption are based on Buddha's teachings,"
Soeun adds. "A person's good acts cannot compensate for the bad
acts. You cannot offset accounts."*

The First Breakthrough: Affinity and Fiat

An organization accumulates knowledge; knowledge builds up and leads to break-
through. Over time this cycle leads to organizational transformation. This is the
basic tenet of organizational change theory explored as early as 1964 in Peter
Drucker's classic *Managing for Results,* in which he stated simply, "knowledge
has to progress to remain knowledge".[20] It is fair to say that later, as ACLEDA
accumulated knowledge, this is exactly the cycle of change that led to organizational advancement. In fact, the cycle of build-up and breakthrough fueled transformation to a commercial bank. But in 1992, the first breakthrough in organizational development happened almost immediately, and through bureaucratic fiat
rather than a carefully constructed strategic plan. Technically, the ILO project

---

[20] Drucker, Peter F. *Managing for Results.* Harper & Row. New York. 1964.

could not administer a revolving credit fund. The ILO staff approached the national staff and asked them if they had any interest in creating their own organization. And here ACLEDA got its first break. His name was Roel Hakemulder and he was the ILO's Small Enterprise Chief Technical Advisor for the SEISP project.

Roel Hakemulder firmly believed in local institutional development. While he was officially there to reconstruct and rehabilitate, Roel held dear the precepts of local empowerment and national ownership of the process of development.

In Channy remembers the first time he met Roel as he arrived at the airport:

> "He was carrying a lot of heavy things, and one staff member rushed up and asked, 'Can I help you', trying to carry everything he held. Roel said 'no, thank you', and we all wondered why, what had our staff done wrong? Our experience was that some experts say 'you carry this, you carry that', and then the expert goes away walking empty."

> "It was the way Roel treated us, treated everybody equally. In Cambodia, if I am the boss, you must do everything for me. The boss gets everything first, and if you are a staff member you get nothing. In ACLEDA we developed a culture of sharing. We share a room, we share the car, and everyone has a duty according to their job description. We listen to each other, we trust each other. And it all came from Roel in the very beginning."

The First Door: The Option to Build

The first door opened, quite unexpectedly, and SEISP staff now had the opportunity to walk through it, and come out with an organization of their own. Roel recalls the project's institutional development strategy:

> "We intended from the start to develop a sense of ownership among national staff. By the end of the project in October 1994, we expected to have tested different strategies for the sustainability of the LEDA network and make recommendations on an appropriate institutional framework. The project developed a nearly reverse strategy. The issue was forced with some urgency in November 1992 by the requirement for the credit component to be implemented through a legally separate institution."[21]

Channy recalls, "It all came so quickly. First, we couldn't believe they trusted us, that the ILO project really wanted us to become our own organization. We had to

---

[21] Hakemulder, "Promoting Local Economic Development", 1997.

show that we trusted them too. And because of that alliance of trust, we gained confidence and power."

The project staff and its international sponsors set a process in motion that was very un-project-like. Later a former ACLEDA staff member reminisced, "I still regret that that decision was not my own. It was such a good idea."

The First Challenge: Owning the Process

Owning the process was not as easy as it seems today. There was a reluctance by Cambodian project staff to speak out. Everything in their history and experience had taught them that it was just better not to say anything than to give the wrong answer. The first discussions were not discussions at all, but awkward meetings where no one said much at all about the future. No free-floating ideas, no brilliant insights, no visionary statements, no one dared to hope. The meetings were exasperatingly painful, silent, stunning and devoid of any ideas. Not a particularly fertile environment for the birth of a dynamic organization, as Channy explains:

> "We needed to break the deadlock. And a logo was the perfect way to begin the discussion. Something everyone should have an opinion about. No one spoke. No one had any idea about what our logo should be. After enduring the silence, we planted an idea, 'Okay, if no one has any ideas, let's choose the pig as our logo. The pig will represent us on our stationery, in our official correspondence, in everything we do; people will see this pig, this symbol of what we stand for. It's decided then.'
>
> Ideas exploded from everyone at once. The pig was acceptable to no one. The discussion went until midnight. People argued and laughed, and joked and finally agreed. But jokes aside, we walked away from that room, that room we had entered with silence, with a new logo, and a glimpse of what this could be ... of what we could be.
>
> We entered that room as SEISP staff and emerged as ACLEDA staff. Our logo was not the pig, but the "hong bird", a mythical golden creature in Khmer folklore that rescues people from drowning. The golden bird stands for prosperity. Something we understand. Something the Cambodian people understand."

The discussion about organizational options began in earnest among SEISP national staff. What would ACLEDA look like?

> "As we saw it" Channy remembers, "we had three options: we could become part of a government agency, establish a private business, or create an NGO. Those who had worked in the government did not want to go back to the drudgery, politics and corruption.

*We didn't see how we could become a private business and survive.
Our clients were poor people. Who would pay for our services?
Where would we get the capital? An NGO seemed to be the best
choice. There was plenty of donor money, and at least we could depend on the donor. But there were only two local NGOs at the time,
and we weren't sure how they started. An NGO appeared to be the
right way to go, so we began our research."*

*And what about the option of becoming bank? "A bank? It was
just too big to even imagine."*

There were no established procedures for registering an NGO. SEISP staff submitted their application to the Supreme National Council and UNTAC and forgot
about it, unsure whether this was the correct procedure, or whether they would
merit a reply. Early one day, a special messenger brought a letter with an official
seal. It was a letter from King Sihanouk confirming the Supreme National Council's official recognition of ACLEDA as a national NGO.

With the awe and excitement that recognition by the powerful presents, Channy
realized, "Now, we are serious."

It is February 1993.

The First Mantra: Beginnings of Corporate Culture

Does vision, that fuzzy concept that calls to mind prophets and Nobel Laureates,
exist from the very beginning of an organization? Management gurus Collins and
Porras define vision as "a dynamic process, when the core ideology of a company
– its core values and purpose – and its aspirations come together to form an envisioned future."[22] Did ACLEDA staff have a vision for the future of the new NGO?

Something important happened in the meeting of the pig and the hong bird that
formed the future: trust. With those first tentative steps, swallowing with great
effort the fear to speak out, ACLEDA staff began a dialogue with each other about
the future of the organization. These were the early beginnings of an internal management council that ACLEDA has kept until this day.

While the story of Roel and the briefcase may now be the stuff of legend, the
power of teaching by example continues. ACLEDA management seeks out staff
no matter what their position. Those who have truly outstanding ways of doing
something serve as teachers to others in the organization.

The ethos of Roel Hakemulder's lesson is not forgotten either. Humility and
politeness are valued. Nay Soksamnang, the manager of ACLEDA's Phnom Penh
branch, emphasizes customer service and courtesy training for all new staff. When
he describes the new staff training program, he grins and shakes his head, "We tell

---

[22] Jim Collins and Jerry I. Porras, *Built to Last: Successful Habits of Visionary Companies*
(New York: HarperCollins, 2002), 221.

them, 'after the training program you will learn how to treat people so well, to respect them, even your parents will be surprised.'"

What does the "voice" of nation building sound like? Is it the lofty exhortations of national pride delivered by a charismatic leader? Yes, but this was not ACLEDA's voice. ACLEDA spoke of "professional pride and the opportunity to build a professional organization". The voice of professional pride became for ACLEDA staff an unrelenting mantra: "If we don't do it together, we will lose it." And so buds ACLEDA's corporate culture, set from an understanding of the basic concept of trust and equal treatment, not from lofty visionary statements, but from determination. The drive to work together was the only option when so many had lost so much already.

* * *

Organizational values and corporate culture generate a lot of respect in the world of microfinance. Sometimes it is called mission; the Bolivians call it "mystica". It is more than loyalty or job security. It is a code of ethics based on the powerful beliefs of the people who staff, manage and lead the organization – a corporate soul that simmers quietly under all financial and managerial decisions of the organization. We talk about the value of leadership and charisma. But what is the charisma of one leader worth without the core values that ride through the stairwells and corners of an organization? "If ACLEDA had only one or two levels of responsibility and only a small group of people who embody our core values," Channy notes, "it would be very difficult to grow, serve the customer and practice transparency."

ACLEDA's core values emerged from its infancy; honesty, trust and a belief in each other. In this early phase, ACLEDA created a management group that would become the company's backbone; they found a method of teaching by example to instill an organizational culture. The complete set of values would develop later and eventually drive the company. "In ACLEDA, we do not tolerate corruption or promote transparency just because of the rules," Channy explains. "Rules can change. First, there were the beliefs, the principles of how we should behave in society and how we should treat others. Then the rules came, to protect those beliefs."

A corporate culture that embraces transparency and strictly enforces a 'no tolerance for corruption' policy may seem like a distant luxury in an atmosphere where bribes facilitate most business transactions. Transparency is the driving force that links ACLEDA's core business values of customer service, permanence in the community and professionalism. ACLEDA Bank staff view transparency as the number one growth factor; expedience is no excuse. Beliefs and values do not end with a mission statement; they are backed by credible actions designed to bring value to customers at all times, even at times of enormous crisis.

At the beginning of ACLEDA's story there was no great entrepreneurial force, no one charismatic leader, no strategic plan, no carefully constructed actions based on research in the market. In fact, ACLEDA emerged almost by accident. What made it different from other development projects that diminish with dwindling donor budgets is that ACLEDA's first steps were grounded in the trust, core values and purpose of a small group of people and technical advisors who believed in them.

Together they would discover what it meant to put those beliefs into practice in a changing policy and market environment as the financial sector developed, and they became an important part of it.

PART II:

Discovery

Every organization has to prepare for the abandonment of everything it does.

Peter Drucker, Harvard Business Review

Prologue

On the Road from Kampong Cham, 1994

It was a long drive from Kampong Cham to Phnom Penh. It was dark and dangerous. Rutted roads disappeared at stream crossings; broken bridges forced jeeps down embankments, into deeper watery holes. The rubble of recent battle smoldered at a crossroads. Bandits drifted through the countryside, appearing suddenly from nowhere, from everywhere. Soldiers, who were never officially demobilized, turned to freelancing as toll collectors, and fired at will, collecting the salary that was months over due, and a pension that would never come. The roads were lawless and bleak.

This was Nay Soksamnang's world. He had navigated these roads for most of his life. The first son of a farming family of ten, Samnang discovered his mechanical talent shortly after his tenth birthday when he realized he could fix the bicycle he rode to school every day. Now, as a professional driver and mechanic, he knew the ways of a road. The way it suddenly turned to mud, when it was impassable despite its serene appearance, when it would punish the vehicle, but still serve. He could fix anything but a broken axle.

Samnang had become a professional mechanic. He honed these skills as a student in East Germany on a government scholarship during the late 1980s. In 1992 he worked for the ILO as a driver. It was a good job, steady and fascinating because his main passenger was Peter Kooi, a young Dutchman filled with stories of unimaginable scope and depth, and the ILO's Credit Advisor for the SEISP Project. The time passed quickly.

Samnang's interest was sparked by the credit officers' jobs. He enjoyed how they engaged with people, how they discussed business, how they thought together with the business owner about the future. What he couldn't observe of the credit officers' duties on the job, he asked them during the long journeys from one branch to another. Samnang remembers thinking, "I like meeting new people, talking to people, challenging my friends and myself to always do better. I thought this is the best job for me."

One day he asked, "Peter, can a driver be a credit officer?"

Peter answered, "In the United States, even a movie actor can be president."

"It was then I had the confidence to apply to ACLEDA for the job," Samnang recalls. "I was very young during Pol Pot's time. I worked very hard just to stay alive. There is no work in the world that was worse than that. Afterwards, I realized I could do anything. I thought, I will be successful in my job. I will be a strong staff member, so I can be a credit officer forever."

* * *

Samnang's first loan was a good loan. It was a small loan to a woman struggling to survive. She borrowed again, and later, again, and built her business. For Samnang, neither rapid disbursement nor the size of the loan was the key ingredient to becoming a successful credit officer; the quality of the loan mattered most to him. And the quality of the loan depended on skill of the credit officer.

> *"When I had my first delinquent loan, I thought, what, what did I do wrong?"*

> *"I learned from others in our seminars, new techniques to determine the cause of the problem. Is it a business problem, a calamity, a deliberate default, or is it unclear? I learned that all of these problems, except one, are within my power to resolve before I make the loan."*

> *"If the business can't make it in the market, I should know this. If the business owner does not have the right skill to run his business, I should know this. If the business owner cannot meet the repayment schedule, I have provided a loan that was too large, or not at the right time. These are things that I should know. I learned from my customers. Sometimes they thought if they had the money they would repay; and if they didn't have the money, well then, they didn't have to repay. I learned to be clear."*

> *"We used to 'give loans' to people who couldn't repay. Why? We put those people into debt. Now they have broken their contracts, broken their word, they are not the same; we helped them fail as business owners and as people. We took away the power of their word. We began to think about customers borrowing money, not beneficiaries receiving a loan. Our responsibility was to provide them with a good service, even if that meant rejecting the loan."*

Samnang's career with ACLEDA rocketed. From 1994 to mid-1996 he worked as a credit officer in the Phnom Penh branch. By mid-1996 he was promoted to deputy branch manager in Phnom Penh, and became branch manager in Kampong Speu in 1998. Under his leadership, the branch became the second most profitable branch in the ACLEDA network. When he had the chance to apply for the deputy branch manager position, Samnang recalls, "I didn't have the confidence. I knew I didn't have the skill." And, becoming a branch manager? "I didn't even think about it."

But Channy saw something else. "Your experience says you can do it. Can you do it? Yes, you can. Study accounting, study management, study planning. These are the skills you will need to manage a branch. You will know how to advise your staff." In Channy explains ACLEDA's staff development policy, "ACLEDA's priority is not seniority, but capacity first, then knowledge and skill. Everyone has to learn, to improve all the time. Some have to train for particular technical areas, others take a business and banking course of study, but the learning never stops."

Today, Samnang is one of the 2,341 ACLEDA staff who values the organization because of what it stands for, and how it has valued them. He is now the Branch Manager of the Phnom Penh branch where he oversees a loan portfolio of USD 16.3 million, a deposit base of USD 3.8 million and 575 staff.[23]

What Channy saw that influenced Samnang's decision was that Samnang was one of the "right people" for ACLEDA. It was who he was, what he believed, how he challenged himself; not precisely what he knew. That would follow.

---

[23] Figures as of December 31, 2004. ACLEDA Bank Audited Financial Statements and Human Resources Department reports.

CHAPTER 3

Exploring the "Marketspace"

A Classic Model

Microfinance came late to Cambodia. By 1993 the world of microfinance had already witnessed the creation of Banco Sol, and its spectacular growth. The resurgence of Prodem as a rural lender with a portfolio of USD 3.6 million and 12,200 clients positioned the organization mere percentage points away from a positive return on equity. Other Latin American microfinance institutions such as ADEMI in the Dominican Republic and ACP (later MiBanco) in Peru experienced robust growth. Grameen Bank in Bangladesh counted two million rural women among its clients and Bank Rakyat Indonesia's Unit Desas served 11 million savers and 1.9 million borrowers. The re-emergence of the Guatemala credit unions as viable financial institutions with 90,000 members and diminishing delinquency pleasantly surprised even the staunchest critics. The numbers dizzied.[24]

Each of these organizations made their first loans long before 1993. Sometimes there was a great fanfare, handshakes and smiles as the cash turned borrower dreams of a better future into investment capital for the family business. Sometimes that first borrower was the springboard for a grand institution, such as Grameen Bank's first client, the bamboo stool maker, who inspired a young economics professor to change the tides of the returns to labor in Bangladesh. The first loan is an exciting moment. Despite any misgivings, the repayment of that loan confirms the organization's mission – its rightness with the world – poor people do repay their loans, we can make a difference.

ACLEDA's first loan was also its first default.

This chapter chronicles the stories of ACLEDA staff's early experiences with products and customers in post-conflict Cambodia. As they learned the art of

---

[24] See Cheryl Frankiewicz, *Building Institutional Capacity: The Story of Prodem, 1987-2000* (Toronto: Calmeadow, 2001), 19; David Bornstein, *The Price of a Dream: The Story of the Grameen Bank* (Chicago: University of Chicago Press, 1997), 289; Marguerite Robinson, *The Microfinance Revolution: Sustainable Finance for the Poor* (Washington, D.C.: The World Bank, 2001), 61; and David C. Richardson, "Model Credit Unions into the Twenty-first Century" in *Safe Money: Building Effective Credit Unions in Latin America*, eds. G.D. Westley and Brian Branch (Washington, D.C.: Johns Hopkins University Press, 2000) cited in Paul A. Jones, *Modernising Credit Unions: The Guatemala Credit Union Strengthening Project, 1987-1994* (Manchester: Association of British Credit Unions, 2002), 30.

lending and business consulting, each staff member brought new meaning to the oft repeated, but rarely followed advice, "listen to the customers." ACLEDA's practice of listening to the customers strengthened, just as many of its products fell victim to this timeless wisdom. These first forays into the "marketspace" honed ACLEDA's perceptions about the importance of the relationship between a retail financial institution and its customers, and later, the marketplace in which they would both operate.

Changes in Attitudes

The intoxicating environment of UNTAC retreated into the hard work of turning ideals into reality. The heady mood lingered long enough for ACLEDA to accumulate knowledge without an overwhelming anxiety about the future or its funding base. There was breathing space for ACLEDA to "confront the brutal facts" about its own operation.[25] There was also rampaging inflation of 150%, continued fighting in the Provinces, and armed robbery without geographical limits. Returned refugees quickly depleted their resettlement stipends with little opportunity to establish themselves on productive land or open a business. And everywhere business was conducted in US dollars, Cambodian riel, and on the borders in Thai baht.

From 1993 to 1995, SEISP was in full swing. With a USD 600,000 loan fund, ACLEDA NGO now served as the SEISP Project credit management agency. It implemented a classic integrated credit and business development model. It provided training to entrepreneurs on a sub-contract with the ILO. But first, ACLEDA staff had to learn the art of business management consulting and training. Foreign advisors and UN volunteers were recruited, first to co-manage the fledgling operation, and then to advise it. The second task for ACLEDA staff, less straightforward than the first, was to sort through all the technical advice that was available to help them.

Who Are We? Who Are They?

It was a confusing time, the newness of the operation and the contradictory messages sent by technical advisors with different points of view served to obscure as well as clarify. But in the confusion, perhaps because of it, staff sought out ways to make sense of the world around them and their own operation, which they were determined not to lose. They learned about what was working and what was not. What to keep and what to discard. And it all centered on their relationships with their clients.

---

[25] "Confronting the brutal facts" is a concept explored in Jim Collins, *Good to Great: Why Some Companies Make the Leap ... and Others Don't* (New York: HarperCollins, 2001), 65-89.

"We tried to follow the technical guidance, but which one?" Soeun recalls. "Our repayment rate was not the best, it was only 80%. There were questions about why the repayment was so·low, so we focused on improving our loan portfolio quality. There was a time when we reached a 100% on-time repayment. And then, there were questions about why it was so high. We must not be lending to the right target group with a repayment rate so high."

"So we relaxed a little bit, and the repayment rate went down," Channy adds. "One of our technical advisors was very happy. But whether the repayment rate was low or high, there were always questions."

"We were supposed to lend to refugees, internally displaced people, widows, demobilized soldiers and graduates of the ILO vocational education program. Sometimes the trainees had just learned the skill and had no concept of how to run a business, even with the training."

Soeun remembers some of the early questions: "Could we turn soldiers into entrepreneurs during one week of training after a lifetime of following orders in the military? How did we expect them to repay the loan? Finally we asked, 'What is the objective of the revolving fund? Do you want us to lend to people who will repay, or the target group whether they will repay or not?'"

"Some of the donors wanted us to lend only to the very poorest, people with no business and no business potential, when others who were just as poor, were also asking to borrow. It didn't make sense to us. We excluded so many people. So we decided to lend to those we thought would repay – those with a business or those who could develop one. There were two types of credit customers in those days, those applications that came through the vocational education program, and those credit clients who we thought were good risks."

"There was one case, a battery maker. He was very poor, but he wasn't part of any target group. He was not a demobilized soldier, or a returned refugee and not part of the vocational education program. We never took the donors to visit him."

Targeted Credit: Bull's Eye or Broken Dart?

ACLEDA staff learned the hard lessons of targeted credit for themselves. So Phonnary is ACLEDA Bank's tenacious Marketing Manager. Her enthusiasm and dedication fly in a constant circle above a resolute core. She is the smarter younger sister who has learned everything that the elders could teach; then she surpassed them. Phonnary was hired in 1993 as a business development training officer after spending three years in Stung Treng, where she worked as a government planning office amid the jungles on the Lao-Cambodian border.

Phonnary remembers her early lending experience with ACLEDA as a newly recruited officer:

> *"I felt so bad when my clients couldn't repay. It was my fault; I made the loan. I should accept the responsibility. My heart ached when I walked into her house. It was a small house on stilts and in bad repair. Through the wooden floor you could see the ground where the animals are kept. There were none. Only dust. On the floor, the rice basket was empty. Her child was lying in the corner, almost lifeless. She cried so softly when she told me she couldn't repay the loan for the ducks she received from the project. The ducks were dead. She was a seamstress, and couldn't really raise the animals despite the vocational training. She spent all her money trying to keep the ducks alive. We made her poorer than she was before, and now she owed a debt."*

> *"She felt obligated to pay, just as much as I felt obligated to help her. She was thinking of running away, leaving behind what little she had. We got her a piecework job with a local tailor; she collected watercress from the river and sold it in the market. She saved 200 riel every week, less than 10 cents, until she repaid her loan. But we knew we could never manage that for everyone. So we learned to be more careful about selection. We no longer wanted to tie credit to the vocational education program. It didn't make sense. Why couldn't we let people borrow for the business they already had, or the one they could develop?"*

Verifying Credit Use, and Then What?

ACLEDA opted early on to manage two loan products: a small business loan in US dollars and a micro loan, or an informal sector loan, disbursed in riel and through solidarity groups. Both products had market appeal, but some features were holding back the quality of product and the performance of the operation. The business development training, so essential in the SEISP project, and clearly a need in Cambodia, stimulated ACLEDA staff to think more about just what they were doing, and how they were doing it.

The small business loan was designed to ensure all loan proceeds were used to support the business venture. ACLEDA loan officers verified credit use on regular visits to the client. It seemed to make sense: a client's business plan was approved for a specific loan amount and for a specific purchase. ACLEDA loan officers were also business development advisors and they wanted to ensure the client followed the business plan.

Channy recalls the story of the looms.

> *"A small family business applied for a loan for the purchase of four looms. We developed the business plan together with the weaver. The loan was approved for the purchase of four looms, but when we went to check, the business had purchased only three looms and used the remainder of the loan for other purposes in the household. Empowered with our business development training, we told the business owner that he would have to purchase four looms to be in compliance with the loan contract. He took our advice and the business nearly failed."*

What happened next was a classic case of microeconomics. The company increased its fixed costs and its variable costs by hiring a new weaver to operate the fourth loom. Production increased but the weaver, who operated in a small market, found the market too limited to absorb the production of the fourth loom. As a result of the increased supply, the price of the woven goods fell.

> *"After a while none of the looms was working because the market was flooded. We made a big mistake," says Channy. "We said, 'Sell the loom'. It was then we realized that our customers may not be able to write, they may not be able to read, but they knew their business better than we did. We knew then that the business advisor does not always know what is best for the customer. We knew then that we were not teachers any more."*

How Many Pigs in a Poke?

ACLEDA also worked with ILO's vocational education program in a few branches. The political imperative of integrating all projects financed by the same donor, forced relationships between credit and vocational education. The new graduates of the vocational education program could expect to become ACLEDA borrowers once they completed a business plan. The process was not automatic, only 48% of the vocational education trainees implemented a business plan and received a loan. But something amazing was happening. Pig-raising became a boom business; prospective trainees and loan applicants flocked to the training sessions for pig-raising. On closer examination, this group of pig breeders also had the lowest delinquency rates. Pig-raising was also the shortest vocational education course on the roster.

But where were all the pigs? They had become chickens, bolts of cloth, provisions in small shops, seeds for rice planting, and small parts for motorcycle repair. Pig breeding was not the boom business it seemed to be on paper. But the shorter training course – the price trainees had to pay to get a loan – was extremely popular.

ACLEDA staff devised the shorter course as a compromise to the mandate of integrating donor-funded project activities. One of the key lessons for the ILO integrated program was that related project activities do not form the basis of an integrated program, despite the appeal of such an approach.

The experience with the vocational education program led to greater insights about the training components for other borrowers as well.

Channy recalls a session with a group of microcredit borrowers:

> "We asked the trainees: Do you want to learn?"
> "No," most of them responded.
> "No? Then why do you spend six days in a class?"
> "Because we want the credit," they replied.
> "Why do we need to sit so long?" they asked. "Why do you provide us with books to record transactions, when we don't use them?"

"We realized they didn't need the books," recalls Channy. "They can record, but in a more convenient way that they understand. We also realized they viewed the business development training as the price they had to pay for the credit."

Many Questions, One Answer

Phonnary was learning similar lessons in a different Province:

> "We began to question, are we teachers and officials, or are we business owners ourselves, providing services to other business owners? If we are, shouldn't that service be more convenient for our customers?"
>
> "Are they customers or are they beneficiaries? We knew they were customers; they paid for the service, so why were there so many restrictions? Why did we determine schedules at our convenience? Shouldn't it be the other way around?"

In far flung Banteay Meanchey, credit officers mulled over the micro loan application process and how to fill out the application honestly together with the client. The application requested the expected income from the business or the project financed by the loan; it also required the identification of the main income earner. But who was the main income earner in a household that was engaged in so many different seasonal activities? Wouldn't it seem like a better idea to look at all the income coming into the family to decide more accurately on the capacity of the borrower to repay the loan?

Vann Saroeun, the Branch Manager in Siem Reap, wanted to know exactly where the line dividing an urban from a rural area was. The ILO project agreed to work only in the urban areas, to avoid conflict with the rural operations of its sister organization, the Food and Agriculture Organization (FAO). Some argued that the only real urban area – an economy where agricultural was not the predominate base – was the city of Phnom Penh, where services quickly developed in response to the huge foreign presence.

"Where is the city limit?" Vann Saroeun asked, pointing to a house that clearly stood over the imaginary line. "If it's here and not there, they will move the house to get the credit." Vann Saroeun ensured that ACLEDA's first strategic plan recognized villages as "sub-urban" areas.

As Samnang enjoyed meeting and talking to people in the heat and dust of Phnom Penh, he saw his portfolio steadily grow, his clients doubled, then tripled. At the time, if an ACLEDA credit officer served 10 to 15 clients a month, that was enough. But Samnang's borrowers came back, applying for larger loans to support their growing businesses. And new clients sought him out as well. There was a surprising momentum. "When we started to think about the people as customers, our portfolio began to grow. It was only a matter of time before we improved our service to become a quick service, an easy service, a service closer to where the customer lived; a service that would always be there. That's what the customer wanted."

Experimenting with Products at the Core

Neighborhood Banks

Community banks had been a main feature of the microfinance landscape in Cambodia since GRET's pioneering work in 1991.[26] In 1994, every international NGO involved in microcredit supported community banks in one form or another. The banks differed in levels of autonomy and control of the sponsoring agency. Mandatory savings and grouping together of five to six solidarity groups were common features of the early community banks. The role of local government, the composition of leadership and the quality and content of educational activities also varied. The community banks also differed in longevity.

ACLEDA originally saw the neighborhood banks as a way to build the portfolio and reach more customers in rural areas in a more cost-efficient way. By late 1995, ACLEDA had established fifteen neighborhood banks within its network. That same year, ACLEDA decided not to encourage their development.

Sokha, the Chief Credit Officer in the Siem Reap branch explains, "The methodology didn't work for us. Of the eight neighborhood banks originally established in Siem Reap, there was only one left in 1997 – the last one in the ACLEDA

---

[26] Groupe de recherche et d'échanges technologiques (GRET) began a rural credit operation in 1991 within the Ministry of Agriculture. It later became Ennatien Moulethan Techonnebat (EMT), a local microfinance organization, and was granted a license as a regulated microfinance institution under Cambodian law in 2001. The company was renamed Amret in 2004.

network. It was always the best neighborhood bank and it worked quite well."
Three months into 1997, it succumbed to political infighting. "People were fighting about money," Sokha notes, feeling partly responsible for adding to an unnec-
essary conflict.

ACLEDA's neighborhood banks were rife with problems. Bank members did
not have the time, interest or the skill to properly manage the banks. As a result,
ACLEDA staff began to invest more time in training and assisting members to
manage their banks, perfecting the administrative arrangement rather than providing micro loans directly to clients.

"Adding another level of organization for the disbursement and collection of
credit increased our costs. At first we looked at neighborhood banks as a way to
decrease costs. That didn't happen," Sokha explains. "The cost of organizing and
maintaining such a large group outweighed the costs of our existing products. We
lost direct contact with the borrower, and no longer had control of many transactions. We began to hear complaints about fraud and theft. We increased the risk of
our borrowers and increased the risk of our entire operation."

By 1995, ACLEDA abandoned the short-lived product. Customers of existing
banks were offered the opportunity to continue borrowing from ACLEDA as
individuals or as members of the smaller informal solidarity groups. But as long
as the neighborhood bank was functioning, ACLEDA would continue to provide
it services.

Perhaps ACLEDA just did not get the community banking methodology right.
Did it give up too soon? ACLEDA staff is unanimously adamant that they did not;
they are equally unambiguous about the lessons the experiment with neighborhood
banks taught them about their own operation and their customers.

First, they learned that just because other organizations could deliver a product,
this did not mean they could. The ACLEDA operation, even in the early years, was
structured to deliver small, individual and non-collateralized small group loans. The
forced savings as a collateral requirement within the larger 30 member neighborhood banks introduced an element into the group loan product that was cumbersome
for ACLEDA to manage. More importantly, compulsory savings created conflict
among the customers, who sometimes lost their savings to strangers over whom they
had little influence. The incentive to save to qualify for a loan, the entry point for the
methodology, was destroyed; the best customers found themselves in a position of
accepting the highest risk. The involvement of village chiefs added a political dimension to the loan process – something that ACLEDA's direct service to borrowers or solidarity groups had avoided. ACLEDA focused on those products with
proven customer appeal, perfecting them first. Later it could diversify.

Secondly, the experiment with the neighborhood banks showed ACLEDA staff
the importance of listening to learn more about their customers' preferences for
financial services. Their predilection to respond to customers conflicted with the
neighborhood bank methodology. From their point of view, the neighborhood
banks distanced ACLEDA from the customer, forced people into an arrangement
that they did not appreciate, and added unacceptable levels of risk and costs to the

borrower. Many micro-loan clients preferred to work through small informal solidarity groups; most preferred to borrow individually, working directly with an
organization specialized in financial services, rather than accessing loans through
another organizational layer. Customers also valued the confidentiality of a professional service, and often resented the involvement of their peers and village
authorities in their financial affairs.

Sometimes the initial promise of a great idea remains unfulfilled. The people
who communicate that message first and most distinctly are those for whom
the promise is made. Soeun recalls, "There were so many complaints about the
neighborhood banks, we saw that we were not providing a good service."

Later, the architect of the neighborhood banks asked Channy, "How can
ACLEDA dissolve the neighborhood banks?"

Channy replied, "We didn't dissolve them; they dissolved themselves."

When ACLEDA stopped supporting its neighborhood banks near the community banking operation of an international NGO, ACLEDA was asked not to work
in the area with the individual or solidarity group loan products. The international
NGO was concerned about the desertion rates in their own community banks as
clients compared services. Channy says, "We thought about the recommendation
to leave the area, and decided not to follow it."

Mandatory Savings

The neighborhood banking methodology introduced mandatory savings to
ACLEDA. Prior to that time, the joint liability of the members was the only guarantee for group loans. Gradually several newer district offices, opening with the
idea of establishing neighborhood banks, incorporated mandatory savings on
group loans. When the neighborhood banks were eliminated from ACLEDA's
roster of services, the mandatory savings fell under the scrutiny of the ACLEDA
group. Their unease about mandatory savings as a full-fledged product never quite
left them.

"We never liked the forced savings product," Soeun recalls. "The customers
didn't like it either. They complained that it wasn't business-like, that it was unreasonable. How do you tell a business person they can borrow a certain amount
of money, but first they have to save for several weeks, and then they have to use
those savings as a guarantee against others' failure to repay?"

"We knew people liked to save. They would save, but in small amounts and
only if we provided a voluntary savings service. Liberty is important for all people, especially liberty over their finances. But we couldn't provide voluntary savings. We had no license, and the calculation of interest would have been too difficult for us to manage on a large scale at that time."

Soeun reckons, as a general principle, mandatory savings as a guarantee can be
successful for some organizations over time, but in the short and mid term he feels
there is too much conflict. "In the long term," he adds, "it is not what the people
really want."

Interestingly enough, in 1996 when ACLEDA removed compulsory savings as a requirement for group loans in several district branches there was no increase in delinquency or default. The last rationale for mandatory savings – a guarantee against default – faded in the minds of ACLEDA staff. By eliminating compulsory savings, ACLEDA reduced costs – costs to the borrower, and costs the institution incurred in managing many small compulsory savings accounts.

Medium-Sized Loans

In 1995 ACLEDA signed an agreement with Caisse Francaise de Developpement (CFD) to manage medium-sized loans, from USD 10,000 to USD 50,000. CFD approved the loans and disbursed them directly to the businesses; the business deposited the installment payments in a special account that was later transferred to CFD. Under a management contract with CFD, ACLEDA provided advice and monitoring to the businesses.

The loan term, originally designed by CFD with a seven-year term, was successfully limited to four years by ACLEDA through a series of negotiations with CFD. At the time, there were no credit services in Cambodia through existing banks, even for this larger sized enterprise. The medium-sized loan product had appeal, but a very limited market.

ACLEDA's experience with the first two customers was a positive one. Yet, by the end of 1995, ACLEDA decided not to renew the contract for managing medium-sized loans for CFD, even though at the time, it was quite lucrative. The product was a stretch for them, demanding a different level of analysis, and leading them away from a primary market they were just beginning to learn to serve. They perceived the costs of offering a new product as too high; the relationship put them in an advisory role, not the role of direct lender. When CFD offered ACLEDA a technical advisor to help manage the product and the institution, ACLEDA decided to opt out of the program.

Throughout the 1990s ACLEDA continued to finance a limited number of medium-sized enterprises. But it was not until later in 1999, when economic growth rates in the country found a match in the business sector, that the product began to find greater market appeal.

Lessons

In the opinion of some analysts, "Cambodia was not yet ready for microfinance." ACLEDA's experience began to demonstrate otherwise as early lessons about customers and products emerged. The first lesson was immediately apparent. Demobilized soldiers, often mobilized for most of their adult lives, were very poor credit risks; they were not particularly solid candidates for entrepreneurship training either. They often willfully defaulted and threatened staff with weapons that were still very much in hand.

During its first three years, ACLEDA made significant progress in overcoming some of the more widely used donor practices that influenced the operation. The staff began to prove to themselves that directed credit was a misguided strategy for the customer and the operation.

They also began to prove that a significant demand for working capital existed in war-torn Cambodia. People were creditworthy; they honored their credit contracts when they perceived credit as a financial service. When people perceived credit as a reward for training or a social welfare benefit, the experience proved equally memorable, but somewhat less honorable.

Two lessons about targeted credit were more subtle. Credit, targeted to a specific group of people who the donor feels are appropriate, may be appealing in theory, but in practice it discriminates against many economically active or potentially economically active people, who are just as poor. They too lack the essential ingredients to grow their business and they too contribute to the economy in a meaningful way. ACLEDA learned the lessons of "inclusion" at a very early phase. The second lesson about targeted credit was a traumatic one. Credit as an input, tied to a specific purchase, can impoverish the very people it is intended to help.

Managing a cash-based operation in times of armed conflict and chaotic violence is a precarious business. Security of the cash, the customers and the staff are central to any operational strategy and technology to deliver the service. In this environment ACLEDA decided that credit officers would not carry cash; they were more easily identified as targets. Transfers from the headquarters to the branch required the utmost confidentiality from those who organized them. Physical security was imperative; branches were located in concrete, not wooden structures.

Lessons about customer preferences surfaced. Customers valued a professional relationship with ACLEDA credit officers and directly with the branch. ACLEDA's branch-based service required the borrower to travel; it was not as convenient as the neighborhood bank. Other features of the products made up for the less convenient village location. They incorporated longer installment payment intervals, monthly or twice a month rather than weekly. At the time, village-based banks with weekly loan repayment intervals formed the dominant model in the region. ACLEDA rejected this model because it imposed unnecessarily high opportunity costs for the borrowers. The opportunity costs of less frequent payment intervals were lower; customers did not have to spend time managing the operations of the neighborhood bank or attending weekly meetings that took them away from their businesses. Customers appreciated the confidentiality and the safety that the branch service provided, valued features often compromised by the neighborhood bank.

The price of credit is but one factor that influences the demand for a product. In the absence of a monopoly, the consumer chooses the most valuable service. It is possible to compete in the market based on the quality of the service, freeing the product of hidden costs that are often a higher financial burden to the client than the interest rate alone. The mandatory savings product fell to the same logic. It served no purpose. It was risky and costly for the customer; it increased the costs for the operation, and it did not mitigate risk for the institution.

What could be interpreted as a fierce independence in this early stage was really about discovering a workable business model; that model centered on a direct relationship with the customer. Working through intermediaries distanced ACLEDA from the customer and its own decision-making. Understanding customer preferences, untied to preconceived methodologies, products or donor imperatives, enabled ACLEDA's early credit operation to grow. Staff found that extensive market research in the early period was really about understanding and listening to customers, really listening.

These were the early questions and discoveries about products and customers, which would later fill the official agenda and the after-hours discussions of ACLEDA's first strategic plans and the workshops in-between.

"We had come to this because we were listening, paying attention and learning", Channy says. "In 1992 and 1993 all staff got training in the "four Ps" of marketing – product, price, place, and promotion. We taught entrepreneurs to understand their markets and apply business principles, but in our own organization we didn't practice this. We taught our customers to pay attention to their customers, why shouldn't we?"

CHAPTER 4:

Crossroads

By early 1993 ACLEDA had a future. The future may have been unclear and
tenuous but it was ACLEDA's future and the staff would push it along until they
figured out what they were trying to achieve. This chapter explores ACLEDA's
first transition from a project to a local NGO. It shows the gradual momentum
towards the second transition from a local NGO to an organization specialized in
the delivery of micro and small enterprise credit. The stories in this chapter illustrate how the organizational infrastructure that enabled these transitions was put in
place. It details the most important processes that led ACLEDA staff to succeed in
their organizational experiment, one that could have backfired just as easily as
they prepared to gamble on the future.

Forging the Infrastructure

Governance

A project requires no governance – strong management, skilled staff, solid systems,
but no governance. An NGO, on the other hand, does. Governance was new for the
ACLEDA team. In 1993 ACLEDA began its research of other NGOs in Cambodia
that operated with a sense of autonomy, not as projects of international agencies.
They looked at Khmera and ADHOC, the only two local NGOs at the time. Each
NGO incorporated a General Assembly made up of staff who voted on all the issues.

"This was the way we could manage ACLEDA," Channy recalls. "Everyone
had a say. I believed this was good governance."

Later ACLEDA would find the General Assembly model of governance, where
all staff had an equal say in the decisions of the organization, and each branch
manager had a seat on the board, was not the best way to govern a large commercial venture. But this first structure served them well. The General Assembly provided a platform for the first ACLEDA to listen to everybody and free itself from
those who would dominate. The branch managers were also members of the
board, hardly a structure that would promote a check and balance in the operation;
but on the positive side, when a policy gained a unanimous vote, there was rapid
and thorough implementation. On the negative side, when a policy was passed by
a narrow margin, branch managers who agreed with it would follow it; those who
disagreed felt that they did not have to comply.

The first governance system established a basis for leadership to be accountable to staff, many of whom worked in remote areas, often cut off from communications with the center as well as the other branches. As a complement to decentralization, the structure fueled exchange of experience among the LEDAs by providing a practical mechanism and a central point for management and administration. As destructive as the governance system would later become, it added to the critical thinking in ACLEDA as an organization. Board members – the branch managers – had to defend their positions on topics ranging from broad organizational policy to the details of branch management. As decision-makers, they engaged in an analysis of their colleagues' ideas and suggestions, compared performance, and crafted together what they thought was best for their individual operations, if not for ACLEDA overall. But at this point, ACLEDA was an amalgamation of the individual LEDAs. The first governance system, with all its drawbacks, also prevented the emergence of a dictatorship and groomed individuals who would become ACLEDA's future leaders, obliging them to prove over time that they had the capacity to lead.

Perhaps most important of all, the General Assembly, as the key decision-making body in the organization, empowered all staff members as owners of the organization. They became so empowered, that they voted themselves out of existence in 1999.

The First Strategic Plan

The first strategic plan in 1994 was buttressed by a Memorandum of Understanding between the fledging national NGO and the ILO. The Memorandum's schedule for installing systems and procedures in the new operation proved to be a powerful tool for ACLEDA's transition from a project to an independent organization. Principled agreements aside, ACLEDA staff trusted that they would in fact emerge as an independent institution; the Memorandum and its detailed performance schedule established the means to make it happen.

The strategic planning started in October 1993, and the final plan was approved in March 1994 by ACLEDA's second General Assembly. The five month interval was not a bureaucratic delay. The process started with each staff member in each branch. Staff opinions about the operation extended beyond their specific duties; their views on the direction of the organization counted as well. In many organizations the theory of equal participation is there; ACLEDA's first strategic plan put into practice its governance concept of organizational democracy. It was here that the concept of accountability emerged – a new concept in Cambodia – where the leader is accountable to the followers, where management is accountable to staff.

The importance of the first strategic plan was lost on no one. This was the staging ground for a quiet revolution, an opportunity to come out victorious by proving they could work as a team and together influence the direction of the organization with what they had learned. It was also a time to balance organization-wide

policies and procedures with increasing decentralization that could rapidly frag-
ment the nascent organization, leading to the creation of fiefdoms and alternative
power bases centered in the branches.

There were different opinions about the future of the LEDAs and the importance of their national association – ACLEDA. Some branch managers envisioned
branches becoming independent NGOs within each Province. In 1994 even
Channy thought he had completed his job in the creation of ACLEDA. The project
was a legally recognized local organization; now he could get back to the business
of managing the Phnom Penh LEDA. And when visitors came to the LEDA in
Kampong Cham and asked to speak to ACLEDA, the branch manager told them
ACLEDA was in Phnom Penh, they would have to go there.

Consolidation of the new organization would be a slow walk up the mountain.
Eventually they would reach a plateau. In 1998 there would be a show-down about
the future of ACLEDA before they could begin a more rapid ascent. But in 1994,
governance and long term vision hardly took precedence in the thinking of
ACLEDA staff. They were thinking about what they were doing every day. Phonnary thought about her clients and how she could improve the product, a product
that must be tied to why some people repaid their loans and others did not.
Channy considered what technical assistance made sense, and why donors be-
haved the way they did. Soeun searched for a way to record transactions that made
sense, and secretly worked on a double entry bookkeeping system, contrary to the
advice of one of the technical advisors who preferred a single entry system for the
level of Cambodian education. And Siphann, a dedicated credit officer in Kampot,
was thinking about whether the soldiers he found as his bicycle rounded the bend
on a deserted road in the rain were Khmer Rouge rebels or government troops.

ACLEDA already had the confidence of its donors, the support of its technical
advisors and a Memorandum that laid out the steps of the transition. Together they
provided the bulwark to build the five LEDAs into one organization. Peter Kooi
recalls the importance of the first strategic plan:

> *"Two years later, when the next transformation began, ACLEDA
> staff looked back at the first strategic plan, and laughed a little. But
> it was extremely important because it forced thinking as a democ-
> ratic team. The first strategic plan was an exercise in team building,
> and in the end what resulted was a pouring out, a cacophony of
> ideas about everything everyone wanted to do, which turned exactly
> into the next project."*

1995: The Crossroads

The first strategic plan, an exercise in team building, was critical to promoting ownership of the new organization. The second strategic plan in 1996 built on that foundation; it focused on sustainability and the organization's specialization in the delivery of microfinance services. In the meantime, ACLEDA traveled to a crossroads.

The crossroads was the end of the grace period. It was time to decide among the growing list of options for the future of the organization. ACLEDA could continue any number of activities that fund raising efforts had been successful enough to start. At the time, even modest organizational capacity inspired donor confidence. ACLEDA's expanding roster of products, pilot projects, training offerings and research sub-contracts each clamored for special attention. But the central question that occupied ACLEDA staff during this period was what they felt they could be the best at doing.

Two options for the future became clear. In 1995 ACLEDA staff and their technical advisors put together a series of workshops to decide whether to continue as an integrated business development organization with a credit component, or whether to specialize in microfinance. They found a recent publication, *The New World of Microfinance*, and organized working sessions around the major topics.

In late 2003, Phonnary pulled out a well thumbed edition of the "New World" and turned to Chapter One. She found a paragraph highlighted in faded yellow and surrounded by notes in Khmer:

> *"This chapter ... considers the prospect of providing financial services – credit and savings – for the majority of poor entrepreneurs throughout the Third World ... from locally generated funds, without external subsidies. Although presently elusive, this goal may be attainable ... "*[27]

A quick flashback and Phonnary cites another faded yellow passage ...

> *"These institutions when placed in the context of the development of a financial system as a whole ... involve the following elements: a market perspective that understands the preferences of the client groups and designs products to meet them, a recognition that savings can be as important as credit ... an insistence that financially viable institutions provide only financial services. These principles require the institution to break even or turn a profit in its financial operations and raise funds from non-subsidized sources. This perspective is a clear departure from the assumptions behind the vast majority of microenterprise programs financed by donors and governments ... "*[28]

"We thought this could apply to us," says Phonnary. "These were the principles that fit ACLEDA. We were the small program the *New World* spoke about. Could we

---

[27] Maria Otero and Elisabeth Rhyne, eds. *The New World of Microfinance: Building Healthy Financial Institutions for the Poor* (West Hartford: Kumarian Press, 1994), 11.
[28] Ibid.

access commercial funds, or develop our own sources to meet the demand? Could we become entrepreneurs and develop services with a market oriented approach? Did we know what our profit and losses even were? If we remained dependent on donors we would spend and finish the funding; that was clear. We were at 20-30% self-sufficiency after three years of operation. If the maximum time period was five years, we had to start planning to achieve 100% self-sufficiency now."

For some ACLEDA staff these new ideas were daunting. If they chose a path independent of donors, it was sure to bring ACLEDA's demise. Many staff left during 1995 in anticipation of that inevitable day. The pessimistic outlook did not correctly auger the future. Two years later, by the end of 1997, ACLEDA broke even and was on its way to reaching the elusive but perhaps attainable goal of which the *New World* spoke.

Phonnary thinks back with only a modicum of the frustration she must have felt at the time, "Staff left because they didn't trust themselves to do a good job."

* * *

The crossroads meetings were organized around the two options to specialize. One presentation centered on the two distinct roads ACLEDA could travel in future. "I remember finishing the presentation," Peter Kooi recalls. "It was very quiet in the room. I waited. Then decided to wait some more until someone spoke."

Finally, Sar Roth, the branch manager from Kampong Cham, spoke, "Why didn't you tell us before that we had the choice?"

Sar Roth, who once gave up his chance for third country repatriation to help the children of Cambodia, is familiar with choices and the long-term impact that they might have. He explains ACLEDA's choice at the crossroads:

> *"From the beginning we knew that people didn't like the training, maybe a few and at the very beginning. But everybody wanted the credit. There was business opportunity for them, but no capital. There were business start-ups and growth-oriented business, people who were already in business but had no capital to expand. We also knew that vocational training was not our expertise. We did not know how to give expert advice on business development; we would always have to rely on foreign experts and donors. When it came to credit, through solidarity groups or individual loans to small enterprises, for business start-ups or expansion, we knew we could be the best institution in Cambodia."*

ACLEDA matched emerging institutional capacity to deliver credit with its clients' demand. In the process, ACLEDA discovered a passion for microfinance.

The crossroads had implications for ILO's expert advisors as well. It would not be an easy decision. If ACLEDA chose business development, Roel Hakemulder would stay; if it chose microfinance, Peter Kooi would become the Chief Technical Advisor. Peter recalls, "Roel and I discussed this together. ACLEDA's choice would be difficult for both of us." But for Roel, who was referred to as the "father of ACLEDA" by ACLEDA staff, the choice was different.

"ACLEDA was going in the direction of building a sustainable microfinance organization, it was clear they would need banking expertise, not a business development advisor," Roel recalls. "Sure, I could have become the project management figurehead, carrying my own brief case back and forth to the office, but I had seen too much of this re-writing of projects to include a position that becomes irrelevant."

"It was the right thing to do," Roel says. "There was an enormous sense of opportunity – the opportunity to do things in the right way, for once. Especially in Cambodia, where there was such an atmosphere of hope, where people expected a lot from us, where the "right thing" had been the exception for quite a while, and where I, for one, felt privileged to be at that time. In your life you get very few chances to do the right thing. It's good to have the chance to do the right thing once."

And so exits ACLEDA's first Chief Technical Advisor, a man with the foresight to know that ACLEDA staff now needed different expertise if they were to achieve their potential. From the very first day in the airport, when he met the people who were to become ACLEDA staff, Roel Hakemulder, became the architect of good organizational bones. In 1995, he did not go away "walking empty", just as he didn't in 1992. He had the chance to do the right thing.

1996: The Future

By almost any definition, the period between the first strategic plan in 1994 and the second one in 1996 was remarkable. The seriousness of the growing number of staff equaled the increasing complexity of their deliberations. From the first period to the next, ACLEDA had experimented with a number of different products through trial and error; the staff now understood what worked and what did not. While ACLEDA continued to operate both training programs and credit services throughout 1996, by the year's end the direction for the future was clear.

As a result of the 1996 strategic planning exercise, ACLEDA decided to become a self-financing microfinance institution. There were many reasons behind this decision; key among them was limited donor commitment at a time when ACLEDA's portfolio began to grow. "Donor commitments were limited to one or two years. We would have liked to access another longer term source of funding, but for us there was no other source," Channy recalls. Unlike other environments where donor resources appear to be without limit and without end, Cambodia had already witnessed the sudden decrease in foreign aid with UNTAC's departure; local jobs vanished with them.

During the strategic planning workshop, each branch manager expressed a desire to become profitable, but no one knew whether or not they could reach that goal, or how. Part of the workshop included a spreadsheet projection, and a very active discussion on the 150 ways to become more productive. After a few hours of playing with the figures and various scenarios using the data from each branch, Cheam Teang, the branch manager from Kampot, suddenly jumped to his feet. "I did it!" he shouted pointing to the computer projections. "Yes, yes, I am profitable!" One year later, Teang's branch in fact, became profitable. It was the first branch to reach profitability in the ACLEDA network. In time others followed, and Kampot never looked back.

The 1996 strategic plan focused on sustainability. ACLEDA branch mangers realized they would have to generate more income and become more efficient. Most branch managers reluctantly agreed to an increase in the interest rate. They worried that a price increase would have a negative effect on their customers, whittling down their portfolios as clients sought out other credit operations. The gamble of sustainability led them to face an impossible situation – a decreasing portfolio and customer base just as they expected customers to pay for their salaries. If there were no customers, there would be no salaries. Many could see only a spiral of doom.

Branch managers returned to their posts with a great deal of trepidation. They had a risky proposition for their customers, a 2% price increase on the small business loan. Customers' reactions surprised even the most anxious branch manager. When clients were polled about the price increase, the majority agreed, with one condition: "decrease the training". Customers often had to close their operations to attend the training seminars; they lost income and at times lost customers to competitors. For them, a moderate increase in the price of the loan was more than enough to compensate for the hidden costs of the training component. The six-day training, which often exceeded the scheduled time, went to a three-day on-time training seminar. Later the seminars were abandoned in favor of individual or group consultations on the principles of cash flow, managing repayment capacity within the business, and the discipline of honoring a credit contract.

Customers thought ACLEDA had improved its products.

As ACLEDA staff began to practice the dictum that customers were paying for their salaries, they became friendlier to borrowers, and began to devise ways to improve the service. ACLEDA began to compete with other microcredit providers based on the quality of the service. The dreams of Phonnary and Samnang – a quick, friendly, convenient, customer oriented service – were coming true.

Sophisticated Consumers

Who were those sophisticated customers guiding ACLEDA staff and their plans?

Cambodia is a country of 13 million people. The United Nations Development Program (UNDP) 2003 Human Development Report ranks Cambodia 130th of the 175 countries on the UN's World Human Development Index.[29] The UN estimates

---

[29] UNDP, *Human Development Report 2003* (New York: United Nations, 2003) and IMF, *Cambodia Poverty Reduction Strategy Paper Progress Report* IMF Country Report No. 04/333 (Washington, D.C.: IMF, 2004).

that 36 % of Cambodians live below the poverty line. Average life expectancy is 54 years, and population growth is 2.6% annually. Women make up a large percentage of the labor force, since 20% of Cambodian households are headed by women.[30] In some regions of Cambodia more than half the households are headed by women.

Maternal mortality is 450 per 100,000 births, infant morality is 96 per 1,000 live births, and half the children under five years of age suffer from malnutrition. Only 32% of the population has access to clean water and 17% of the population has access to sanitation, resulting in a high incidence of disease. Tuberculosis and malaria are the main causes of death. HIV/AIDS is endemic; the actual number of HIV-positive Cambodians is unknown, with some estimates showing 2.8% of the general adult population. Some 30% of the population is illiterate, less than 10% are engaged in skilled occupations, one-third of the population aged five and above has no education and only 20% have completed schooling beyond primary level; only 4% complete lower secondary school. The per capita GDP is USD 284.[31]

These are the statistics for 2002-03. Ten years earlier, in 1993, the statistics were less heartening.

Cambodia is a country of small and micro businesses. Agriculture is the main economic activity today, as it was in 1993. Estimates indicate that 80% of rice farmers are also engaged in off-farm economic activities. The majority of the national labor force, more than 60 percent, is self-employed. Households in rural areas are generally engaged in several economic activities, combining agriculture and microbusiness. In 1995 an ILO study for the World Bank estimated that 95% of all households in Cambodia engaged in some micro or small enterprise activity. A 1995 study by the Cambodian National Institute of Statistics noted that income from agriculture in the rural areas accounts for just 3% more of the total income than micro business does. For Cambodia as a whole, business accounts for a much greater share of household income than agriculture.[32]

Are They Poor?

Like many nations, poverty in Cambodia is complex and has many origins. Twenty years of war, from which no area was spared, is at the top of the list. Landmines and unexploded ordinances continued to disable three people a day as

---

[30] World Bank, *Cambodia from Recovery to Sustained Development* World Bank Report No. 15593-KH (Washington, D.C.: World Bank, 1996), 19.

[31] These statistics are from *National Poverty Reduction Strategy 2003-2005* (Phnom Penh: Council for Social Development, Royal Government of Cambodia, December 2002).

[32] Statistics from the National Institute of Statistics and the ILO/World Bank study are cited in Hakemulder, *Promoting Local Economic Development*, 9.

Table 4.1. Poverty Lines in Cambodia

Area	1993-4	1997	1999
	Riel per capita per day	Riel per capita per day	Riel per capita per day
Phnom Penh	1,578 (USD 0.63)	1,819 (USD 0.52)	2,470 (USD 0.63)
Other Urban	1,264 (USD 0.50)	1,407 (USD 0.40)	2,093 (USD 0.54)
Rural	1,117 (USD 0.45)	1,210 (USD 0.35)	1,777 (USD 0.46)

Notes: Figures reflect riel per capita per day, and exchange rates at the time.
Source: Poverty Profile of Cambodia, 1997 and 1999. Ministry of Planning.

late as 2002, considerably down from 1996 when eight people a day were killed or injured[33]. But poverty is also caused by poor health care, low agricultural productivity and lack of access to agricultural land on which 85% of the population depends. Low levels of education, lack of basic infrastructure, significant corruption and leakage in the system, and the new course of impoverishment – HIV/AIDS – contribute to poverty.

Poverty in Cambodia is not equally distributed throughout the provinces. Extensive expert surveys launched since 1994 established a poverty line in Cambodia; the people who fall below it tend to live in the rural areas as shown in Table 4.1.[34] They are likely to reside in villages in the Provinces of Siem Reap, Banteay Meanchey, Prey Veng, Kampong Chanang, Pursat, Svay Rieng and Otdar Meanchey where villages are isolated by poor communications and transportation or have experienced massive destruction due to war and late raging battles in the mid and late 1990s.

Very poor people are engaged in agriculture; they are also self-employed. They have fewer than six years of formal education, and are more likely to have been of primary school age during the Pol Pot regime and the disruptive years that led up

---

[33] Cambodia is one of the most heavily mined countries in the world. Official estimates range from 4 to 6 million mines and UXOs planted from 1979 through 1997. Records show that from January 1979 through the end of 2000 mines and UXOs injured or killed 49,413 people – over half were civilians and children. In 2002 and the first half of 2003, three people per day were injured or died as a result of landmines and UXOs. Landmine Monitor 2001: Cambodia. Third Annual Report 2000-2001. Available from the Electronic Mine Information Network at http://www. mineaction.org.

[34] Statistics in this section are cited from surveys conducted in Cambodia since 1993. For a complete poverty survey see, Nicholas Prescott and Menno Pradhan, *A Poverty Profile of Cambodia*. World Bank Discussion Paper No. 373. (Washington, D.C.: World Bank, 1997); John Knowles, *A Poverty Profile of Cambodia – 1997* (Phnom Penh: Ministry of Planning, 1997); *Cambodia Socio-Economic Survey, 1999* (Phnom Penh: National Institute of Statistics and Ministry of Planning, 1999) and *Cambodia Poverty Assessment*. World Bank Report No. 19858-KH. (Washington D.C.: World Bank, 1999).

to it. The poorest households support five to ten family members. The incidence of poverty increases with household size.

Research over a two-year period based on household surveys in eight rural villages in three Provinces looked at the amounts different segments of the population borrowed from the informal credit market.[35] The research found that those below the poverty line and just above it used moneylenders more often than those who were considered wealthy or very wealthy, who could rely on family members. Villagers below the poverty line as well as non-poor villagers borrowed amounts up to riel 50,000 (USD 18). Both groups also borrowed amounts between riel 150,000 and 250,000 (USD 55-92). The majority of those below the poverty line borrowed amounts of USD 55 and below, and the majority of those above it borrowed amounts over USD 92.

An extensive poverty profile carried out in 1997 found the value of outstanding loans to be a promising poverty indicator.[36] Households below the poverty line had outstanding loan balances of riel 137,000 (USD 40) and those in the lowest quintal riel 130,000 (USD 38).

ACLEDA's Customers

In 1996 ACLEDA provided a profile of its clients spanning the first four years of operation as shown in Table 4.2.

At the end of 1995, the year which marked ACLEDA's decision to become an organization specialized in the delivery of credit, loan distribution statistics show that 69% of ACLEDA's clients sought loans below the equivalent of USD 50. (See Table 4.3 for details.) The average outstanding loan balance of the micro loan clients was equivalent to USD 31, indicating that the majority of micro loan borrowers were well below the poverty line, and many of them were in the lowest quintal.

The average daily per capita income of ACLEDA's micro and small business borrowers may come as a surprise to observers of the operation, who tended to discount ACLEDA's outreach to the very poor, perceiving it as an organization that worked in the higher end of the microcredit market. The average daily per capita income of ACLEDA's micro borrowers was riel 937 (USD 0.37), below all national poverty lines for the period. The average daily per capita income of ACLEDA's small business borrowers was riel 1,875 (USD 0.75), just above the national poverty line of USD 0.63 per capita per day. (See Table 4.4)

---

[35] Pascal Bousso et al., *The Micro-economic Impact of Rural Credit in Cambodia* (Paris: GRET, 1997), 13-15.

[36] Knowles. *A Poverty Profile of Cambodia*, 39-40.

Table 4.2. ACLEDA's Client Profile, 1993 – 1996

	Micro Credit Clients	**Small Enterprise Credit Clients**
Female	99.6%	77%
Male	00.4%	23%
Average age	34	35
Average years of schooling	n.a.	5.9
Average family size	6	6
Heads of household	90%	79%
Previously unemployed		25%
Average daily per capita income	Riel 937	Riel 1874
Business start-up		35%
Business expansion		65%
Production	10%	35% (75% female)
Agriculture	10%	23% (80% female)
Trade	80%	23% (88% female)
Services		19% (60% female)
Median disbursed loan size	139,339 riel (USD 40)	
Average outstanding loan balance end 1996	USD 52 USD 43 (inflation adjusted)	USD 457 USD 374 (inflation adjusted)

Source: Provided by ACLEDA

Table 4.3. Distribution of Loan Sizes, December 1995

Disbursed Loan Size in USD	**Number of Active Clients**	**% of Total**
< 50	4,491	68.7%
50 – 100	54	0.8%
100 – 300	576	8.8%
300 – 1000	1,171	17.9%
1000 – 2000	201	3.1%
2000 – 4000	42	0.6%
4000 – 10,000	3	0.05%
TOTAL	6,538	100.0%

Source: Provided by ACLEDA

Table 4.4. National Poverty Lines (1993 – 1994) and Daily per capita Income of ACLEDA's Borrowers

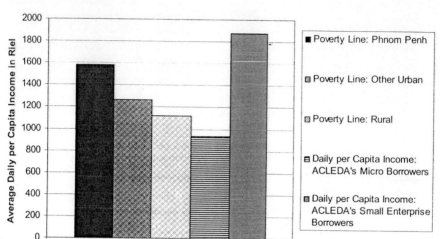

Sources: National Poverty Survey, 1993 – 1994, cited in Poverty Profile of Cambodia, 1997 and 1999. Ministry of Planning. ACLEDA impact surveys, 1995.

Impact assessments over the first 18 months for the small business operation found that incomes of entrepreneurs had increased by an average of 65%. Expanding businesses as well as start-ups created on average two jobs per enterprise, including the entrepreneur and family members. Two in-depth impact assessments were carried out for the micro lending or informal sector operation. Again, about one year after the provision of the first assistance, an average income increase of 45% was found among micro lending clients. The first study found that 67% had increased their income; the second impact assessment found that 84% of the clients had increased their income. Improvements were also found in ownership of assets, school attendance, medical care, and housing.[37]

Far from ACLEDA's first foray into lending in 1993, when the first loan ended in the first default, things started to seem right with the world. Poor people could borrow to build their businesses, and they would repay their loans.

Shifting from Targets to Markets

ACLEDA learned that targeting specific groups of people – demobilized soldiers, the disabled, widows, internally displaced persons and returnees – was an exclusionary strategy. It was not a particularly effective one for reaching great numbers of Cambodians who had no access to credit. As the first two years of operation

---

[37] Hakemulder, *Promoting Local Economic Development*, 30-31.

ended, ACLEDA looked for borrowers who could productively use credit to expand or start a business, tiny as it might be, and whoever they were. And there were many.

The shift to a market-oriented approach was propelled by the idea that the targeted credit program excluded the majority of Cambodians who were self-employed, the poorest segment of society. By the time poverty-targeting measures became the advocates' holy grail of microfinance, ACLEDA was moving away from the idea of targeting people for who they were; rather, it targeted people for what they could achieve, no matter how poor they were. Invasive means tests and participatory poverty measurements too closely resembled the previous targeting of particular groups in society – an approach that did not serve them well in the early years. They wanted a more dignified approach to service provision; they designed products to reach the market.

Two products were designed for two distinct market segments – poor households with economic activities, and more formal small businesses. Neither group had access to credit through formal financial institutions. The micro loan product, delivered through solidarity groups, required no collateral and no minimum loan amount. Repayment intervals every two weeks allowed for small installment payments well within the reach of the household. This product had its greatest appeal to those below and close to the poverty line. The small business loan required collateral, featured monthly installment payments, and was offered in US dollars. This product appealed to customers who were not below the poverty line. Their incomes placed them somewhere in the range from below the poverty line, to slightly above it, to those who would be defined as well above the poverty line. Over time, these businesses would grow, creating additional jobs, and benefiting the poorest people who sought employment, preferring not to test their entrepreneurial skills right away.

The social welfare approach to credit, where credit allocation decisions are based on who is the poorest, conflicted with ACLEDA's budding market-oriented approach. What didn't make sense to ACLEDA staff was that if people were buying the financial services, why should they limit lending to several groups within a much larger market of poor and low-income people? As long as there was demand for their products, repayment capacity and significant results, why should they resort to an approach that failed them in the past? As long as capital was available, why should they ration it by using a donor's criteria designed to exclude other groups? There seemed to be another strategy available: they could enlarge the capital base to serve a greater number of people.

Interestingly enough, after ACLEDA became a licensed financial intermediary, a specialized bank, it reached ten times the number of micro loan customers it reached in 1995.

Perhaps there was something to this new, market-based approach.

Performance

Looking back, ACLEDA staff is almost embarrassed by performance at the end of 1995. If at this point in time, ACLEDA had been a microfinance institution, the first year's experience would have been disappointing. But ACLEDA was not a microfinance institution; it was an integrated business development project. The operation had recently grown from a project targeting demobilized soldiers to a local NGO that would serve a broader population disenfranchised by war. ACLEDA's donors paid little attention to the credit operation or its performance. The aim was directed to rehabilitation in a war-torn country. The task was to create "immediate impact" by providing assistance to micro and small enterprises. An historical account summarizes ACLEDA's first rationale:

> *"The creation of employment and additional income had to be realized as soon as possible to improve living conditions, contribute to reintegration and reconciliation, and therefore eventually the consolidation of peace. It was important for the project's supporters to do something urgently for those most affected by the war."*[38]

While there was concern about operating in the mode of a development project, from which ACLEDA might never recover, early performance reflects the structure of the development project that ACLEDA was. Only slowly did ACLEDA begin to evolve into an organization of substance. During this period, ACLEDA staff members doubled as the national project staff of the SEISP, an integrated business development and credit project. The cost structure reflects this. The early ACLEDA designed products and opened branches in response to donor expectations; financial performance reflects this aspect of the operation as well. Later, by the end of 1996, incremental growth in outreach, productivity and financial performance show as staff began to realize a greater responsibility for the future of their own organization. But in 1995, the organizational focus is not yet clear, the purpose driving the business is missing.

Let us compare ACLEDA's performance over the first three years with that of an equally young and dynamic organization – Prodem, the forerunner to BancoSol in Bolivia. The time period for the comparison between ACLEDA and Prodem differs by five years, as shown in Table 4.5. The different environments in which they operated served up different challenges. Nevertheless, there are striking similarities – and differences – that point to some common features of microfinance organizations during early stages of growth. Overall, the differences in performance reflect the two different operating strategies and their underlying organizational philosophies.

---

[38] Hakemulder, Promoting Local Economic Development, 14.

ACLEDA's outreach and portfolio expansion performance is similar to Prodem's in the early years. Both organizations are working in an environment that shows a large, pent-up demand for credit. The number of active clients doubles or triples with each year of operation. The size of the outstanding portfolio parallels the growth in the number of active borrowers for both organizations. ACLEDA's average micro loan balance is three times lower than Prodem's, reflecting the relatively smaller size of the enterprises, and their ability to absorb working capital. However, ACLEDA's greater attention to small enterprise lending increases the portfolio to match Prodem's.

This is where the similarity between the two organizations ends. High costs, high levels of delinquency and low cost recovery are features of ACLEDA's early operation, features that are absent during Prodem's early years.

In comparison, ACLEDA's administrative costs are much higher. The relatively higher costs of the operation reflect the lack of infrastructure in Cambodia, as well as the higher security measures imposed by war. By 1994 ACLEDA had lost 5 vehicles at gun point. Terrorist and sabotage attacks regularly escalated into war in the Northwest of the country. Branch offices often closed, and operations were limited during much of 1994.[39] However, the cost structures reveal more about the two organizations' different business models and organizational growth strategies during the early years. ACLEDA's performance statistics are indicative of its model for providing business development training and credit to a restricted group of people. The growth strategy relied on donor financing to build up branch infrastructure and to expand to a greater number of provinces almost immediately. Investments in fixed assets and staff training increased costs. As the number of branches grew, so did the costs of communication among the dispersed LEDAs and their national association.

Prodem chose to build economies of scale within two branches, focusing on credit. This enabled the organization to reach higher levels of efficiency as the cost per dollar lent rapidly decreased. The number of active clients per credit officer outpaced ACLEDA's by a two to one margin during most of the period. One of the most telling indicators of these two different strategies shows up in the financial productivity of credit officers. On average ACLEDA's credit officers managed a slightly higher portfolio than Prodem's credit officers, but credit officers made up only 41% of ACLEDA's staff, compared with 77% of Prodem's staff.

Attention to delinquency shows a marked difference in the two organizations. Prodem adopted a "no tolerance for delinquency" policy from the outset. ACLEDA struggled with the notion that a higher level of delinquency was related to the poverty level of its clients. The features of directed credit, explored in the previous chapter, weighed heavily on the quality of the portfolio in ACLEDA's early operation.

---

[39] ILO. Small Enterprise and Informal Sector Promotion Report. 1994, 16.

Table 4.5. Comparison between ACLEDA and Prodem: The First Three Years

	ACLEDA			Prodem		
Outreach						
	1993	1994	1995	1987	- 1988	1989
Active Clients	1,475	2,344	6,539	1,737	3,830	7,395
Micro	*1,160*	*1,189*	*3,426*			
Small	*315*	*1,155*	*3,109*			
Medium			*4*			
Growth Rate		*1.59*	*2.79*		2.20	1.93
Active portfolio (in USD)						
Total	234,067	376,123	1,248,659	158,000	414,000	933,000
Micro	*36,876*	*23,601*	*149,451*	158,000	414,000	933,000
Small	*197,191*	*352,522*	*1,026,825*			
Medium			*72,383*			
Growth Rate		*1.61*	*3.32*		2.62	2.25
Average loan balance (in USD)						
Micro	*32*	*20*	*44*	91	108	126
Small	*626*	*305*	*330*			
Medium			*18,096*			
Branches	5	6	11	1	1	2
Financial Performance						
	1993	1994	1995	1987	1988	1989
PAR >30 days [a]	21%	17%	9%	0	.40%	.19%
Operational self-sufficiency [b]	6%	18%	25%	n.a.	63%	92%
Financial self-sufficiency [b]	6%	13%	24%	n.a	40%	42%
Cost per USD lent	1.06	.72	.34	1.21	.10	.13
Efficiency						
	1993	1994	1995	1987	1988	1989
Portfolio per credit officer	12,319	15,672	30,455	6,990	29,791	28,793
Portfolio per staff	8,360	5,614	12,487	8,316	17,250	26,657
Number staff	28	67	100	19	24	35
Number credit officers	19	24	41		12	27

Notes: a. Portfolio at risk greater than 30 days. See technical note in the appendix for definition and method of calculation. b. See technical note in the appendix for definitions and method of calculation
Sources: ACLEDA financial reports (1993-1995). Cheryl Frankiewicz, The Story of Prodem (Calmeadow: 2001) 9.

In the age of quick impact projects, "less priority was given to financial sustainability, and long-term dependence on donors was initially considered inevitable".[40] The fundamental philosophy, and the idea that relying on donor funding was inevitable, drove the early performance in cost recovery.

The different environments in which Prodem and ACLEDA operated certainly go a long way to explaining the difference in costs. Yet it is the striking difference in organizational philosophies, their business models and expectations that shadow the performance of each of these young organizations.

Expectations

In an ironic sense, ACLEDA was protected from performance critiques by its status as a small enterprise and employment generation project in a post-conflict country. Current skeptics may look back and say, of course, that was Cambodia, it was easy to build a microfinance institution; there was nothing there to dismantle. Analysts at the time said, Cambodia is not ready for microfinance. In other words, don't expect too much. The expectations were low because to anticipate otherwise would set the bar too high.

Yet the lack of external expectations created breathing space to pay more attention to building the organization. In 1993, critical thinking emerged among ACLEDA staff about just who they were and what they were doing. The type of questions, so maddening to the first ACLEDA staff, arguably formed the foundations of business analysis, strategic thinking about objectives, purpose, customers and markets. ACLEDA embraced a learning culture from the outset. One could argue that they had no choice. But that would be wrong. ACLEDA could have followed the well trodden path of any number of organizations in Cambodia where the "boss gets everything". They could have reserved the inner circle of senior management by establishing a power base that would use and abuse the system. They could have trained employees just enough to function in their jobs and complete the objectives of the project, asking no questions and getting no answers. They could have followed the norm, but chose a more difficult path – they chose to lead, not to follow.

Their technical advisors supported them. Roel Hakemulder believed in local institutional development. Despite the taboo of building an institution in a time of emergency relief, he could not let temporary measures override his firmly held beliefs about the rightness of local ownership in fostering development. And Peter Kooi had the financial and commercial skills to get them there. In those conversations between Peter Kooi and Nay Soksamnang, as their vehicle traveled the perilous road from Kampong Cham to Phnom Penh, whether they knew it or not, a meritocracy was born.

---

[40] Hakemulder, Promoting Local Economic Development, 37.

ACLEDA staff focused on what they understood, what they learned from the people who were their greatest teachers – their customers. They retreated from ideas that found no market, products that found no customers, and methodologies that held no dignity. They rejected demands from product sponsors that appeared unreasonable. They let their abilities and their ideas about how they could improve their operation lead the way. Small improvements – what they thought was important – determined what they attempted. And these small improvements led to great changes.

*   *   *

With the modest performance of 1993-1995, the ACLEDA NGO was to take ownership responsibilities to a new dimension. So profound was this first transformation from project to local organization, if not in performance, certainly in attitude, that ACLEDA staff barely remembers a time when they were not free to make their own mistakes. ACLEDA began to act like a business with a customer focus and a concern about the business's ability to deliver. By 1995, the ACLEDA NGO found meritocracy, a learning culture and a determination to become the professional organization. Later, concern about improving performance and efficiency in all aspects of the operation was added to the foundation.

The first transformation, distant though it may be, paved the way for subsequent transformations and sparked a tentative sense that if this were possible, perhaps anything was. If this could happen, perhaps anything could. And if the expectations for the future of Cambodia were low, expectations within ACLEDA were high and began to accelerate. Potential to contribute, values and business insight, the qualities for which the first LEDA staff were recruited, saw them through this first period of transition from a project to a local NGO. Now they expected to build it.

CHAPTER 5:

Latitude to Grow

Changes in attitude led to the latitude to grow. ACLEDA's expansion is rooted in the commercial approach to microfinance. The concept of listening to customers became the keystone of that approach. What ACLEDA came to understand was that customers, not donors, were the future. Changes in ACLEDA's products reflected this understanding,. This chapter discusses the first building blocks the led to that change. It links the changes in attitude to the latitude to grow, unveiling the mystery of ACLEDA's formula for growth.

Performance: 1994-1997

ACLEDA's performance dramatically improved when in 1995 it decided to become an organization specialized in microfinance. With a clear purpose, ACLEDA's portfolio tripled, as did its outreach. Yet overall, the financial performance continues to show the legacy of a donor project and the high cost of operating in a risky environment where banks fail, exchange rates fluctuate, and the costs of security and neglected infrastructure are high.

Table 5.1. Active Portfolio and Borrowers, 1993 – 1997

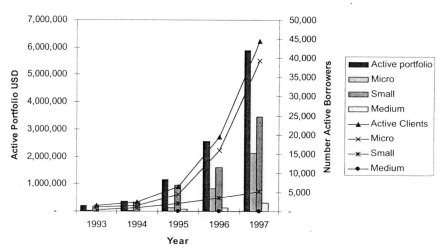

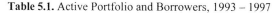

Source: ACLEDA Portfolio Reports and Audited Financial Statements, 1993-1997.

Table 5.2. Composition of Portfolio and Borrowers of Micro, Small and Medium Loans, 1993 – 1997

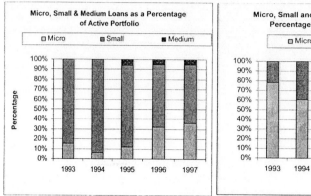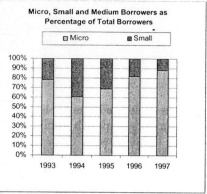

Notes: The percentage of medium sized loan clients is less than 1%
Source: ACLEDA Portfolio Reports, 1993-1997..

From 1994 through the end of 1997 ACLEDA's portfolio more than doubled every year and the number of active loan customers matched this pace as shown in Table 5.1. The rapid increase in portfolio size is due to two factors: the large increase in the number of micro loan clients, and the growing value of the small business portfolio. As expected, the value of the small business portfolio is greater than the value of the micro loan portfolio. However, the rapid expansion of the micro loan portfolio accounts for a larger and increasing percentage of the total active portfolio over the four year period.

When it comes to the number of borrowers, the reverse is true. The number of micro credit customers outpaces the number of small business customers, accounting for a greater and increasing percentage of the total clientele over the four-year period as shown in Table 5.2.

ACLEDA's striking outreach and dramatic portfolio growth occurred once the organization decided to specialize and follow a more market-oriented approach. The 1995 loan portfolio of just over USD 1 million and 6,539 active borrowers grew six-fold by the end of 1997 to a portfolio of just under USD 6 million, which financed loans for 44,533 active borrowers. Eighty-eight percent of ACLEDA's customers borrowed micro loans with an average outstanding balance equivalent to USD 54.

Average outstanding loan balances appear to increase during the period, but when they are adjusted for inflation, the real value of the micro loan in 1997 is equivalent to USD 41 in 1993 currency. A common measurement for depth of outreach is to compare the average loan balance per borrower to GDP per capita. The average loan balance for the micro borrower by the end of 1997 was 25% of GDP per capita, indicating deep outreach to poor and low income people. While

Table 5.3. Nominal and Real Value of Micro Loans, 1993 – 1999

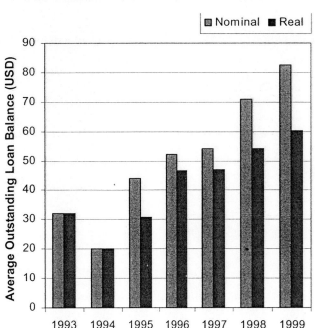

Notes: Average outstanding loan balance calculated from ACLEDA audited financial state-ments, 1993 – 1999, and portfolio reports over the same period.
Sources: Inflation, IMF, Inflation data are obtained taken from line 64x of the International Financial Statistics, International Monetary Fund, various years, for 1995 through 1999. Inflation data for 1993-1994 obtained from World Bank, Cambodia: From Recovery to Sustained Development (Washington, D.C.: World Bank, 1996), 7.

the very low average loan balance as a percentage of GDP per capita may appeal to donors interested in increasing poverty outreach, it is also an important factor for how ACLEDA approached its market and planned for growth. Micro loan custom-ers were keeping up with inflation and perhaps participating in the buoyant growth rates experienced by the Cambodian economy from 1993-1996, when real GDP growth averaged 5.5% year. The organization did not cap loan size, which would force lower average outstanding balances as a matter of policy. ACLEDA attempted to match loan size with the borrower's repayment capacity. Over the five-year pe-riod, as shown in Table 5.3, the microcredit borrowers kept up with inflation.

Within the organization, productivity and efficiency began to improve. Physical and financial productivity of credit officers approached or exceeded the bench-marks of best practice microfinance institutions throughout the world. By the end of 1997 credit officers served on average 560 micro borrowers in solidarity groups; credit officers serving individual small businesses counted on average 165 borrowers. The combined averages are shown in Table 5.4.

Table 5.4. Productivity, 1993 – 1997

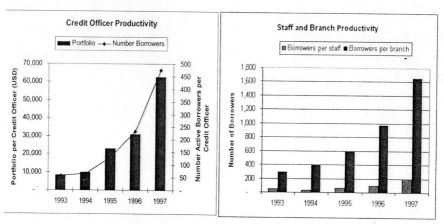

Source: ACLEDA Portfolio Reports, and Human Resource Department Records and Reports, 1993 – 1997.

High operating costs continued to burden the operation's advance toward profitability. While there were dramatic improvements in administrative efficiency compared with prior years, by the end of 1997 recurrent non-financial operating costs hovered at 39% of the average portfolio. (See Table 5.5 for trends.) There is little increase in cost recovery in early years. This reflects the project heritage and a financing strategy that donor dependence was inevitable; only partial cost recovery was thought to be possible through a combination of the operational income from lending and subcontracting business development and training services. The gap between operating income and operating expenses narrows when ACLEDA staff decided the organization could become self-financing, learned the fundamental factors that influenced it, and put policies in place to achieve it. (See Table 5.6 for details.)

Donor financing of shortfalls in operating income slowly disappears as the organization advances. An interest rate policy is adopted that will lead the organization to cover its costs with operating income from lending. Table 5.7 below shows the trend in nominal and real yield on portfolio during the period, and the companion table, Table 5.8, shows profitability ratios over the five year period.

Many of the operating costs are burdens imposed by the Cambodian environment, the high cost of communications and transportation. There were extraordinary losses due to war and a weak financial system, such as exchange rate losses and special provisions for accounts held in de-licensed and closed banks. These amounts were never recovered.

As discussed in Chapter 4, high costs were also associated with ACLEDA's growth strategy: an extensive strategy which relied on new investments in new branches was chosen over a more intensive strategy to penetrate the local market through existing branches, taking advantage of reduced costs. For each year, about

Table 5.5. Efficiency, 1993 – 1997

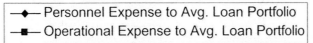

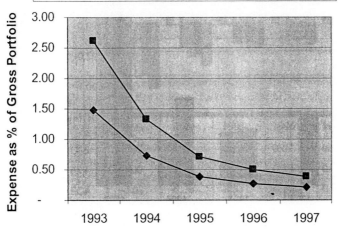

Source: ACLEDA Audited Financial Statements, 1993 – 1997.

Table 5.6. Operating Income and Operating Expenses, 1993 – 1997

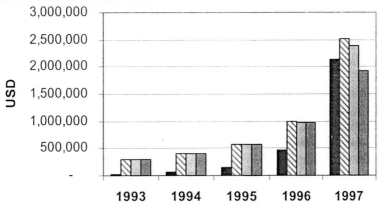

Source: ACLEDA Audited Financial Statements, 1993 – 1997.

Table 5.7. Nominal and Real Yield on Gross Portfolio, 1993 – 1997

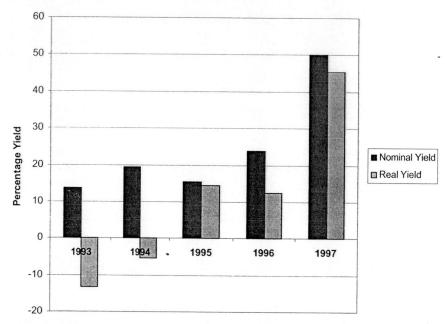

Sources: Inflation data are obtained taken from line 64x of the International Financial Statistics, International Monetary Fund, various years, 1995-1997. Inflation data for 1993-1994 from World Bank, Cambodia: From Recovery to Sustained Development (Washington, D.C.: World Bank, 1996), 7. ACLEDA Audited Financial Statements, 1993 – 1997.

40 percent of the administrative costs are investments in the next year's physical and human infrastructure, which only began to produce income after 1997. During this period ACLEDA invested heavily in staff training, another policy which benefited the organization's growth and efficiency in subsequent years, but accounted for high costs during this period.

Net loan assets to total assets begin to climb by the end of the period. By the end of 1997, 74% of total assets were dedicated to the loan portfolio, up from 24% of total assets in 1993. The policy to increase infrastructure caught up with business growth and the economies of scale found in expanding the number of clients within existing branches. As ACLEDA focused on sustainability, measures were adopted to contain costs and mine efficiencies in existing human and physical infrastructure.

In summary, there were four main financial factors that keyed future growth. First was the dramatic increase in financial and physical productivity – of credit officers, staff and branches. Secondly, the portfolio yield grew as interest rates were adjusted for inflation and the costs of delivering the services. Third, transaction costs for customers were reduced, making the lower-cost credit products more appealing in the market. The fourth factor was investment in the future.

Table 5.8. Profitability Ratios, 1993 – 1997

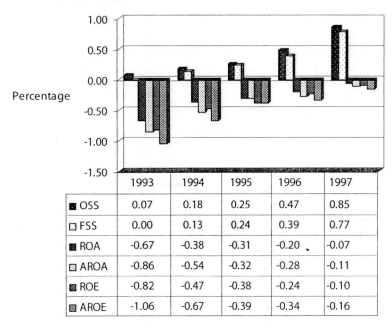

	1993	1994	1995	1996	1997
■ OSS	0.07	0.18	0.25	0.47	0.85
▢ FSS	0.00	0.13	0.24	0.39	0.77
▨ ROA	-0.67	-0.38	-0.31	-0.20	-0.07
▨ AROA	-0.86	-0.54	-0.32	-0.28	-0.11
▨ ROE	-0.82	-0.47	-0.38	-0.24	-0.10
▨ AROE	-1.06	-0.67	-0.39	-0.34	-0.16

Note: Operational Self-sufficiency (OSS), Financial Self-sufficiency (FSS), Return on Assets (ROA), Adjusted Return on Assets (AROA), Return on Equity (ROE) and Adjusted Return on Equity (AROE) are calculated using the methods described in the Technical Note.
Source: ACLEDA Audited Financial Statements, 1993 – 1997.

Underlying each of these growth factors were the decisions that made them possible – decisions that could only be made by a fundamental shift in the way the organization perceived itself.

Corporate Soul

What drives a young organization to commit to the challenges of growth and change? Why do some succeed in making transitions appear effortless, while others settle on self-imposed limits at the first sign of change? What factors make transition and transformation possible? Mission? Capital? Capacity? Financial performance? Competition? Context?

ACLEDA's story offers some insights into the dynamics of change in young organizations that are relevant to any environment, particularly those organizations operating in settings that offer few advantages. ACLEDA began in a post-conflict country as a small donor-designed integrated business development project with a USD 600,000 revolving loan fund. ACLEDA Bank Plc is now the largest retail bank branch network in Cambodia's history; it has created value in the financial sector and to society beyond the important microfinance goals of deep customer outreach and financial sustainability of the institution. The breadth and quality of leadership, the strength and energy of the organization's values and the way the team of people embraced the dynamics of change were the elements that enabled ACLEDA to succeed.

ACLEDA's history is one of continuous change. In Channy likens the many organizational transitions to climbing hills:

> "We climbed the first hill as a project to a local NGO. When we got to the top, we saw that the results were better. But we saw the next hill in front of us. The hill was bigger, but we were more determined to climb from a local NGO to an NGO specialized in microfinance. When we got to the top, we saw that the results were better. So we decided to climb the mountain that was in front of us, the mountain that would lead to becoming a specialized bank."

That climb enabled ACLEDA to achieve what no other NGO in Cambodia achieved. Within two years of becoming a specialized bank, ACLEDA became a fully licensed commercial bank. The climb started with shared values and has been sustained by the energy those values create within the organization. That energy motivated the original ACLEDA staff and now attracts a new generation of Cambodians who wish to be a part of it.

1993

ACLEDA's early transitions were more soulful than formulaic. In the earliest period ACLEDA developed a set of core values that translated into attitudes – the way staff thought about their operation is illustrated below in Figure 5.1. Starting from the left-hand side, the table shows how basic values influenced attitudes about how to run their operation. These attitudes influenced organizational practices and systems that they put in place. The set of values, attitudes, practices and systems underpinned the corporate goal – or mantra – of the organization.

In 1993, ACLEDA's mantra summarized what was urgent and important to the organization at the time: "If we don't work together, we will lose it." The key values were the personal codes shared by the group that made up the SEISP project staff: trust, honesty, equal treatment, and a commitment to do your best.

These values translated into attitudes of openness to new ideas, the rightness of transparency, the importance of consensus, and the recognition that training and capacity building were critical to their survival. Values took root in the organization in three areas – management, governance, and staff development. In the earliest period, systems are not comprehensive; practices do not fall into a neat set. Laying the bricks, not cutting the ribbon, characterizes the first stage of organizational development.

Mantra 1993: *"If we don't work together, we will lose it."*

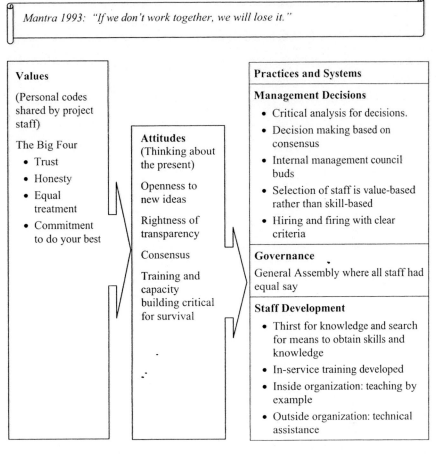

Values	Attitudes	Practices and Systems
(Personal codes shared by project staff)	(Thinking about the present)	**Management Decisions**
		• Critical analysis for decisions.
The Big Four	Openness to new ideas	• Decision making based on consensus
• Trust		• Internal management council buds
• Honesty	Rightness of transparency	• Selection of staff is value-based rather than skill-based
• Equal treatment	Consensus	• Hiring and firing with clear criteria
• Commitment to do your best	Training and capacity building critical for survival	**Governance**
		General Assembly where all staff had equal say
		Staff Development
		• Thirst for knowledge and search for means to obtain skills and knowledge
		• In-service training developed
		• Inside organization: teaching by example
		• Outside organization: technical assistance

Figure 5.1. Values, Attitudes, Practices and Systems

Practices and systems were products of those values, not the other way around. While their strategies and practices changed dramatically over the years, each change was grounded in the set of core values that strengthened over time. Good business strategies made the course navigable and accelerated the momentum. Systems enabled ACLEDA staff to see what the organization had accomplished, where it was going, and where it might be possible to chart new courses. But systems did not dictate the fundamental direction. Values did.

1994-1996

Figure 5.2 shows how the organization deepened the values, attitudes, practices and systems from the earlier SEISP project period to support an evolving local organization. Far from the accidental beginning, in 1994-1996 ACLEDA staff began to define what they could be best at doing, not just what they could do and raise donor money to support. They discovered their enthusiasm for microfinance, and were advised by expert technical assistance in tools of the trade.

The new organizational mantra, again summarizes what was urgent and important to the organization: "If we listen to customers we can build it."

Values that are individual codes of ethics in the project phase became a set of shared values within the organization. They set in motion a culture of trust, a meritocracy, and the accountability of leadership to staff and staff to each other. The focus on trust, equal treatment and transparency worked within the organization because there were clear examples of the way people were given a chance and promoted from within. Values were translated into practices that gained credibility through the consistent actions of management.

Attitudes about how to run the operation strengthened.

- ACLEDA found a balance between rejecting blueprints and re-inventing the wheel. It actively sought to bring knowledge back into the operation by learning from others, both from within the organization, and outside it. Knowledge became the fuel propelling the organization forward, but that knowledge had to match ACLEDA's ideals. Imported knowledge or copying the technology of others often moved the organization along a torturous, but reasonably preventable detour, until it once again re-aligned. The main path for ACLEDA was bound by its understanding of its customers on the one side, and its own capacity to deliver on the other.

- Honesty, equal treatment and trusting people to do their job empowered staff. Staff policies were developed and agreed to by all the staff during this period. Everyone knew the rules; they also understood the consequences of breaking them. They recognized that the opportunities for corruption in a cash-based business were endless, and even more so when loan customers were accustomed to traditional methods of doing business. Transparency in business with customers was considered to be of utmost importance. And when the rules were broken, there was a consistent application of the policies, open to the scrutiny of the entire organization – the staff who governed the organization.

- Staff development continued as a priority, not as an afterthought. Staff acknowledged that current capacity might limit their immediate response, but that was no excuse for the future. Training and capacity building in the 1993 project period were perceived largely as survival toolkits. In the later period, staff development and professional growth were viewed as keys to fulfilling organizational purpose.

- Consensus, an ideal that everyone should participate in decision making and also be held accountable for their actions, enabled an internal management council to develop that guided organizational decisions about the future. A set of rules developed to protect these beliefs. Systems were put in place that reflected the rules and ensured accountability, which all held in high regard.

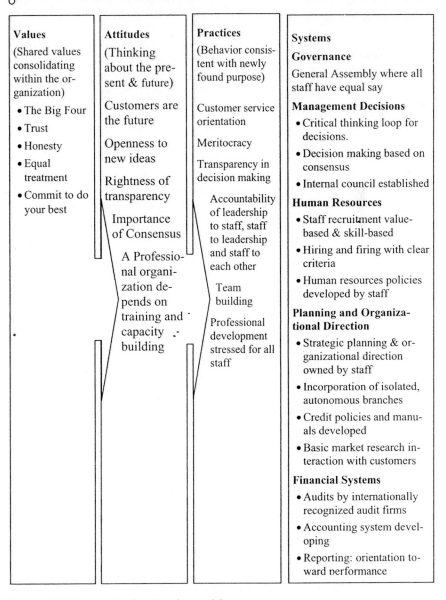

Mantra 1994-96: "If we listen to customers, we can build it."

Values
(Shared values consolidating within the organization)
- The Big Four
- Trust
- Honesty
- Equal treatment
- Commit to do your best

Attitudes
(Thinking about the present & future)

Customers are the future

Openness to new ideas

Rightness of transparency

Importance of Consensus

A Professional organization depends on training and capacity building

Practices
(Behavior consistent with newly found purpose)

Customer service orientation

Meritocracy

Transparency in decision making

Accountability of leadership to staff, staff to leadership and staff to each other

Team building

Professional development stressed for all staff

Systems

Governance
General Assembly where all staff have equal say

Management Decisions
- Critical thinking loop for decisions.
- Decision making based on consensus
- Internal council established

Human Resources
- Staff recruitment value-based & skill-based
- Hiring and firing with clear criteria
- Human resources policies developed by staff

Planning and Organizational Direction
- Strategic planning & organizational direction owned by staff
- Incorporation of isolated, autonomous branches
- Credit policies and manuals developed
- Basic market research interaction with customers

Financial Systems
- Audits by internationally recognized audit firms
- Accounting system developing
- Reporting: orientation toward performance

Figure 5.2. Values, Attitudes, Practices and Systems

This period shows the adoption of new systems required for an organization with rapid staff growth within a widely dispersed branch network.

- Staff policies on hiring, review and firing are comprehensive and fit the purpose of the organization.

- Strategic plans engage each staff member and pull the organization together. Even though the first plan pulls the organization in many directions, it is owned by the staff and is a key tool in building a democratic team. The second plan affirms a clear direction for the organization.

- Credit policies and manuals are developed and re-designed based on experimentation with products and the features that appeal to customers.

- Audits are undertaken by internationally recognized firms.

- Performance related reporting for a credit operation is taken more seriously in the later part of the period. Earlier reporting is focused on employment generation and training. Prior to 1996 branches kept only expense records. As the credit operation becomes the core business, financial reporting is developed.

Taking Ownership

ACLEDA would continue to change, and with every advancing degree of sophistication, it would demand a greater level of skill from its staff. Those who couldn't keep up, those who couldn't change or wouldn't avail themselves of the educational opportunities ACLEDA offered, would, at some point, have to go. As early as 1993, they had seen staff departing for higher-paying jobs. Some left because they did not want to be part of a local NGO when an international organization offered more promise and prestige. But a day was coming when ACLEDA would present the decision for staff to leave, not the other way around.

There would also come a time when the first staff would be out-paced by a younger generation who had enjoyed more opportunity to study, opportunities denied to their predecessors. ACLEDA did not opt for a quick fix strategy; instead investment in staff development gained the attention it rightly deserved. ACLEDA would continue to value experience learned on the ground, and staff whose values and work ethic matched the organization's own.

ACLEDA was founded as a professional service organization. The next step was logical: ACLEDA had to continue to become a professional organization. This basic tenet came from the beliefs of senior management. It was reinforced by their actions. It came from Soeun, who worked late into the night, and then studied computer technology and English so that he could make sense of the wealth of new information he found there. It came from Channy, who completed his MBA at night and on weekends. It came from Roel Hakemulder in the very beginning. It now comes from new staff – accountants, customer service representatives, tellers, loan officers. "We hire them young, and train, train, train," says Tiv Dynare, who is part of the new generation and the chief accountant in the Prey Veng branch.

"New staff comes to ACLEDA with basic knowledge and the motivation to learn. They gain experience by working with others," Samnang, ACLEDA's Phnom Penh branch manager, says. "I like this new staff. I used to be one of them."

As organizational achievements grow, so do the challenges. The MIS still plagues the management of performance. Even though there is now a computer in every branch, the technology is new and requires proficiency in a foreign language. Managing multiple currencies, multiple products and managing the system itself continue to be struggles for ACLEDA staff. Advances are hard won.

The economic denominator driving the business is still unclear in 1996, but coming into focus, as ACLEDA staff begin to understand the business they want to build. The dramatic growth in response to customer preferences breeds a major liquidity crisis, where demand for credit outpaces supply. A waiting list develops, and with it concerns grow about increased delinquency that could be brought on by diminished customer confidence in the timeliness of ACLEDA's services and its very permanence as a business. Out of the first crisis of growth (which is discussed in the next chapter) ACLEDA's strategy to build capital, not to ration it, is reaffirmed.

ACLEDA's mantra changed as the organization changed. What seemed impossible only three years before was now clearly within reach. Aspirations aside, ACLEDA staff began to understand what it was that they really could be best at, not merely what they intended to achieve according to donor objectives. And, if the mantra at the beginning of the organization was: "If we don't work together, we will lose it," the second mantra became: "If we listen to the customers, we can build it." ACLEDA's drive for sustainability was based on their shared purpose to build a lasting organization, not the relentless pursuit of sustainability that many MFIs blame for poor planning, erratic growth and leaving poor borrowers behind.

As it ventured into the marketplace for the first time, what ACLEDA understood, as many fail to do, was that its customers, not its donors, were the future.

Lessons

Chapter 3 related discoveries about products and customers that were so essential to ACLEDA's early growth. As they began to manage a more sophisticated organization, ACLEDA staff also made important discoveries about transitions from an integrated project to an organization specialized in the delivery of micro and small enterprise credit. There are five broad lessons that deal with the donor relationship, specialization, technical assistance, the environment and the commercial approach to microfinance.

- First, independence from donors meant dependence on the market. A donor driven organization, by design or happenstance, has to overcome many obstacles to function effectively in the marketplace. The drive to secure additional funding comes with a price – it is often the independence to make business decisions. Once ACLEDA believed that continued donor support was not inevitable, and had the tools to project its own profitability, it then became a matter of putting the systems and people in place to achieve it.

  – The transition from a donor project to a local organization is not an automatic process. The donor, accustomed to being in control, may have difficulty in relinquishing it. Fostering local ownership of a process and a local institution is often more difficult for a donor to manage than a short-term credit project. It implies responsibility over the long term, conceding to decisions that may conflict with the donor's own, and the patience to wait out a steeper learning curve. But there are greater rewards, and the learning curve may not be as steep as the donor anticipates.

  – Performance indicators, even at the earliest stage of development, reflect management decisions. Management decisions are rooted in the values of those who make them. While it is tempting to think that values can be engineered, they fall outside the reach of donor policies and legislative mandates. Values refuse to be mandated; they are built through interaction with the environment and other people. This lesson is important for donors and quick fix campaigns that face the unfortunate dilemma of mandating values and tying them to markets. Remedies that include pushing increasingly demanding performance on weak project structures, or flooding a project with money in an attempt to purchase values the donor thinks are important, are likely to fail.

- The second broad lesson is one of specialization. ACLEDA's experience illustrates that specialization in microfinance from the start would have enabled ACLEDA to focus on what rapidly became the core business. Systems and procedures that were later developed led to dramatic increases in productivity, outreach and sustainability. There was a large, pent-up demand for credit in post-conflict Cambodia. Although business development training may have been a need, it was not effectively translated into a demand by self-employed Cambodians. The flexibility of the project design, the confidence the UNDP and the ILO showed in the Cambodian staff and their international experts, enabled ACLEDA to respond to the abundant demand for credit in the lower segments of the market.

- Accessing the right technical assistance is the third broad lesson. Although ACLEDA had its share of the wrong technical assistance, the right technical assistance "from the very inception" and throughout the formative years, was fortuitous. A flexible, ethical, non-bureaucratic approach to institutional development led to just that. The successful transition from an integrated project to an organization specialized in the delivery of micro and small enterprise credit, a weighty proposition, depended on an established sense of identity. Together ACLEDA staff and their technical advisors built the incentives and the capacity for project staff to manage their own change.

- The lack of government control and the absence of a strong banking system in the "half-war, half-peace" of Cambodia during most of the 1990s were factors that did not prohibit ACLEDA's early growth. The security situation certainly dictated where ACLEDA could and could not work; it also increased costs, affected performance and created an aura of apprehension pervasive to all operations. Improved security and consolidation in the banking system would later promote a stronger, deeper growth and reduce the external risks associated with it.

    The decimated human resource base of post-conflict Cambodia did not prevent a well managed and capably led local organization from emerging. The strategy called for selecting people with business insight and the desire to learn matched with abundant investment in staff development and trust in local management.

- Finally, ACLEDA's experience shows that a commercial approach to microfinance begins with a change in attitude about borrowers. They are no longer "takers" of benefits; they are "makers" of services and the prices they are willing to pay to buy them. Unless this fundamental shift in attitude takes place within an organization, the prospects for its future commercial growth are unattainable.

*   *   *

The transformation of microfinance organizations is often likened to the metamorphosis of butterflies. The metaphor is a compelling one, but the genesis of organizational transformation is the hard work that leads to growth; it sparks the conditions for organizational "build-up and breakthrough", the classic concept of organizational growth. With the achievements of growth, transformation depends on a gamble that the future will be better than the present. Between breakthrough and transformation there is an often tumultuous and surprising odyssey.

PART III:

Velocity

"Picture a huge, heavy flywheel – a massive metal disk mounted horizontally on an axle, about 30 feet in diameter, 2 feet thick and weighing about 5,000 pounds. Now imagine that your task is to get the flywheel rotating on the axle as fast and long as possible. Pushing with great effort, you get the flywheel to inch forward, moving imperceptibly at first ... [it] begins to move a bit faster ... you keep pushing in a persistent effort ... a consistent direction ... [it] builds up speed ... builds momentum ... faster with each turn ... then, at some point – break-through!"

Jim Collins, Good to Great: Why Some Companies Make the Leap... and Others Don't

"There are safety concerns associated with flywheels due to their high speed rotor and the possibility of it breaking loose and releasing all of its energy in an uncontrolled manner."

Jason Rayner, University of Price Edwards Island, Physics Department

Prologue

Kampong Cham – The Other Side of the River: 1996

Behind the fence, as far as the eye can see, the rubber plantations of Kampong Cham grace the entrance to the Provincial capital. They are neat and well kept, almost ghostly in the half-light of dusk. Their income has dwindled steadily since the mid-1960s. In 2003 they await the extensive research, privatization and investment that will revitalize contributions to the commodity market.[41] The plantations appear somber and quiet, a far contrast to the bustling ACLEDA branch where customers are making savings deposits, paying loan installments, and sending wire transfers to business associates and family members in distant parts of Cambodia.

Located in this fertile farmland, the bread basket of Cambodia, the Kampong Cham branch is one of the oldest branches in the ACLEDA network. In 1996, with the branch established and positioned for take-off, enthusiasm for expansion grew. Kampong Cham boasts 1,758 villages with almost 1.6 million inhabitants; the largest population of all of Cambodia's 18 Provinces.[42] And, a river runs through it.

Prospects for growth in 1996 were robust, if not bullish. In 1996 Kampong Cham was active ground for many donors; credit projects in the area flourished. Sar Roth, the former manager of the Kampong Cham branch, remembers the time with the same excitement and clarity as he remembers trading with his mother as they traveled by ox cart from house to house, or helping his father cut bamboo to build the houses of Kampong Cham. Many of those houses still stand today; some tip well above the water line in a normal year of inundations, others are located far from the water, accessible only by ox cart, by foot, by bicycle.

Sar Roth recalls the flourishing microcredit operations in Kampong Cham. "There were a lot of credit providers in the same area, but the demand was so great we agreed among the three major providers to work in specific areas. This was our thinking at the time," he says. In a large untapped market the first growth strategy for all microcredit providers was to divide market share by geographic

---

[41] Cambodia. Action Programme for the Development of Agricultural Sector in Cambodia 2001-2010 (Phnom Penh: Ministry of Agriculture Forestry and Fisheries, n.d) cited in Fertilizer Advisory Development and Information Network for Asia and the Pacific (FADINAP), Agro-Chemicals Report, Vol. II, No. 1 January-March 2002. (Bangkok: FADINAP, 2002), 29. Available from http://www.fadinap.org/cambodia.

[42] Prakas No 493 PRK, on Number, Name and Boundaries of the Communes and Sangkats of the Kingdom of Cambodia, 30 April 2001. (Phnom Penh: Ministry of Economy and Finance, 2001).

area – not to compete, but to cooperate. The artificial division would be short-lived. "We operated in the same districts for three years but gradually, as we all expanded, many of the villages overlapped," Sar Roth notes.

The first taste of competition emerged not out of market saturation, but from the very policies that were set to coordinate credit operations by location. PRASAC, a large integrated agriculture and rural development project, was the major provider of agricultural credit in Kampong Cham. ACLEDA and PRASAC had collaborated since 1995, first in the training of credit officers, and later through a management sub-contract. As they each rooted and developed, the differences between the PRASAC and ACLEDA loan products, policies and management widened. PRASAC's focus on disbursement and laxity about repayment frustrated ACLEDA loan officers, who were taught to emphasize the importance of analyzing repayment capacity and honoring the loan contract. With a different approach to development, PRASAC soon earned notoriety among many NGO credit operators. They were critical of its subsidized interest rates and lack of attention to repayment and sustainability.[43]

In 1996 a new initiative developed in Kampong Cham, following the rapid impact strategy at the heart of the PRASAC project. Increasing disbursement pressures on the under-spent USD 44 million project budget led to an interesting proposal: every family would receive a 50 dollar loan if they joined the village bank. The people of Kampong Cham delighted in this gift from a generous donor.

"Eventually, many people borrowed from both ACLEDA and PRASAC. It became increasingly difficult for people to repay loans from both organizations," recalls Sar Roth with some disappointment. "Some borrowers simply decided not to repay either loan. Some people repaid us because of the strong loan contract, and then they could not repay PRASAC." Sar Roth remembers complaints from the village chief. "'In ACLEDA it is not easy to get a loan,' he told me. 'ACLEDA requires repayment and gives a big headache to the village chiefs.'"

The number of villagers with bad loans grew over time, cultivating a serious repayment culture that was difficult to reverse. The culture of default affected

---

[43] For an interesting critique of the early PRASAC see a study carried out at the joint request of the European Union and the NGO Forum on Cambodia. The study notes "PRASAC – Programme de Réhabilitation et Appui au Secteur Agricole du Cambodge (Rehabilitation and Support Programme for the Agricultural Sector of Cambodia) – is a rural development programme focusing on irrigation schemes, domestic water supplies, credit schemes and small enterprise promotion. It comprises the major part of current European Community development assistance to Cambodia, with a budget of approximately USD 44 million. PRASAC displays serious weaknesses in design and planning, primarily because the developmental sectors in which it works are not amenable to a 'rapid impact' approach. The sustainability of its programme is jeopardized both by the uncertainties over PRASAC's future after June 1997, and lack of clarity surrounding the institutions PRASAC is trying to promote. These problems are particularly acute in the credit sector." Chris Dammers, et al., Differing Approaches to Development Assistance in Cambodia: NGOs and the European Commission (Phnom Penh: NGO Forum on Cambodia, August 1996)

ACLEDA's current loan customers, as well as prospects for identifying new borrowers. "It became so difficult we couldn't move," recalls Sar Roth. "In some areas we failed completely. We decided we would have to leave those areas, and work where no one yet operated, where there were fewer people. Our strategy at the time was to collect the debt we could, finish in the overlapping districts and open our branch on the other side of the river."

But some people wanted to continue to borrow. They wanted to borrow more than 50 dollars and they wanted a service that would be there whenever they wanted it. Recapturing the market was a slow, painstaking process, as Sar Roth remembers:

> *"We held discussions with each borrower, explaining that if they repaid all their debts, they could borrow from ACLEDA. If they continued to repay on time, respecting the loan contract, they could borrow more than once and eventually for larger amounts. At first they didn't believe us. We were also very careful with loan approval – only those with no outstanding debts and current repayment capacity would be approved."*

> *"We started slowly, with two or three people at a time. As the others saw, many repaid their loans to PRASAC to become ACLEDA customers."*

In areas with large default and continued subsidized lending practices, ACLEDA had no choice but to leave, returning only to collect bad debt. "We started in a new market," Sar Roth notes, "increasing our costs and leaving people behind. But we didn't leave them completely. Many people followed us across the river."

Throughout 1996 and 1997, following the USD 50 loan distribution, ACLEDA's Kampong Cham branch experienced high delinquency. The on-time repayment rate for micro loans dipped to 76% from monthly average on-time repayment rates of 97% during the prior 12-month period.[44] Eventually, in 1998, 5.60% of the micro loan portfolio was written off. The costs of branch relocation added to the default rates were estimated to have cost ACLEDA over USD 150,000[45] – a little over 40% of the value of the portfolio outstanding in the Kampong Cham branch at the end of 1996, and about half of the total outstanding portfolio of the PRASAC Kampong Cham branch at the end of 2002.[46]

Today the ACLEDA Kampong Cham branch has fostered 14 district offices and village service posts on both sides of the river. The quality of the portfolio, its size

---

[44] ACLEDA used two formulae to measure repayment rates during this period. The on-time repayment: amounts paid on time/amounts falling due for the first time; and a cumulative collection rate: amounts received since the branch began/all repayments that had fallen due by the date of measurement.

[45] Peter Kooi, interview by author.

[46] ACLEDA Kampong Chan branch portfolio report end of June 1996 and PRASAC audited financial statements of 2002.

and diversification made it one of the outstanding branches in ACLEDA's 2003 line-up.[47] And PRASAC? In 2002 PRASAC created the PRASAC Credit Association. Registered with the Central Bank, the association aims "to create sustainable access to financial services for rural communities and microenterprises."[48] Unlike its predecessor, the PRASAC Credit Association is no longer the unfair competitor of ACLEDA, but an ACLEDA Bank customer.

*   *   *

In post-conflict Cambodia, many credit operations relaxed repayment requirements and offered subsidized loans. The landscape featured donor-sponsored government projects where low portfolio quality was the norm, and large integrated development projects with credit components, where other activities were viewed as more important than the professional delivery of financial services. "Post-conflict environments draw out the charity of many donors," notes Peter Kooi. "This is understandable in an environment where there is so much suffering; it is difficult to appear impervious to it."

Heated debates about subsidy, common in the offices of Paris, Brussels and Washington D.C., played out in rice fields and small shops of Kampong Cham. As operational differences and mentalities collided, friendly agreements to divide areas of operation fell victim to a widening gulf in views about subsidy and sustainability.

The subsidy debate is essentially one about vision. The farsighted perspective looks toward a future where a microfinance operation can provide access to financial services to as many people as possible over the long-term. Proponents of this view argue that people pay for a service they value. The near-sighted perspective clings to the idea that distribution of resources to as many people as possible in the shortest amount of time – whether the resource is a cow or a bag of seed, or a loan – will have immediate impact on the lives of poor people. Proponents of this view often think that people must pay something for the gift, otherwise they won't appreciate it and somehow they value it less. It is hard to imagine that a poor family in post-conflict Cambodia would place little value on a gift of USD 50. In essence, PRASAC's early strategy was correct in one sense: people did value the fifty dollars. But why a loan was chosen instead of the gift it was intended to be is still a mystery.

In Channy is somewhat philosophical about the practice of lending and the people that do it. He explains that some people let their emotions cloud their reason. "Many people cannot deal with delinquent borrowers. I once worked with a UNV technical advisor, whom I respected very much. She liked working in the

---

[47] As of December 2004, the Kampong Cham branch had an outstanding portfolio of USD 5.5 million with 11,719 active borrowers. The portfolio at risk greater than 30 days was 1%. The yearly write off rate was 0.19%. ACLEDA Credit Control Report, December 2004.

[48] PRASAC Audit Report. 2002.

field, the contact with the people. Everyone liked her. But when she went with us to visit delinquent borrowers, she would feel so sorry. She would take out her money and give it to them to pay the loan. We finally said to each other, "Don't take her with you when you visit the customers. People get confused."

The first crisis of growth was externally stimulated. But this was not the only crisis that either the Kampong Cham branch or ACLEDA as a growing institution would experience. Others would follow — some would be brought forth by factors outside the organization's control; but others would emerge from within.

During this period of rapid growth ACLEDA learned how to combine a customer orientation that would produce expansive growth with risk management techniques that would produce sustainable growth. And if the mantra during the previous period was, "If we listen to customers, we can build it", the mantra during the growth period added the corollary: "If we build the systems, we can sustain it."

CHAPTER 6

Confidence: The "Flywheel" Turns

Elusive growth, coveted growth. Mystical, magical, visionary growth. The momentum, the build-up, the break-through. The advancement, the achievement, the success. Growth!

Rapid growth of the type ACLEDA experienced was not an automatic process, nor one without risk. It was based on a balancing act, balancing the commercial orientation of putting the customer first with a strong aptitude for risk management. Sustainable growth is based on the daily tasks of constructing systems, organizing and re-organizing departments, writing and tearing up policies, accepting changes that limit authority and enhance oversight, hiring, training and firing staff.

Sustainable growth has incessant demands; it requires difficult management decisions and the will to create and destroy systems that no longer fit the magnitude of the operation. In ACLEDA's case, sustainable growth mocked the retreat across the river; later, it summoned the staff to confront the brutal facts about their own organization.[49] The stories of sustainable growth are the less glorious and heart-warming tales of putting bricks and mortar in place. The bricks and mortar of institutional infrastructure may not be glamorous, but they yield important lessons. They are, after all, the foundations of growth.[50]

There were two distinct phases of growth in ACLEDA's transition from a multisectoral NGO to an organization specialized in the delivery of microfinance. Both of them were fueled by increasing capacity to manage the institution. The first growth stage 1996-1997 enabled the organization to grow bigger; it was based on the clear strategic focus of becoming a dedicated microfinance institution. Clarity of purpose freed the organization to develop along one track as it came to the crossroads; it prompted ACLEDA to build a structure of reasonable soundness in support of that purpose.

The second stage enabled the organization to grow better, deeper; it fused the customer orientation, established in the first stage, with the strengthening of risk management systems throughout the organization. The leap between the first and the second stage of growth called for a recognition that the track they built may have been secure enough for the passing of a motorcycle or an ox cart, but would not support a bullet train.

---

[49] Jim Collins coined the term "confronting the brutal facts" in Good To Great (2001).

[50] Craig Churchill's *Managing Growth: The Organizational Architecture of Microfinance Institutions* (Bethesda, Md: Development Alternatives Inc., May 1997) is an often overlooked, but valuable paper on microfinance organizational development and change.

Nowhere more than at branch level can one see these patterns of growth and how sensitive a lending operation is to external events and internal policies. This chapter explores the phenomena of ACLEDA's expansive growth period, telling the stories of branches in crisis and the radical overhaul of organization-wide systems that clamored for attention. It discusses the fund raising strategies, the adequacy of systems, and difficult decisions that were made by the people who managed the organization.

The following chapter places ACLEDA in the dynamic Cambodian context. It examines the policies and preferences of leaders in national government and donors that supported microfinance. The chronicle centers on what they were thinking about microfinance at the time, how that thinking evolved, and why the evolution was important for building an inclusive financial sector in Cambodia.

Capacity to Expand: The First Growth Period – Bigger, 1995-1997

ACLEDA's growth during the mid-1990s owed much of its momentum to Cambodia's small and microentrepreneurs. The early ACLEDA became adept in providing products with market appeal and a service valued by customers. Fundamental pieces were in place as a platform, but not as a guarantee of future growth. As illustrated in Figure 6.1, the platform for growth established itself in sequential steps: a collective commitment to the organization's values, attitudes on how to run the business that were consistent with those values, a clear focus on the core business, and establishing the basic systems that would support the operation consistent with its values and core business vision.

The progressive path to growth, as shown in Figure 6.1, began with a deep understanding of customers' preferences about products and services. Growth broadened with investment in human and physical infrastructure that enabled future expansion. It accelerated with an increase in physical and financial productivity and an interest rate policy that covered the costs of lending. ACLEDA's plans targeted building up equity and expanding sources of funds by leveraging equity.

One of the basic assumptions during the early period, which later proved to be correct, was that attracting additional capital would depend more on the organization's capacity to manage sustainable business operations than to disburse massive amounts of credit following a quick impact strategy. ACLEDA followed a long-term strategy based on the dictum "capacity leads, capital follows". The illustration below, Figure 6.1, shows the early platform for growth and the progressive steps that enabled it.

With a promising base for growth established, growth indeed followed. The total active portfolio increased sevenfold from USD 351,000 at the end of 1994 to USD 2.5 million by the end of 1996. The portfolio doubled each year for the next two years, reaching the heady figure of USD 15.5 million by late 2000 when

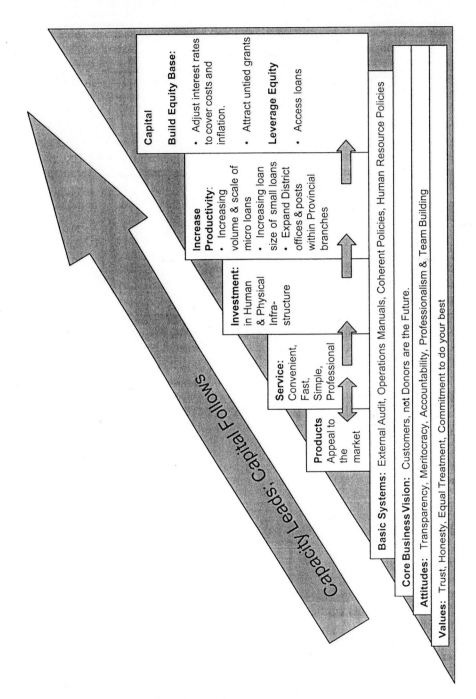

Figure 6.1. The Early Platform for Growth

Table 6.1. Growth in Borrowers and Portfolio, 1993 – 2000

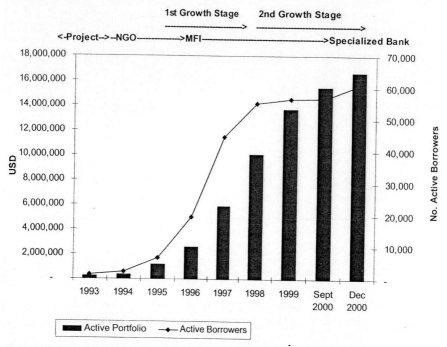

Source: ACLEDA Portfolio Reports and Audited Financial Statements, 1993 – 2000.

ACLEDA transformed into a specialized bank licensed by the National Bank of Cambodia. (See Table 6.1 for growth trends.) The intervening years called for the skilled work of technicians and the deftness of management as ACLEDA weighed and negotiated each node of an increasingly complex matrix of growth.

The Great Liquidity Crisis: 1996

In 1996 a liquidity crisis developed as ACLEDA's business expanded much more rapidly than the capital available to finance the growing portfolio. As waiting lists to borrow grew to three months and then to six months, ACLEDA staff worried that waning customer confidence in their ability to continue borrowing would fuel delinquency.

With little excess liquidity in any branch, and the near impossibility of inter-branch cash transfers over dangerous roads, ACLEDA began to disburse only as much as it collected daily from borrowers making installment payments in each branch. There was no other choice. ACLEDA's expectations of continued expansion were sorely dashed as portfolio growth rates, which hit an all-time high mid-year, decreased throughout the last seven months of 1996. Lending capital for small enterprise loans – the largest share of the portfolio – decreased most.[51] (See Table 6.2 for trends during the year.) Cash management and scrutinizing daily balances became a priority in each branch. A liquidity crisis is not perhaps the best inspiration for laying a brick, but it did serve as a strong foundation for the fundamental shift from disbursing loans to managing a business, a business that would falter if a solution was not quickly found.

As constraints on capital affected ACLEDA's other mature branches, the Kampong Cham branch re-established itself on the other side of the river. Other recently opened branches were also ready to expand operations – Kampot, Takeo, Sihanoukville, and Pursat. Plans were on the drawing board to open new branches in Kampong Speu and Kampong Thom; plans that would have to be put on hold until additional funding could be found.

Liquidity Crisis into Solid Plans: Lessons

When a growing microfinance institution confronts a liquidity crisis, certain facts become clear. First, there is never enough money to serve current commitments and start new ventures. Second, the funds that are most stable and most easily controlled are retained earnings. Third, the surest way to preserve current capital is to control delinquency and default. And finally, reliance on donors is not an effective long-term strategy to finance growth.

Table 6.2. Monthly Disbursements in 5 Mature Branches

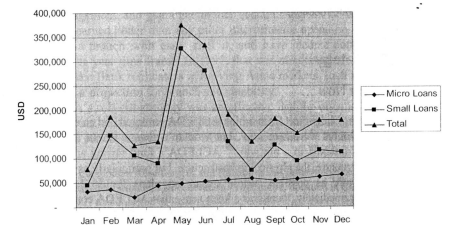

Source: ACLEDA Branch Portfolio Reports, 1996

---

[51] Portfolio growth statistics are for ACLEDA's mature branches that had been operating since 1993. The branches include Battambang, Banteay Meanchey, Kampong Cham, Phnom Penh, and Siem Reap. Source: ACLEDA monthly portfolio reports at the branch level for small and micro loans, 1996.

What all these facts led ACLEDA to discover was that the basic systems that were enough to spark growth – even fuel it – fell short of ensuring sustainable growth. Business planning would have to complement strategic planning. Interest rates needed to reflect the full cost of lending to prevent operational losses as well as to contribute to building an equity base. Costs would have to be contained just at the moment when fixed costs, apparently not related to the direct production of income, such as more sophisticated systems, would increase. Information technology and an MIS would need to be developed that could provide timely information for decision making to management at all levels of the organization. The information systems created in the past responded to ACLEDA's donors' concerns about accountability to their constituents; they were not appropriate for managing a stable business operation with designs on increasing efficiency. Nor were the systems proficient at anticipating cash flow projections required for growth; they did little to send an early warning for the great liquidity crisis of 1996.

Now that the organization had the capacity to grow, there was an acute awareness that capital constrained the operations. As a donor dependent organization with no option to borrow on the local market, ACLEDA had little choice but to try to find donors who could provide capital untied to specific geographical areas or target groups. Throughout the mid-1990s ACLEDA raised donor funds on a branch-by-branch basis. This strategy allowed individual branches to prosper, but promoted uneven organizational growth and a lumpy cost structure as expansion won favor over consolidation. If the strategy continued, it would promote a mismatch of capital available to the demand in the area. Re-thinking the future, ACLEDA sought donors who would invest in the institution and the dream of what ACLEDA could become.

Funding Strategy

They Are Here Now ...

From the beginning, the project from which ACLEDA emerged had an opportunistic donor strategy. Donors were here now, but wouldn't always be. In fact in 1993, donors were in Cambodia in a big way.[52] ACLEDA's fund raising appeal was to finance the infrastructure, the physical infrastructure, but particularly as much of the human infrastructure as possible. While expansion plans for 15 LEDAs were scrapped almost immediately, there was a keen sense that ACLEDA could be first to

---

[52] At its peak UNTAC had a budget of USD 1.8 billion. Donor pledges to Cambodia from 1992 to 1995 were USD 2.29 billion. Disbursements represented only 61% of total pledges at some USD 1.394 billion. Grant Curtis. *Cambodia Reborn?: The Transition to Democracy and Development* (Washington, D.C.: Brooking Institution Press, 1998): 77-78. UNDP in Cambodia had a budget of USD 105 million from 1992-1996. Sam Barnes and Alain Retiere, *Peace Building from the Ground Up: A Case Study of UNDP's CARERE Programme in Cambodia 1991-2000* (Phnom Penh: UNDP/Cambodia, March 2001), 10.

get a grip on the market and deploy a first rate team. Quite ingenious for the time, ACLEDA developed a "branch for sale" strategy and marketed it widely to donors and integrated development projects in Cambodia.

Branch for Sale

From 1994 to 1996, with institutional funding secure through the ILO/UNDP project, financed by the Government of the Netherlands, ACLEDA developed a complementary donor strategy. The basic idea was to sell branch locations in a donor's area development project. It was an attractive offer for large integrated development projects like CARERE and UNFPA; they could focus on their objectives to build local infrastructure and provide health services.[53]

Donors with an interest in a particular geographical area sought out ACLEDA to open credit operations to bring peace and prosperity to small farmers and female-headed households in areas not completely abandoned by the Khmer Rouge. Royal Dutch Shell financed the set-up of the Sihanoukville branch; they aimed to address the problem that small businesses needed working capital to expand and consume more fuel. Smaller NGOs with specialties outside of credit found the idea compelling as well; they could employ their own scarce resources exclusively in their areas of expertise without adding a burdensome credit component.

So successful was the "branch for sale" strategy that from 1994-1997 ACLEDA had as many as 22 donors, many of whom funded, in small amounts, specific branches, products and the delivery of services to special target groups.

The formula was straightforward: ACLEDA would open a branch, offer professional management, and guarantee branch sustainability. In the early growth stage, ACLEDA learned better than any other microfinance operation in Cambodia how to roll out a branch with ease, staff it, and have income contributing to costs within a three-year time frame. In 1997, that was almost unheard of in Cambodia. Even Grameen Bank replicators in thriving Asian markets, such as the Philippines, had a 10-year projection for branch sustainability.

ACLEDA's roll-out strategy was so effective that the organization covered all of its recurrent costs with operational income by the end of 1997, and that was in a growth period where 21 new offices were opened.[54] While costs of the new

---

[53] CARERE, Cambodian Resettlement and Rehabilitation Programme, and later re-named the Cambodian Rehabilitation and Regeneration Programme, operated in Cambodia from 1992-2000. CARERE was engaged in local economic development and building local governance systems. It supported the expansion of ACLEDA's district branch network from 1994-1996. CARERE, now institutionalized as the government's Seila Program, continues work in building local governance in Cambodia to this day. UNFPA, United Nations Population Fund, opened a permanent office in Cambodia in 1994, and provided funding to ACLEDA in 1996 and 1997.

[54] The calculation includes financial costs and all operational costs, with the exception of currency loss, and a special provision expense for doubtful accounts ACLEDA maintained with Cambodia Farmers' Bank. The bank ceased operations in 1997; its license was suspended by the National Bank of Cambodia. The USD 267,932 ACLEDA held on account was never recovered.

openings were significant, ACLEDA borrowed a concept from the Bank Rakyat Indonesia and opened district offices and posts that fell under the management of Provincial branches. This allowed deeper expansion into the rural areas and small towns, without the considerable investment in fixed costs that a new full-fledged Provincial branch would require.

In theory, the branch for sale fund-raising strategy made sense; practice proved a bit more difficult. Some initiatives succumbed to politics, as local authorities were reluctant to relinquish decision-making power over disbursing small amounts of money to local constituents. Other branch locations that were inspired by a donor's special interest in an area where there was no market continued to languish without a market; those offices were subsequently closed. Some initiatives fell victim to issues of control, such as the contract with PRASAC. The contract came to an end when a proposal called for a merger and co-management of the institutions, under the name ACLEDA PRASAC. The proposal was rejected by the closely held and independent ACLEDA.

Lastly, as In Channy notes, the branch for sale strategy may have served them well in raising funds for an NGO operation, and a waiting list of customers may have appealed to donors who wanted to place funds quickly, but this was not a prudent way to manage a financial institution.

... And One Day They Will Leave

Prescient, ACLEDA knew that donors would leave one day. This insight based on the UNTAC experience in 1993 proved to be correct.. In 1997, after the bloody coup that toppled the splintered coalition government, many donors left Cambodia. This quick closure was not lost on ACLEDA. The idea that donor money is unreliable, perhaps doubted by many at the time, once proven true yet again, added fuel to the quest for sustainability. The interest rate hike discussed in the strategic plan of 1996 almost seemed too low. The aim was now to become sustainable quickly, to become more efficient, to become commercial and independent of donor funding. The real danger of losing what they had built loomed large.

The Risk Takers: A New Round of Donors

In 1996 three donors were on the horizon — Sida, KfW and USAID. Each of these donors shared ACLEDA's new perspective of an increasingly commercial approach to microfinance, and each of them believed in an institutional rather than a project approach to microfinance. What distinguished these donors from others at the time is that they recognized they were investing in the future of a microfinance institution, not merely supporting a project's list of activities that would have a short-term impact at the beneficiary level. In 1996 they were all ahead of their time.

What made them different? First, they recognized that they could act as good investors, but they would be poor implementers. They understood that the institutional approach rested on identifying an organization with potential and supporting it to reach its own goals, goals that were compatible with their own. Secondly, they recognized that as investors, the organization's business plan was of primary importance; they did not seek to design a project for the organization to carry out, nor did they seek to influence operations with respect to clients, products, or areas of service. Each of them had skilled staff, knowledgeable about microfinance. Perhaps most importantly, their institutional mandates would not compromise a technical approach in favor of a political one.

Three donors played important roles in easing the capital constraints, with a mix of different instruments. Sida's contribution is notable for being the first significant non-designated grant, one that contributed to building equity; it was not targeted to geographical areas, specific branches or target beneficiaries. Matching equity with liabilities, KfW – acting on behalf of the German Federal Ministry for Economic Cooperation and Development (BMZ) – approved a loan for DEM 5 million (USD 2.8 million) which leveraged ACLEDA's equity for the first time. USAID provided a small grant to ease the liquidity crisis.

Sida's support of the early ACLEDA operation was a departure from the earmarking of the past. Sven Svensson recalls Sida's equity grant as a calculated risk that fit Sida's rural development policies and responded to a great need for a bank that supported Cambodia's micro and small entrepreneurs. "We chose not to earmark geographical areas or clients. We did not decide on the borrowers; ACLEDA did. We didn't analyze the individual enterprises they supported; ACLEDA did. If we approved of the general idea of the organization, the business plan and the organization's management, why not support the institution's work? We looked at the overall operation, and were confident that we could expect the work of the organization to continue without earmarking. We analyzed the overall portfolio and the policy of the bank. Our monitoring was then focused on institutional performance, not just one activity."

What KfW's project manager, Dr. Joachim Trede, saw in ACLEDA was "a diamond in a desert of stones". "I could not understand why others could not see it at the time," notes Dr. Trede. "To me it was very obvious. There was a history of transparency, external audits, a strong management team, and a robust market apparent in the waiting list of customers that ACLEDA could not fulfill."

KfW recently had started operations in Cambodia and was looking for projects with the capacity to support sustainable development and to alleviate poverty. They searched for an institution with the capacity to manage significant funding, as KfW provides funds, not stand-alone technical assistance. From KfW's perspective, the continuity of expert technical assistance and the capacity of the institution to manage the loan matched KfW's instruments and investment philosophy.

Toni Ferrera, USAID's Project Officer, saw ACLEDA in a similar light, but found a different problem. In 1996, USAID in Cambodia supported local NGOs under umbrella grants to international NGOs. The ACLEDA grant would be different; a direct relationship with USAID would be established. The small amount of money, USD 250,000 to ease the liquidity crisis, created a double bind. Ms. Ferrara recalls that the small grant was attractive for a new relationship with a local NGO, and USAID's Microenterprise Development Office could explain in clear, technical terms why such a small amount of money would back big potential in building the financial system. She also recalls the imperatives of the time:

> *"We were under such pressure to support a variety of projects in post-conflict Cambodia, with a limited staff who had no expertise in supporting the development of financial institutions. There was resistance to adding to the management burden, especially for such a small grant that would require special arrangements. It was clear for ACLEDA there would be no value added through an umbrella arrangement. But there would be hoops to jump through, a pre-award audit, an opinion on registration with USAID, procedures to establish pre-eminent capacity. We called on the services of contract officers, technical assistance from the Microenterprise Development Office, USAID's staff training program in microfinance, lawyers and auditors to make this happen."*

Risk-taking in a donor agency is a by-product of procedure, policies and mind-set. Risks can be mitigated by the presence of other donors and the confidence the local organization inspires, but ultimately the flexibility of a donor to respond depends on its way of doing business and mind-set. There can be a trade-off between additional management burdens in the short term, and responding flexibly to what is appropriate for the local organization. USAID directed existing capacity to finding new solutions; it responded flexibly with changes in instruments that otherwise would have hindered an appropriate response to ACLEDA's stage of growth.

Why did they do it? "Working in Cambodia made you want to do something positive for the future. The Cambodians who worked hard for a better future made you want to do it," says Toni Ferrara. "ACLEDA had the potential to grow and make a significant contribution to the way the financial sector operated; one that included poor and low-income people. Our main thinking at the time was: 'This would be good for Cambodia', not why we couldn't do it."

Sven Svensson balanced the risks of the environment with the potential for the future. He notes that the talks about MFI mergers with a national development bank made for a risky environment; and the financial robustness of any microfinance operation might decrease in a fragile and unpredictable economy for small and microenterprises. What was appealing to Sida was the potential for the future of Cambodia's entrepreneurs. "The idea that the funding would multiply, maximizing the long-term development effects was positive," he notes. "It mobilized the energy of the people; they put in time, work and inventiveness. The clients were convinced of supporting the bank; we supported the initiatives of the people in the context."

Joachim Trede focused on the soundness of the institution, looking beyond the financial projections, articulating the idea that financial performance is a function of institutional strength, not the other way around. "It was the expression of the general attitude of the institution, the professional staff, the commitment, the competence and integrity you could see there. You can always ask for more figures, statistics and projections, which ACLEDA had ... but at a certain point, you have to believe."

Charity oriented? Not really. Compassionate, yes. At some fundamental level each of these donors believed in what ACLEDA could accomplish for the people of Cambodia; they bought into the dream of ACLEDA. And they, like ACLEDA, bought into it for the long-term. In 1999 KfW would make a second soft loan, through the government of Cambodia. The Sida equity capital would be preserved and grow within the institution, just as Sven Svensson predicted. And USAID together with UNDP and the Mekong Project Development Facility would pull together a transformation project based on ACLEDA's business plan in 1998.

The new donors invested in ACLEDA as an institution. They held out the tempting promise of fulfilling ACLEDA's objective – to become a sustainable microfinance organization serving poor and low-income Cambodian entrepreneurs.

The three years from the arrival of the new round of donors to their departure in 2000 ushered in a new era for ACLEDA – the era of enthusiasm for building better systems. The enthusiasm was not misplaced; every system needed improvement.

A PC in Every Branch

"Peter created a small program – "Int-clac"– that was very helpful between the no records period and the Quick Books period." Chhay Soeun, Finance Department Manager

When Terry Mach arrived at ACLEDA in 1995, each of ACLEDA's branches had an old desk-top computer. One day of the month the computer was lavished with attention as each staff member fought for a turn to pound out the monthly report; on the other 29 days it suffered from neglect.

Terry Mach's journey back to his homeland took 13 years, transits through refugee and repatriation centers in Thailand, a stiff climb through Australia's educational system, and a brief foray into the job markets in Singapore. A bright young man with a background in accounting, statistics and computer programming, Terry fell hard in the job market in the early 1990s that saw the retrenchment of the computer industry and veterans in the field scrambling for positions.

In 1992 he returned to Cambodia, enticed by a job offer with the ILO vocational education program. "I didn't know what to expect. I was too young to remember much of Cambodia. But I remember my first days back. You could hear mines exploding. You could hear shots in the night. It was still quite risky."

The MIS had plagued ACLEDA's operation for years; working on one design or another they always came up short. But rapid growth made computerization imperative; it was becoming increasingly difficult to manage the growing operation. "I used to see Terry frequently, dusting off computer key boards at the ILO Vocational Education Programme office," says Peter Kooi. "We needed help with the computerization of ACLEDA. I knew he was knowledgeable and well prepared, but I never suspected he was such a whiz kid." Terry was recruited to develop a computerized MIS system. Almost an outsider, he spoke Khmer with an accent, and had forgotten how to write the script.

Terry quickly focused in on designing a system without the benefit of having personally done the prior analysis. "I was concerned about the dust, the humidity, the airflow, purchasing the right hardware, designing the software, writing the program and testing it with those who would use it. ... And, I kept asking for more money. If you prepare for computerization, you have to be prepared to spend money."

More money was not something management wanted to hear at a time when controlling costs was a priority.

"You know, change is a scary thing," says Terry. "It creates more work initially. People have to change their way of doing things, their way of managing things. No one saw the benefit at the time, only the problems. And there were so many problems."

Quick Books, the program in use, did not track multiple currencies or the multiple products that were the core of ACLEDA's daily business. Several branches regularly conducted business in three currencies. The solution at the time, one which irritated the young computer professional, was to have one branch operating five different programs – one to run each of the products and currencies, and one to consolidate the manual currency conversions.

But progress was slow. Finally, after too long a time with no apparent results, management held a meeting to cancel Terry's contract. The problems with the system multiplied at a pace to match the costs. Staff complained, management was doubtful; Terry felt adrift, saddled with a system analysis that he didn't perform. Terry remembers management asking, "Is it a user problem, a system problem, a training problem, or a Terry problem?" "Peter convinced them to give me three more months to solve the problems," says Terry. "I knew I had to work out the bugs."

Taking his key from management, Terry kept asking himself the question: "Is it a user problem or a program problem?" "I knew I had to change the program or the user, if I kept the user I would be forced to change the program; if I kept the program I would be forced to change the user. I finally met it in the middle. I changed the program and the user."

The main problem Terry confronted was trying to develop the information management system, improve it, and computerize it at the same time. "If you focus on requirements of the system first, then you can make the improvements. Some of the improvements were practical solutions, for example the calculation of the interest rate. But most of the problems required management solutions; the design had to focus on the way the system inter-acted with the business." The

ACLEDA program in use was statistical, not financial. "What we needed was a system that managed the loan from the beginning to the end. We needed to develop a new system, not improve the existing one."

What does management need? "Management needs accurate figures, fast figures," says Terry, "but the program was centralized, requiring data input at too many levels. It was not fast, it was inefficient, and there were too many mistakes." Finally he thought, "If things happen at the branch, let the system operate at the branch."

"One thing I knew, and on the theory that that was right, the system should have minimal requirements for data input at headquarters. I didn't know what the headquarters needed at first, but I knew if I got the branches right, it would be okay. The work happened there; the design of the system had to be done there."

By the end of 1996, half the ACLEDA operation was computerized. "It was very messy and massive," recalls Terry. But with the first half completed and operating relatively smoothly, the Click Loans program, designed by Terry Mach, provided management with fast accurate information for the first time in ACLEDA's history. Interest in computerizing the other half of the operation was high, and a support team was hired.

"That was when I did a systems analysis," recalls Terry. "I really understood how to standardize the system to reflect requirements of the entire organization. I still had problems, but I knew what the problems would be." By early 1997, the Click Loans program was finalized and gradually becoming operational throughout the organization.

Terry designed a homegrown system. "It was a *bottom-up approach*," he says, "not *outside-in* and because of that there are experienced people in every branch. We rationalized the reporting system and organized those who did it. We increased productivity; the credit officers could spend time concentrating on their customers, not reporting, or making calculations. Because of the program, we could recruit credit officers who didn't need to be mathematical experts, but people who were good with people. Accountants made fewer mistakes. As the points of data entry decreased, systemic error was easier to detect and random error decreased. Mistakes were caught quickly, problems did not develop undetected. Management got accurate information, fast information. They could pay attention to running the business, not correcting errors."

Terry went on to design other systems, payroll systems, Click Savings – the counterpart to Click Loans, staff administrative systems, and branch reporting systems as he moved steadily, if not so quickly at first, to bring ACLEDA from a monthly reporting system to a daily one.

The Click Loans and Click Savings programs were designed for speed and accuracy, not for security, as the ACLEDA Bank's GLOBUS system is today. GLOBUS will replace Click Loans and Click Savings as each branch comes online. Regrets? Not in the least. "Information technology leads the business," says Terry. "It changes the thinking, and then the way the business operates changes. Technicalities are removed, and people can start thinking about the business, not the calculations. Productivity increases, new products are possible. This is positive for staff, management, the organization and the customers."

When Terry Mach landed in Australia in 1981 he was a sixteen-year-old with third grade education. He could barely speak English, and had forgotten how to write in Khmer; a teenager without a country walking in a strange new land. His age determined the grade he would attend in the Australian school system. Terry would be selected for grade 12. He recalls his thinking about this dubious honor:

> *"I had three years of education before I left Cambodia, not the best education, and nothing in between. I begged them not to put me in grade 12, otherwise I knew I wouldn't make it ... School was difficult for all of us Asian kids. The change was difficult. We weren't accepted. We couldn't cope with it; and most of us gave up. All the kids I knew quit school."*

And how did he get through? "I just tried harder than everybody else."

And Now, It's a Calf

The short foray into neighborhood banking provided an important lesson in risk management: that creating too many products too soon was riskier than creating one product too late. During the period of growth, ACLEDA focused on two products, the solidarity loan with a group guarantee, and the individual loan for small businesses backed by collateral. Tweaking core products became necessary as experience with borrower behavior led to another advance in balancing customer orientation with risk management.

From the outset ACLEDA provided small business loans to individuals. The loan was disbursed in US dollars and backed by collateral or a third party guarantee. With a generous collateral policy, ACLEDA accepted traditional forms of collateral, such as land as well as assets purchased by the loan, equipment, or any item of value, including livestock.

Channy tells the story of the cow that found the fountain of youth:

> *"One of our borrowers applied for a loan to purchase a cow. He soon fell delinquent on his monthly payments. Every time we visited him, the cow got smaller and smaller, until one day, when we went to get the cow, it had become a calf. Finally, when we confiscated 200 ducks, the designated collateral on the loan, we knew we had to change our policy."*

Pattern Recognition

Sometimes, the origin of a crisis is not clear-cut between external causes and internal weaknesses. What is certain is that an external crisis uncovers underlying weakness in an organization. An external crisis presents opportunities for things to go wrong, and for people to take advantage of the situation.

In 1997 and throughout much of 1998, the Siem Reap branch was hard hit by the continuing battle between the Cambodian People's Party (CPP) and FUNCIN-PEC. The district office in Puok, difficult to reach in normal times, was completely cut off from the Provincial branch for almost 18 months.

"I saw a small mistake on a report, and I began to investigate," says Vann Saroeun, ACLEDA's long-time manager of the Siem Reap branch.

It was difficult to notice something odd in the behavior of the Siem Reap branch during the fighting of 1997. Many of the trends, though logical after analysis, at first appear as strange and unexpected trends. A sharp dip in on-time repayment almost immediately following the outbreak of the July 1997 war was expected. It was also not odd that the rural financial services would have a somewhat greater time lag for repayment performance to improve, as distance presented higher risks for travel.

What was unexpected, and illogical, at first was the number of high prepayments as people traveled to the branch to safeguard any cash from advancing troops. On reflection, that behavior appears eminently logical. But something else was clearly going on in the Puok district office. After record high disbursements, delinquency, almost negligible for years, began to soar. A reported 100 % repayment rate since the office's inception, dropped to 80 %. It wasn't only the total amount of delinquency that claimed attention, but the greater number of loans that had fallen into arrears, and the number of defaults recorded, a clear sign bucking the trend. What was also odd – a small mistake – was that a borrower, who was previously recorded as having repaid the loan, was now listed as a defaulter.

Vann Saroeun called in the internal audit department, headed by the intrepid Kim Sotheavy. Slight, mild-mannered and talkative, Kim Sotheavy has earned a reputation for fearless drive to uncover "odd trends". She holds an uncompromising position on fraud and corruption.

"The scheme got too big for them, and eventually they made a mistake," says Sotheavy. "This was a case of collusion among the three staff members in an isolated district office. It could have gone on for much longer, but the branch manager's diligence lead him to notice, and ask the internal audit team for help to investigate the office, and interview borrowers." That was a rare attitude in the early days, when most branch managers thought of the internal audit team as the police. What Vann Saroeun understood was that without the internal audit team he would lose control.

"When we arrived we closed the office and the safe. The office had reports that indicated cash balances, but the cash was not there. It took us almost a month to document the extent of the fraud. We interviewed every borrower, checked every receipt." Some borrowers had repaid their loans, but were listed as defaulters. Other borrowers simply didn't exist. Ghosts.

The fraud cost ACLEDA 49 million riel, USD 12,000. The jailed staff members paid a much higher price, and so did the Siem Reap Branch.

"They destroyed the whole team," says Vann Saroeun.

*   *   *

The internal audit department plays a pre-eminent role in risk management, although it is not always perceived as one of the most glorious departments in a banking institution, For the ACLEDA MFI, an NGO, this was a new step toward improving systems. The enthusiasm for such a systemic change was not shared by all ACLEDA staff. The change produced conflict with branch managers who until that time operated independently, often with a great deal of power.

As ACLEDA grew from a staff of 27 to a staff of over 1,000, and from 5 branches to 27, internal audit became a prominent feature on the organizational chart. The technology and the computerized MIS made pattern recognition possible within a short period of time. Financial audit, IT audit and operations audit are on the ACLEDA internal audit department's menu. Reporting directly to the Audit and Risk Committee of the Board, the internal audit department works together with each department — human resources, credit management, marketing, finance, treasury, the IT department and each branch in ACLEDA's network.

At the point in transition from the almost limitless authority of the branch managers to an organization-wide system to enhance overseeing and manage risk, the internal audit department had the utmost support of management. "At first we had to convince branch managers that we were not the police. We are not the police," says Sotheavy. "We work with branch managers to help solve problems, not make them. We help them maintain control. We come with evidence; we are clear, we are objective and we are independent. This protects them and the organization."

Vann Saroeun agrees.

Corruption!

The small pick-up truck loaded with goods weaves down the streets of Phnom Penh as if on a drunken lark. It speeds up, quickly makes a turn and disappears down a side street. The driver is not intoxicated. He is trying to avoid the police, who will charge him a tax. During the day he could be stopped five or six times. Each time he digs deeper into his pocket for the wad of 500 riel notes that he has prepared for his trip, then he tries his luck at the next intersection.

It is difficult to speak about corruption in any society. It makes people blush, it makes them angry. People in Cambodia speak about corruption with candor. As one observer of the scene put it, "the only thing that is transparent in Cambodia is corruption." A recent investment climate survey conducted by the World Bank noted, "Cambodian firms identify corruption as their leading constraint to the operation and growth of Cambodia."[55] "Cambodia's bribe tax is more than double

---

[55] A recent World Bank report notes, "Four-fifths of the private sector sampled acknowledges the necessity of paying bribes, and 71% of large firms report that these payments are frequent. The private sector estimates that unofficial payments cost firms an average of 5.2% of total sales revenue." World Bank. *Cambodia: Seizing the Global Opportunity: Investment Climate Assessment and Reform Strategy for Cambodia* (Washington, D.C.: World Bank, August 2004), 14.

that found in a parallel investment climate survey in Bangladesh, which rated last in the 2002 Transparency International Corruption Perceptions index of 102 countries."[56] The results of a national survey on public attitudes towards corruption reported that "84 % of Cambodians felt bribery is the normal way of doing things, 58 % did not think that corruption makes things run smoothly, some 90 % believe that corruption hinders national development, and a massive 98 % believe that ending corruption is important." Equally striking, 75 % of those surveyed felt that paying a bribe was just as wrong as asking for a bribe.[57]

In a 1995 speech at a conference on Corruption and its Impact on National Reconstruction and Reconciliation, Finance Minister Keat Chhon estimated that the state was losing up to USD 100 million a year to corruption, primarily because of illegal logging, rubber exportation and fishing.[58] The price of low-level corruption, undocumented and underestimated, must be more.

On any one day the "cost of doing business" for a small trader could easily amount to 1 % of a USD 100 loan, a phenomenal amount when compared with the interest rates charged by any MFI in Cambodia, or by moneylenders who are so often reviled. School children regularly pay teachers to pass them, even when their grades merit advancement. Government officials ask their staff to purchase televisions for them as gifts. Savers who make deposits in banking institutions expect to pay a commission to the teller for the safe deposit of their money. Borrowers often pay extra fees to village chiefs to sign the documents for their loans; some microcredit organizations have institutionalized this practice so that the chiefs automatically get the fee, and become an integral part of running the village bank.

Piv Thary, the cashier in Prey Veng branch, tells a story of customers expecting to pay extra fees despite their feelings that paying a bribe may be just as wrong as asking for one. "They come with small deposits, or to repay their loans, and they have an extra amount. They push the notes forward, saying 'this is for you, do I owe more?'"

"I tell them, 'no this is your money. Would you like to deposit that amount too?'" The customers are astounded. They think, she made a mistake, but they come back, and deposit more.

---

[56] A World Bank Group Consultation Summary in 2004, *Towards a Private Sector Development Strategy for Cambodia: Investment Climate Assessment* (World Bank, International Finance Corporation, Mekong Project Development Facility and Public-Private Infrastructure Advisory Facility, n.d):5-6. The summary notes a rough estimate of bribes paid by the manufacturing and services sectors "amount to around USD 120 million."

[57] See "National Survey on Public Attitudes towards Corruption" (Phnom Penh: Center for Social Development (CSD), 1998). The survey disaggregates results by income level, occupation and gender. Available from CSD http://www.bigpond.com.kh/users/csd.

[58] Center for Social Development. Conference Proceedings. (Phnom Penh: Center for Social Development, 1995). Accessed June 2004. Available from CSD http://www.bigpond.com.kh/users/csd.

"It makes me feel good that I belong to the ACLEDA staff. This is why I joined," she says. "I like working for a Cambodian organization that is different, one that has no tolerance for corruption; one that helps people keep their money safe."

Comprehensive banking services are new to Prey Veng, says Son Sai, ACLEDA's branch manager. "We're developing the practice of honest banking from the beginning. People appreciate the service. Transparency within the organization makes my work feel bright; staff and customers feel confident. We advance ACLEDA's reputation for transparency. We will be an example of an institution in Cambodia that works hard to keep corruption out."

The Prey Veng branch was established in January 2001. By December 2004 the branch had an outstanding portfolio of USD 2.4 million, serving just over 7,300 borrowers. Customer deposits reached USD 400,000; they are small accounts, averaging USD 120. A local transfer service represented USD 8 million of business during the year. Customer confidence and appreciation built the Prey Veng branch.

... And Transparency

Just as external events can reveal weaknesses, so can they heighten an organization's internal strengths, stripping down lofty goals to reveal the values at the core. The arrival of the first tranche of the KfW loan provided just such an opportunity.

As Chhay Soeun stood at the counter of the Foreign Trade Bank waiting to withdraw the proceeds of the loan that had arrived in ACLEDA's account, the teller asked, "Would you care to give me something extra?"

Soeun says this type of behavior is all too frequent in Cambodia, from tellers who ask savers for a percentage of their deposits to cashiers who require borrowers to pay an extra fee from the proceeds of their loans.

"I said, 'I cannot pay an extra fee. I will need an official receipt'", recalls Soeun.

The teller, somewhat taken aback, became coolly indifferent, impassive. "If you want your money, then you can withdraw it only in small bills." And then a logical appeal, "It would save you time if you took larger notes. Then you would not have to spend the entire day counting it."

And it did take all day to count the money. Three hundred thousand dollars in one, five and ten dollar bills takes an extraordinarily long time to count. "But I would not pay the bribe. I could not pay it." At closing time, Soeun carried a great sack of money out through the door.

Many people would have paid the bribe, chalking it up to the costs of doing business, or justifying it as an efficient use of time, a cost saving measure. Why did he refuse to do it? Because Soeun believes that you cannot have corruption at any level, let alone participate in it. As he explains, corruption is a slippery slope. "Once you start you cannot stop." How do you justify paying a small bribe to a teller to issue you larger notes as a more important cost of doing business than lending to a Provincial governor without the expectation of repayment just to make operations smoother? You cannot. They are the same. How do you accept corruption in the banking system, collude with the practice, and go back to your own institution to strictly enforce a 'no tolerance for corruption' policy? You cannot.

Soeun is adamant if not exactly fearsome when he says, "It took a lot of effort to build ACLEDA, and we will not destroy it."

* * *

There are fundamental values that are more important to an institution than the generation of profits; and some of these carry a heavy price. If those values strike a strong path right down to the core, the organization gladly pays for them. These are not just high-minded ideals that look impressive in a mission statement. On a very practical level, values and actions must match. Otherwise costly contradictions build between the values an organization says it holds and the decisions the organization makes. What is at risk? For ACLEDA, the mismatch of values and actions would destroy the integrity of the systems, the fairness of policies, the morale of the people who run the organization, and ultimately, the confidence of customers.

In the early period ACLEDA learned that there was a huge return in aligning values and actions. The growth period reinforced this lesson. Transparency is the most basic value.

Cheam Teang, a gifted mathematician and Head of Treasury of ACLEDA Bank, says "the culture of transparency is the bank's key to success", not expediency. Sotheavy agrees. "The internal audit helps achieve higher performance at the branch level by controlling fraud and managing risk. It helps each branch and the organization provide the best quality service to our customers. It protects them." Terry Mach struggled for years to ensure the systems could produce the kind of information that supported ACLEDA's drive for transparency. In Channy believes "Transparency is a growth factor."

The Changing Capital Structure

The solution to the 1996 liquidity crisis enabled a steeper growth path. With secure institutional funding in place, ACLEDA's portfolio grew to USD 13.7 million by the end of 1999. KfW's soft loan and the Sida grant of USD 2 million were employed to generate a portfolio five times the size of portfolio in 1996. By the end of 1999, ACLEDA's adjusted return on assets was 8 %; the adjusted return on equity was 11 %. The organization had accumulated retained earnings that made up for the cumulative losses since 1993. While still financed mostly through accumulated donor equity, by late 2000, when the organization transformed into a specialized bank, 11 % of the assets were funded through retained earnings, and 30 % were funded by soft loans as shown in Table 6.3. What appears to be a modest change in capital structure in 2000 was only a precursor to what was to come.

Table 6.3. Capital Structure: Earnings, Shares, Commercial Borrowing, Soft Loans, Public Deposits and Donor Equity

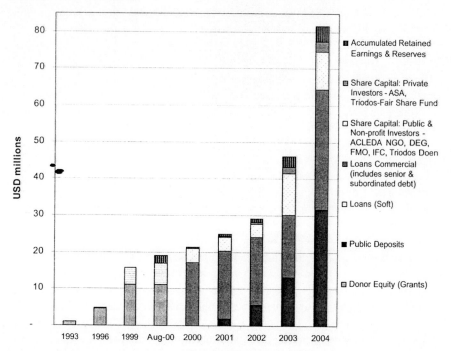

Source: ACLEDA Audited Financial Statements, 1993 – 2003 and un-audited Financial Statements for the year 2004.

CHAPTER 7:

Union

Comrades: Policy and Regulation

By early 2000 the micro credit operators in Cambodia enjoyed a new status. They shared it with the National Bank of Cambodia (NBC) that assumed new authority through a microfinance supervisory unit. Shored up by technical assistance agreements with the Asian Development Bank (ADB), the Agence Française de Développement (AFD) and the World Bank, in 2000 the National Bank of Cambodia issued a set of regulations as part of the new Banking and Financial Institutions Law of 1999. NGOs were now able to transform into licensed financial intermediaries. The new law incorporated a tiered licensing and regulatory framework for microfinance, including a specialized bank license allowing MFIs to provide services other than credit, such as deposits and transfers.

By 2003, observers in the region recognized that, "With these measures being in effect since the late 1990s, it can be said that among South-East and East Asian transition countries, Cambodia has put in place the most *supportive* fundamentals as to policy framework for micro-credit development (but not necessarily in terms of savings mobilization), though local capacities and institutions are yet to be substantially developed."[59]

How do decision-makers push forward policy to build an *inclusive* financial sector? We see the financial sector, whether it is bank-centered, as it is in Cambodia, or broader, as established regulatory and supervisory frameworks, legal statutes, and financial policies that govern the behavior of banks and non-bank financial institutions in the market. We rarely glimpse the debates of decision-makers as policy options develop and choices are made.

In Cambodia the framework that would consider poor and low-income people as worthy actors in the formal financial sector was five years in the making, amid substantial exchange, rumor, false starts and controversy. The main point of contention centered on the extent of government control over the nascent but rapidly growing microfinance organizations. This period in the history of microfinance in Cambodia is remarkable for the extraordinarily open dialogue as microcredit operations, their donors and national policy-makers struggled to find unity in discourse.

---

[59] Ryu Fukui and Gilberto Llanto. "Rural Finance and Micro-Finance Development in Transition Countries in South-East and East Asia" (paper prepared the International Workshop on Rural Finance and Credit Infrastructure in China, Organization for Cooperation and Development (OECD), Paris, France, October13-14, 2003), 3.

None agonized more over government policy decisions than the leading micro-credit organizations of the time — CRS, GRET and ACLEDA. Many in the National Bank of Cambodia, supported by the IMF, pushed forward radical positions that enabled bold supportive legislation. Experts in the field argued broad philosophical views about the welfare state, as well as more narrow legal positions about the ownership of bilateral donations. Yet the tumultuous period paved the way for the passage of the law on microfinance, one that would force or inspire NGOs to contribute to the formal financial sector or opt to provide other much-needed development assistance. The debates eventually mellowed with a unified answer to one basic question — is microfinance charity or banking? In the interim the debate would hit a resounding crescendo.

This chapter traces the evolution of the policy and regulatory framework for microfinance in Cambodia. It considers the role of national dialogue in framing the issues within the country context. The chapter also continues the story of ACLEDA's evolution within the changing regulatory environment. The value of the right kind of technical assistance for sustained growth of a microfinance institution within the broader financial sector is discussed. The chapter concludes with the story of change at ACLEDA's most fundamental level – the system of governance – the last hurdle ACLEDA had to clear as the organization prepared to make the leap into the formal financial system.

Growth of Microcredit Programs in Cambodia

By the end of 1999 close to 90 NGOs operated credit programs in Cambodia. They ranged from small one-person operations to the 25 more established NGOs that reported basic figures to the National Bank of Cambodia on a voluntary basis. Two major government programs figured prominently – the UNICEF-supported credit project within the Ministry of Women's Affairs that was winding down, and the EU-supported PRASAC project through the Ministry of Agriculture that was going strong.

Table 7.1. Borrowers, Portfolio and Percent of Households Covered by MFIs in Cambodia, 1995 – 2002

	1995	**1997**	**1999**	**2001**	**2002**
Borrowers	50,000	225,030	334,145	427,663	449,100
Portfolio (USD millions)	3	15	23	30.2	38
Households Covered (%)	3%	10%	14%	15%	17%

Sources: CCRD, RDB 1995-2002.

At the end of 1995, the total outstanding micro loan portfolio in the system was reportedly USD 3 million. In a short three years, by the end of 1999, it was a fraction under USD 23 million, serving about 14% of the households in Cambodia.[60] (See Table 7:1.) The combined portfolios of all microcredit operators accounted for roughly 11% of the private-sector domestic credit in Cambodia at that time.

The unexpected rates of growth caught many of the microcredit programs by surprise and caught the attention of government agencies that no longer ignored microfinance as an insignificant activity. At the time, 12 microfinance organizations and projects held 95% of the total micro and small business credit available in Cambodia as shown in Table 7.2. ACLEDA, the largest microfinance organization, contributed 60% of the total credit available, while the greatest number of borrowers was shared between ACLEDA and EMT.

Table 7.2. NGOs and Government Credit Projects Reporting to the NBC (Dec 31, 1999)*

	Portfolio (USD milions)	% Portfolio	Borrowers	% Borrowers
ACLEDA	13.70	60%	58,355	17%
EMT (formerly GRET)	1.83	8%	56,646	17%
CRS-TTP	1.35	6%	31,589	9%
PRASAC**	1.25	5%	28,000	8%
CCB – World Relief	0.90	4%	13,631	4%
HatthaKaksekar	0.60	3%	3,741	1%
World Vision Int'l	0.57	2%	17,303	5%
Seilaniti	0.57	2%	11,725	4%
MOWA**	0.24	1%	19,470	6%
ANS	0.30	1%	7,737	2%
CHC	0.23	1%	3,424	1%
Concern	0.22	1%	17,300	5%
Total Large Programs	21.76	95%	284,821	80%
35 Other reporting NGOs	1.04	5%	65,224	20%
Total	22.80	100%	334,145	100%

Estimates at the time indicate an additional 25 NGO credit programs did not report.
** *Government Projects.*
Sources: NBC 1999; NGO Forum 1999; ADB March 2000.

---

[60] Early figures on the extent of microcredit operations in Cambodia are sketchy due to the poor quality, consistency and scope of reporting. By mid-2002 about 60 small NGOs were still unregistered, although the bulk of microfinance was provided through ACLEDA, licensed as a specialized bank, 3 licensed MFIs and 24 registered NGOs.

Enter the Credit Committee for Rural Development

Created by ministerial decree in 1995, the Credit Committee for Rural Development (CCRD) was tasked with the development of a coherent policy and strategic direction for rural credit. One aim was to settle perceived problems with a relatively large, growing and unwieldy NGO microfinance sector. Chaired by the Minister for Rural Development, the CCRD included the Minister of Agriculture as the deputy chair, and members drawn from the Ministry of Economy and Finance, the Ministry of Women's Affairs, the National Bank of Cambodia and three NGO representatives with sizable micro credit operations — CRS, GRET and ACLEDA.

Officially responsible for training and disseminating information to NGOs on policies and strategies for rural credit, the Technical Unit of CCRD buzzed with financial intrigue and political adventure. Run by Mr. Tea Eav Ho, who had spent years in Nigeria providing expert advice to the Ministry of Finance, CCRD made its presence known within the NGO community almost overnight. Talkative and quick, Mr. Tea Ho provided a fresh face and a welcome relief to his more reserved colleagues. Together they crafted the first short-lived rural credit policy for the Kingdom of Cambodia.

The debates within the CCRD Technical Unit, which could have been cautiously diplomatic, were animated and often heated. During his short presence on the Cambodian microfinance scene, Mr. Tea Ho served as the epicenter for the ideological crossfire of the time. Perhaps his lasting contribution to the microfinance regulatory environment was to encourage the open and frank debates that occupied much of the more vocal microfinance advocates, as well as those who quietly worked behind the scenes. His accomplishments were no small feat in a close-knit microfinance community that often generated rumor and supposition, and largely acted on it.

At the time, opinions on the CCRD vacillated between viewing it as a minor irritation that had to be dealt with and as a significant force tasked with tightening the rein on the way micro credit would develop in Cambodia. Regardless of the views at opposite ends of the spectrum, the majority felt the CCRD served as a useful forum for NGO communication with government about pending regulation. On a more practical level, the debates that started in 1995 lasted throughout 1999, eclipsing CCRD's own institutional life. In the process, the members of CCRD, government officials and NGO credit operators alike created an atmosphere of open exchange that attempted to separate political designs from technical input into national policy, and largely succeeded in this over time.

Considerable attention centered on striking the balance between control of the microfinance NGOs and the promotion of financial services to the rural areas. A major preoccupation of the CCRD was the "institutionalization of rural credit". However, different perspectives abounded about just what institutionalization really meant. Would credit operators fall under a regulatory authority? Which one? Would they have to abide by strict guidelines with respect to institutional form and structure? Would their current operations become illegal? Would they be required to federate as branches of a central body, or could they remain independent organizations as long as they adhered to specific levels of performance?

It was clear that the Technical Unit of the CCRD preferred a much more heavy-handed level of control than did most of the microcredit NGOs. Perhaps there was real confusion about the distinction between the concepts of coordination and control. This confusion, or difference of opinion, contributed to developing suspicions that CCRD's ultimate goal was not to coordinate or supervise, but to own and perhaps manipulate for political purposes all microcredit operations in the Kingdom. Whether or not these suspicions were based on careful analysis of the facts, or on heightened anxiety, the proposals put forth by the Technical Unit, did little to assuage them.

The First Policy on Rural Credit

The CCRD generated a Policy on Rural Credit to accelerate the provision of rural credit and resolve the perceived problem with a lack of discipline in the microfinance community. The laudable aims to expand financial services throughout the country and to enhance the sustainability, efficiency and professionalism of the existing microcredit organizations belied the more operational proposals put forward by the Technical Unit. The first policy reserved CCRD's right to "determine an interest rate at the minimum level appropriate to the financial situation of the country". It also stipulated that all funds for on-lending received from bilateral or multi-lateral donors were owned by the government, and "managed, used and protected by the operators".[61] The policy did concede that interest income would remain the responsibility of the operators.

In one fell swoop the February 16, 1996 rural credit policy effectively nationalized all local and international credit operations in Cambodia, and simultaneously placed them in receivership. Oddly, the policy that was circulated as "finally considered and adopted by the CCRD" was never officially vetted or approved by the members of the CCRD. The efforts of the Technical Unit in pushing ahead the policy were viewed by some as usurping the powers of the committee. Criticism abounded in the widening circle of credit operators, donors and government agencies; some pointed to a process that appeared to break down; others claimed the policy was riddled with serious contradictions. The policy met a wall of resistance in the microfinance community as those who could never agree on much of anything, now agreed on one thing: the policy would never see the light of day.

Technical drafts of a new banking and financial institutions law within the NBC, and the emergence of the Rural Development Bank from an idea into a USD 4 million pledge by the government, overshadowed the CCRD's already waning

---

[61] CCRD Technical Unit, Policy of the Royal Government in the Field of Rural Credit in the Kingdom of Cambodia (CCRD, Phnom Penh, March 1996, photocopy), 6-7.

authority. When donors were attracted to the new best thing, the CCRD Technical Unit found itself without a budget to set much of an operation in motion. Slowly, the politically charged committee faded from the centerpiece of the microfinance policy and regulatory forum to the responsibility of the Supervision Office of Decentralized Banking System Bureau within the National Bank of Cambodia. Many, including the NBC, thought microfinance, as a banking activity, naturally belonged there.

In the interim there was a brief flirtation with the idea of federating, centralizing and regulating microfinance NGOs under the auspices of what would become the Rural Development Bank.

Enter the Rural Development Bank

The seed of the Rural Development Bank (RDB) was in fact buried in some of the first seminars held by the CCRD Technical Unit in 1995. An obvious preoccupation with creating a loan fund for rural credit overshadowed concerns about establishing the rules of the game for micro credit operators or building a professional microfinance sector.

> *"Based on discussions and consultations with different experts about rural credit, the Technical Unit of CCRD proposes to the Royal Government to establish the Rural Credit Fund for operating along with the Social Fund with financing from CFD, World Bank, AsDB, EU, international organizations, friendly countries and domestic commercial banks ... It's the best way to increase agricultural production and to develop rural area[s] ... We would like to ask the Council for the Development of Cambodia and the Ministry of Economy and Finance to intervene with [the] above mentioned institutions and countries for ... financial aid for operating the above proposed Rural Credit Fund as soon as possible. The Technical Unit will take all responsibilities for managing and coordinating this Fund."[62]*

The plans for the creation of a rural development bank advanced throughout 1996 and 1997, and with them the main controversy intensified about whether the government should provide and control microfinance and rural credit or whether a private sector approach ought to be promoted. Once again, the CCRD put forward the idea that all NGO assets in fact belonged to the government of Cambodia, on the theory that international donors had provided funding for the people of Cambodia.

---

[62] *Proposal on Policy for Rural Credit Development in the Kingdom of Cambodia.* Results of the Seminar on Rural Credit 05-07 June, 1995. (CCRD, Phnom Penh, June 12, 1995, photocopy), 12.

In their view, the government, as the people's representative, was the lawful owner of all donated assets.

CCRD proposed a plan for the coordination of rural credit that would designate a rural development bank as an umbrella under which all NGO operations would become federated cooperative banks. They would reside there as stockholders of the rural development bank, but retain the technical support from existing NGO operations. All existing NGO credit programs would transform into formal financial institutions regulated and supervised by the proposed rural development bank under the authority of the National Bank. The plan would require NGOs to scale back their operations, target particular sectors, and centralize into one perfect model loosely based on the *mutual* system popular in some government and donor quarters.

The uproar in the NGO community that now had considerable ownership and growing credit portfolios resounded across the continent. So serious was the situation in 1997 that a concerned microfinance professional wrote a quick memo to a supportive donor:

> "... the plan is for the RDB to take over <u>all</u> rural finance operations, a proposition confirmed in a CCRD document of February 1997. There was even talk of "nationalizing" the existing credit operators! This is all in accordance with the CCRD concept of forcing operators to federate and be controlled by RDB. The plan is for the RDB to control and channel all donor assistance for rural finance ..."

As early as May 1996, 20 credit operators issued a joint analysis of the CCRD's draft policy. The main concern was not with the creation of specialized rural financial institutions, nor with falling under a supervisory and reporting authority. The concern centered on the proscribed and centralized nature of the proposal which would effectively exclude many promising institutional models. Those microcredit operators based in rural Cambodia argued that the lack of financial management capacity could result in the formation of a weak rural financial system if member-owned cooperatives were to be the only legally recognized form of organization. The supervisors expressed concern that all credit programs would be required to incorporate as financial institutions regardless of their size and scope of activity. Looming large was the question of government or NGO ownership of loan capital received from international donors. There were also rumors that the RDB may be organized in response to perceived donor financing available through the Asian Development Bank.

If the RDB was designed in response to perceived funding available from the Asian Development Bank, it came as a surprise to the ADB. In an April 1997 letter, the ADB noted the imminent arrival of a technical assistance mission fielded with the purpose of assessing rural savings and credit.

> *"The TA will assess the Government's proposal to establish a rural development bank together with alternative mechanisms for development of rural credit and savings, and make recommendations on viable and sustainable institutional mechanisms. At this stage, the Bank, and many other donors are concerned about the current proposal to establish a rural development bank. The experience in most of the Bank's developing member countries shows that it is extremely difficult for state-owned rural development banks to have autonomy, and achieve financial viability and sustainability."[63]*

In January 1998, in the middle of steadfast controversy and without a clear mandate, the Rural Development Bank was officially created with a capital pledge of USD 4 million from the Ministry of Economy and Finance.[64] The new banking law was still in draft form. The old debates and suspicions resurfaced, and a new one was brought to the forefront. Among donors and operators alike there was suspicion that shortly before the scheduled July 1998 elections the RDB, constituted as a government-owned rural finance retail bank, would be used as a political enticement to get people to the polls and cast their votes in exchange for a loan.

Enter the NBC MFI Supervisory Unit

The Specialized Bank and MFI Supervision Office was originally established within the National Bank of Cambodia as the Supervision Office of Decentralized Banking System Bureau.[65] Funded by the AFD, the office was established in November 1997 to supervise compliance with the licensing, regulatory, and reporting requirements of microfinance institutions. It is true that the NBC was not focused on rural credit or microfinance throughout the early years. There were larger challenges in the banking system that required urgent attention. But it became clear that the CCRD, as a committee with an uncertain life span and few staff, could not effectively discharge the duties of a supervisory body.

Most remarkable from the archives of studies, position papers, draft policies and their ensuing rebuttals, stands the Horus report on "Institutionalization of Microfinancing Institutions in Cambodia". Presented in August 1998 well after the elections, the creation of the RDB and the National Bank's specialized bank and microfinance division, the report raised historical issues to an audience that was now prepared to combat them with evidence, logic and insight about the future of microfinance in Cambodia. In the interim, the NGOs worked together with the NBC to ensure that attention focused on microfinance and rural credit as an important and growing banking activity within Cambodia and the proposed, if somewhat misplaced, role of the CCRD in supervising it. The NGOs found champions within the National Bank.

---

[63] Asian Development Bank letter to H.E. Keat Chhon, Minister of Finance. April 9, 1997.

[64] Sub-Degree No. 01 A.N.K dated January 21, 1998.

[65] Prakas No. B 8-97-129 PK, dated November 25, 1997.

The main issues on the table dealt with prudential or non-prudential regulation of the MFIs, fair competition among all financial institutions, and capacity building for MFIs to strengthen governance, systems and profitability. The specific issues on the table ranged from the type of institution that could legally operate in the marketplace to the ownership of donated funds. The position put forth by In Channy to counter the main recommendations of the Horus report was registered by eager and interested NBC officials. Those arguments tipped the scales in favor of market-based microfinance, consistent with the NBC's private-sector approach to banking and financial institutions.

The differences in political view and ideological bent about state ownership or private sector development now fell to the more practical issues of whether or not a banking activity should be supervised by the banking authority, a technical institution, or a loose, politically organized committee supported by a technical unit. Even Mr. Tea Ho, the Director of CCRD's Technical Unit, was convinced that a supervisory function could not remain in a coordinating committee that included members from the very agencies they were expected to supervise. Shortly thereafter, he joined the NBC's Specialized Bank and MFI Supervision Office.

The National Bank's future vision for microfinance in Cambodia was extraordinary for the time, as well as a significant departure from the history of state-owned banking in Cambodia. If the vision remained anchored in the past, or if the supervisors followed an approach favored by some microfinance international experts at the time, then an entity not affiliated with the NBC or an APEX institution similar to the Rural Development Bank might make sense.[66] Both options were considered during the often turbulent debates supported by a flurry of experts with different points of view.

The banking authorities in Cambodia had another vision of the future of microfinance. The dismal state of the formal banking system contrasted with the strong growth of the MFIs, who were now viewed as important players in the financial sector, if not exactly commercial powerhouses. The banking authorities were interested in building a banking system in Cambodia that would include poor and rural people, not isolate them further from the formal financial system. In the end, the NBC opted for a tiered regulatory framework that included prudential regulation and supervision for specialized banks and licensed MFIs, and a non-prudential regulatory and reporting regime for small-credit-only operations.

---

[66] See for example, Paul B. McGuire, John D. Conroy and Ganesh B. Thapa, *Getting the Framework Right: Policy and Regulation for Microfinance in Asia* (Brisbane: Foundation for Development Cooperation, 1998), 52-59 that notes "one promising avenue for ensuring that microfinance institutions operate on a sound basis is through the lending policies of second tier microfinance institutions. Another approach to establishing performance and reporting standards for MFIs is through self-regulation." Also see Rachel Rock, Regulation and Supervision of Microfinance Institutions: Stabilizing a New Financial Market. CGAP Focus Note 4. (Washington, D.C.: CGAP, 1996), 3. that notes, "As the microfinance industry develops in individual countries, superintendencies will need to organize themselves to regulate it. Some are creating specialized MFI departments. A less costly alternative might be to contract out reviews to experts familiar with MFI operations."

The Future and Past Close in on the Present

Why so much attention to the issue of regulation in the nascent microfinance industry in Cambodia? The law on specialized banks and MFIs was one of the main factors that led NGOs to become a permanent feature of the formal financial system. During the five-year struggle the NBC and MFIs together hammered out a framework that made sense in Cambodia. The NBC was concerned above all with the safety and soundness of the financial system in Cambodia. The microcredit NGOs were concerned about the advent of restrictive regulations that they would find impossible to meet under the best of circumstances. They were also concerned about directives that would put them out of business. Where they found common ground was in the number of Cambodians who remained outside the financial system, and the recognition that NGOs were increasing their outreach and depth to the unbanked population in unprecedented numbers.

Amidst the politics, the divergent expert advice and assorted donor preferences, cooler heads prevailed. Throughout the period, the issue of ownership of accumulated donor assets could be seen as a thinly disguised attempt to capitalize the RDB. But underlying the discussions was the basic issue of state control of a rational system of neatly organized village-level cooperative societies affiliated to a government-owned APEX bank. This distinctly imported approach had a certain appeal; there was a hunger for systemic neatness and state control in an otherwise chaotic country.

Political ideologies about state control gave way to practical concerns about an environment that could neither provide the appropriate membership vigilance nor, at the time, the appropriate supervisory function on the national level. The experience of the state-owned cooperatives of the 1980s weighed heavily in the decision about the direction the "institutionalization of rural finance" in Cambodia would take in the 21st century. Within the NBC Supervision Unit was a new generation of Central Bankers who favored a private approach to banking. There were also those made from an older cloth who remembered the failures of government-affiliated cooperatives and the disastrous consequences of state ownership of the banking sector in the 1970s.

From a regional perspective, the ADB was in a position to support, together with the Ministry of Economy and Finance, a Rural Development Bank that would contribute to building a financial infrastructure, absent in Cambodia at the time. The RDB statutes were amended in 1999 to constitute it as a specialized bank and wholesale lender to retail microfinance and rural finance organizations. Since 1998, the RDB ceased all retail credit activities to focus on wholesale lending.[67]

---

[67] Development of Rural Finance: Role of Rural Development Bank. 2004. Presented by Chairman and CEO of RDB, H.E. Son Koun Thor at the 5th Asia Network, Phnom Penh, Cambodia, November 2004.

The early discussions about regulation and supervision of microfinance yield critical lessons about the importance of a fluid national dialogue with all actors who can influence the direction and behavior of the financial sector. The stakes are high. Hammering out the framework and the timing with clear goals in the forefront is crucial to building a financial sector that works within the country. The story from Cambodia confirms the cautions about the "rush to regulate", just as it confirms the importance of listening to the voices of national experience.[68]

According to Tal Nay Im, the General Director of the National Bank of Cambodia, "lending and deposit mobilization are banking activities, and fall under the supervision of the banking authorities". There is no clearer approach than that. "The purpose of the regulation was to extend banking services to the people of Cambodia, to enable the institutions to become a sustainable part of the financial system for the long term."[69]

The Right Technical Assistance

> *"We don't need a banker to run the credit component in our project, anyone can do that," said the rice specialist to the banker. The banker replied, "It must be the same with rice. All you have to do is grab the seeds, throw them on the ground, watch them grow and then eat them."* Peter Kooi

What does technical assistance have to do with growth? Ask a donor that is concerned that all funding goes into the loan fund, and they will tell you technical assistance is not important. Ask a government official in charge of a loan negotiation with a multilateral bank, and he will tell you technical assistance is only important if someone else pays for it. Ask ACLEDA, and they will tell you, technical assistance has everything to do with growth, but only the right kind of technical assistance.

Peter Kooi was the right kind of technical assistance. Following Roel Hakemulder's preoccupation with finding talent and national ownership of the development process, Peter Kooi focused on letting talent bloom, deepening the institutional structure with strategy, logic and a commercial approach. John Brinsden, a former Standard Chartered banker, focused on molding talent and experienced microlenders into bankers. Together they forged a bank that did not grudgingly lend to poor people or need a government quota system as an incentive to lend to

---

[68] See Robert Peck Christen and Richard Rosenberg, The Rush to Regulate: Legal Frameworks for Microfinance. Occasional Paper No. 4. (Washington D.C.: CGAP, 2000).

[69] Tal Nay Im, Director General National Bank of Cambodia. Author interview, December 2003.

them, but a bank that would seek out poor and low income people – the unbanked – as valued customers.

Was each of these technical advisors exceptional? Probably, but what was most fortuitous for ACLEDA was that they each came at the right time, and they each knew that process and discussion were more important than power. They each stood on the work of their predecessors and built on it; they did not detract from it. Most importantly, as ACLEDA developed through each stage of growth, the systems and staff capacity to manage and develop them served up a solid footing for the next generation of changes.

Why was technical assistance effective? When asked, Soeun, who has had his share of experience with technical advisors, says with one or two exceptions all the technical assistance from short-term consultants to resident advisors was important. Even if 90% of the assignment was a waste of time, ACLEDA looked to outsiders for ideas, searching for the diamond in the mud. They were open. Vann Saroeun remembers, "When we started we didn't know how to lend. But we learned." They were open to new ideas, and they analyzed whether the advice made sense for their organization. Many microfinance initiatives fail as they are rooted in an ideology or methodology that effectively closes the organization to new ideas. If they don't fail, they stagnate. There is no institutional innovation.

One of the key lessons ACLEDA learned from its technical advisors was that increasing institutional capacity creates greater opportunity. Perhaps the most important skill that the resident technical advisors transferred to ACLEDA staff was how to think through and solve problems of the growing organization, meshing homegrown ideas with lessons from international experience. ACLEDA developed an internal council of seasoned managers, one that could be trusted, one that thought first of the organization, its customers and its place in society. Rarely did those in positions of power abuse their authority for their own betterment. And when that did happen, as it is apt to happen in any organization, there was a revolt within the organization that jealously guarded its independence, professionalism and honor. Those values guided ACLEDA through the second growth period.

Capacity to Sustain Growth: The Second Growth Period – Bigger and Better, 1997-2000

ACLEDA moved through the late 1990s like a bullet train. What appeared to be an endless growth track, one that could only accelerate with each persistent push of the mammoth flywheel, led ACLEDA to the edge of a gaping abyss. The second growth phase, much more sophisticated than the first, took the organization almost by surprise.

Hand in Hand: Ownership & Governance

It is no secret in the world of microfinance that NGOs do not have a commercially accountable ownership structure that parallels the world of banking.[70] An NGO is often well governed, guiding the fulfillment of corporate mission and protecting the assets. However, the governing board of a non-profit organization acts as a steward of donor money; the board of directors does not represent or consist of owners who have capital at stake. This lone feature – the fragile connection between ownership and governance – emerges as the centerpiece as microfinance steps from the non-profit world to the world of commercial banking.

Absence of owners with capital at risk deserves all the attention it receives. It is the main structural hurdle for many NGO microfinance institutions that aspire to become commercial players as they strain against capital limitations and organizational confines in search of new and better ways to grow. Banking authorities as well are concerned about the capital adequacy of all institutions within the financial sector, particularly those that pose a risk to the financial system due to their sheer size and as managers of other people's money. Banking authorities favor financially healthy owners who provide both vigilance and accountability and, ultimately, the security that large amounts of capital engender. NGOs, even those with abundant accumulated donor equity, are unlikely to be able to call on their donors with the agility and authority required to shore up capital for growth, or in times of crisis.

In Cambodia, during the mid-1990s, the ownership of donated assets was challenged just at the time many MFIs ascended through their initial growth period. Ownership of capital became the principal topic of the microfinance legal and regulatory debates. Much less attention was given to governance of MFIs, although the closely related topics of governance and ownership were often confused. An item in an expert report prepared for the NBC argued that "without capable owners [of capital], an institution is deprived of clear objectives, of recourse or support in case of difficulty, and goes astray."[71] Establishing causality between ownership of capital and whether an institution "goes astray" is a tenuous knot to tie. Yet the forging together of ownership and governance, neglected by many institutions emerging from a pattern where technical management dominates, became the key concern of ACLEDA from 1997 throughout 2000.

---

[70] There are many good publications on the ownership and governance challenges of NGOs that dedicate themselves to microfinance. See Elisabeth Rhyne, Mainstreaming Microfinance: How Lending to the Poor Began, Grew and Came of Age in Bolivia (Bloomfield, Conn: Kumarian Press, 2001): 105-106. Also see Maria Otero and Michael Chu, "Governance and Ownership of Microfinance Institutions" in *The Commercialization of Microfinance: Balancing Business and Development*, eds. Deborah Drake and Elisabeth Rhyne (Bloomfield, Conn: Kumarian Press, 2002).

[71] Horus Bank and Finance, Report on Institutionalization of Microfinancing Institutions in Cambodia: General Conclusions (Phnom Penh: August 1998), 20.

It is now widely recognized that "good governance is what successful MFIs have in common."[72] On the other side of the coin, fragmented, financially weak, or concentrated, self-interested ownership structures are indeed what many failed MFIs have in common.[73] Ownership structure largely determines the type of governing board an MFI will have, even though the duties of any governing board are similar, regardless of ownership structure. Governance is more than closely related to ownership; as the growing ACLEDA found, governance and ownership go hand in hand.

While the ownership of capital dominated external discussions, within ACLEDA governance became the critical issue. ACLEDA's governance structure emerged from the early days when the central concern was to ensure everyone had a voice in decision making and to prevent the dominance of a group of powerful individuals. At the time, the governance structure allowed for the consolidation of organizational mission and corporate culture as ACLEDA operated with a common bond among professionals – a new and different way of operating in the Cambodian environment. The governance system did consolidate a sense of ownership among all staff; but if ACLEDA was to advance during the second growth stage, it was apparent that governance had to change.

Prior to transformation, ACLEDA's governance structure, which evolved only slightly, operated similar to a staff cooperative. A general assembly of all staff approved strategic plans and the organization's constitution. By constitution, each branch manager was guaranteed a seat on the governing board, as was one member of the headquarters technical support team. The board of branch managers elected the General Manager of the organization, who in turn appointed other members of an Executive Committee. In theory the Executive Committee acted as the general management of the organization, holding branch managers accountable

---

[72] Otero and Chu, Governance and Ownership, 229.

[73] When discussing the failure of rural banks and licensed microfinance operations in Peru, Filipe Portocarrera, a researcher for the Inter-American Development Bank, notes that "in each and every case of failure, shareholder structure played a crucial role," cited in Damian von Stauffenberg, *How Microfinance Evolves: What Bolivia Can Teach Us*, Microenterprise Development Review, vol. 4, no. 1 (Washington, D.C.: Inter-American Development Bank, 2001), 7. Jean Steege's *The Rise and Fall of Corposol: Lessons Learned from the Challenges of Managing Growth* (Bethesda, Md.: Development Alternatives Inc., 1998) notes one of the main factors contributing to Corposol's collapse was a concentrated ownership structure made up of self-interested parties from the organization. The Asian Development Bank recounts the 2004 closure of Bank Dagang Bali by the Bank of Indonesia. "Bank Dagang Bali (BDB) had been a model institution with a long history in microfinance lending ... BDB's business relations with Bank Asiatic, compounded by personal relations between the families of the two principal shareholders of the two institutions, appear to have contributed to financial problems and mismanagement in both institutions. Poor governance and irregularities in lending practices over the past 2 years in BDB and Bank Asiatic led to losses of Rp1.2 trillion ($140 million)." Asian Development Bank, *Country Economic Review – Indonesia* (Manila: ADB, December 2004), 8.

for performance. The Executive Committee held the ultimate responsibility for appointing and dismissing personnel, including branch managers.[74] In reality, the Executive Committee was accountable for organization-wide performance to a board made up of branch managers who could appoint as well as dismiss the Executive Committee.

The Executive Committee had little authority other than moral suasion to implement change. In effect, the branch managers became the powerful governing body of the organization. Some preciously guarded their branches and resented overseeing by the Executive Committee or specialized departments such as internal audit, particularly when branch performance lagged. Other branch mangers were endowed with a more expansive world view, and felt responsible for the organization as whole, not just the performance of their specific branch. The rift in the governance structure became so critical in 1997 that several branch managers thought their growing operations would make a promising base to establish their own NGOs at the Provincial level. As discussions about transformation of the NGO into a bank spun from casual conversations to the main topics of management meetings and staff workshops, anxieties about the future of the organization, the revenue stream and job security resurfaced.

Conflicts of Interest and Conflicts

Once thought of as a structure that ensured expansion, cohesion and national ownership, the growing ACLEDA became confined by the very structure that had brought about its greatest strength — the people who ran it. It was now left to those people who had developed and nurtured systems, and claimed them as their own, to change them for the evolving times and the trajectory of ACLEDA's growth.

Management by committee no longer held the promise of strength in greater numbers; rather, it was gradually viewed as a mechanism that clouded accountability as staff competence accelerated. If the General Assembly's diminished powers to appoint the board was viewed as a major stumbling block in effective governance, this was equaled only by a heightened concern with the inherent conflict of interest, as branch managers appeared to be supervising themselves.[75] As In Channy notes, "at that time if ACLEDA wanted to change the composition of the board, the only option would have been to fire branch managers." And it was the branch mangers themselves, in their capacity as directors, who would act on this covenant.

To outside observers, governance seemed to be an insurmountable problem for the future of the organization, one rife with contradictions and open to abuse. In

---

[74] Statutes, Article 11. ACLEDA Organization: Micro Financial Institution for the Poor. (Phnom Penh: March 1997).

[75] Hendrik Prins, ACLEDA: Transformation Study. (Phnom Penh: May 1997), 23-24.

practice, the system worked reasonably well for ACLEDA during the first five years of operation as the independent LEDAs consolidated into one organization. A technical study on the prospects for ACLEDA's transformation noted:

> "... the existing constitution and management structure has a number of constraints compared to the usual structure in a commercial organization. One must recognize however, that the structure has been effective in practice. With all staff being members of the General Assembly, there is a strong sense of "ownership" within the organization. A strong consensus is developed before decisions are taken. Whilst not formally accountable to the General Assembly, directors take into account views of members of the General Assembly."[76]

There was no question in Channy's mind as early as March 1997, as he addressed the Fifth General Assembly of ACLEDA staff, that ACLEDA's future depended on a transformation to a legally recognized financial institution.

The entire ACLEDA staff was greatly influenced by their first visit to BRI in June of 1996. With the continuing flood of visits over the next three years, this influence strengthened. ACLEDA's beliefs were reinforced by the perspective of Peter Kooi, who considered the merits and challenges of the transformation of their comparatively small and subsidized NGO to a national branch network based loosely on the BRI model, but without state ownership. How that would be possible in Cambodia rested equally with the National Bank of Cambodia and ACLEDA's General Assembly.

ACLEDA staff and management prepared to vote on the future of the organization to become a specialized bank through a series of workshops held during 1997 and 1998. Voting in favor of the proposition meant they would approve the five-year business plan, vote themselves out of power, and relinquish control of the organization to a board of external directors who would be appointed at the discretion of the shareholders. In keeping with ACLEDA's tradition of consensus building, the workshops were designed to analyze the prospect of transformation from different points of view. They communicated the genesis of the idea, ideas on how they could reasonably accomplish it, the options they had and the risks that might emerge.

Guns on the Table

If Channy expected a modicum of opposition to a transformation plan that would remove branch managers from power, he was not disappointed. The growing strength of the headquarters was already requiring higher performance standards

---

[76] Prins, ACLEDA: Transformation Study, 25.

from branch managers, as well as new demands, such as regular reporting, stricter staff policies and compliance with the newly established internal audit department. It was probably no coincidence that the main opposition to the transformation, and the growing centralized system of accountability, came from branch managers who regularly underperformed. An internal audit of the Battambang branch uncovered credit officer fraud amidst troublesome branch performance; the Sihanoukville branch was already under audit, and the Takeo branch was likely to fall somewhere at the top of the random internal audit list.

In December 1998, prior to the General Assembly meeting, the Executive Committee and the Board met to discuss business and prepare for the assembly. The General Assembly would discuss and vote on the transformation and the creation of the Staff Association, which would allow staff to participate in the new ACLEDA Bank as shareholders. Perhaps the branch managers could see the writing on the wall, when Channy decided against the decision of the board to reconsider the firing of a fraudulent credit officer. "We do not keep people who steal," Channy explained. The manager of the Sihanoukville branch already felt threatened by this new system of stronger risk management and central control; he was bound to be disciplined for allowing sloppy cash management procedures in his branch, something recently discovered by the internal audit.

There was a small silence in the boardroom as branch managers shifted in their seats. They saw the branch manager open his bag, just enough to show the gun. "I have my gun" he said as he started a litany of criticism directed to the internal audit department. "No one can do that to me" he proclaimed, as a second branch manager showed his gun in support. Vann Saroeun, the Chair of the Board and a veteran of a helpful internal audit in Siem Reap, recalls, "They played the gun, and it was terrible."

Channy remembers knowing the meeting would be tense. Prior to the meeting, he asked everyone not to bring guns. "We knew some people carried guns in those days, and we expected the meeting to be difficult because we were going to discuss business and the future of the NGO", Channy says as he explains the announcement's inception. "You cannot have someone with a gun in a meeting where debates are sometimes heated. It is unprofessional in an NGO or a business; it threatens the free discussion of ideas; and, it is against the law." Trouble might come soon if they have guns, reasoned Channy, they might fight each other during the General Assembly meeting that was scheduled in one month's time.

The last official board meeting of branch managers, and certainly the most dramatic, again saw the majority of branch managers in unity against those who would destroy the organization. The trade-off was clear: retain power to direct the organization, or protect the organization's uncertain future. Consistent with ACLEDA's past, they chose the future. With approval of the Chair of the Board, and the consensus of the Executive Committee, the branch managers who carried the guns to the meeting were fired.

The Hands Went Up

Even as ACLEDA teetered under the strain of an outdated governance system, the organization stirred with quiet changes – changes that were more substantial than the explosive events which preceded them. In two years time, the NGO operation would look insignificant in comparison. The two-day General Assembly in early February 1999, where each of ACLEDA's staff voted on the future of the organization, proceeded without further incident. An overwhelming majority voted to approve the five-year strategic plan that called for the transformation of the NGO into a licensed financial institution falling under the regulatory framework of the NBC.[77] The General Assembly of ACLEDA staff, the supreme body of the organization, voted to abolish itself and its governing board, granting the transition team full authority to carry out the transformation plan. The minutes noted, "The assembly finished happily and successfully at 6:15 PM."[78]

In effect, from February 1999 to October 2000 when a new board was installed, ACLEDA had no formally recognized governance structure from either the NGO world or the business world. For almost two years, the organization was managed and governed by the transition team who oversaw operations and worked on new by-laws, articles of association and the shareholder agreements for what ACLEDA would eventually become.

The governance system of ACLEDA, melting down since mid 1997, finally collapsed under the weight of ACLEDA's own mounting success. It was only a matter of time before the massive operation exposed weaknesses in all systems. Advances in operations and management, human resources, finance, MIS, internal audit and risk managements systems, allowed the organization to grow bigger. At the time, a governance structure that established clear roles and responsibilities and the corresponding accountability mechanisms were the remaining obstacles to allowing the organization to grow bigger and better.

The changes proposed were not incidental, nor were they seamless steps to the next phase of organization. The imminent end of the NGO held great emotional significance for all ACLEDA staff; it also raised their economic stake in the operation. When staff pledged to put their own capital at risk, the ACLEDA Staff Association became the founding shareholder of the new regulated financial institution. They bet on an uncertain future. The uncertainty was countered by the promise that what they had accomplished together was only the beginning of something much better. They trusted that promise, and each other. They defended that promise against those who would divide and destroy. Out of the turmoil emerged a leader and a management team whose capacity was matched by integrity.

---

[77] Minutes from ACLEDA's Six General Assembly, February 20, 1999.

[78] Minutes from ACLEDA's Six General Assembly, February 20, 1999.

The Failure of Recipes

From the dramatic changes in governance, an organization-wide MIS, and the advent of specialized risk management departments to the small changes in loan terms and collateral policies, growth challenged just about every aspect of the ACLEDA operation. It was as if every carefully stitched seam bulged from a great pressure building within. The flywheel. Would it break loose and release all its energy in an uncontrolled manner, or would it continue to accelerate, to the point of break-through?

Sometimes the thinking of the microfinance community is overly optimistic about the prospects for sustained growth, as well as sanguine about the hard work that goes into building the solid foundation that makes sustained growth possible. The question that has been asked since the beginning of the microfinance revolution is, "why is there such a huge gap between supply and demand for financial services, when low-income entrepreneurs have high repayment rates, when these entrepreneurs have shown their willingness and ability to pay higher-than-market interest rates to gain access, and when the most successful intermediaries have shown that lending to this group can be profitable once volumes are reached?"[79]

The question was asked throughout the 90s as examples of institutions showed both profitability and deep outreach to poor and low-income people. Microfinance experts consider that one of the main reasons why he gap is so large is the lack of solid retail institutions that serve the market and have the capability to expand. But this is only one answer to a much larger question.

Without basic policies and systems it is clear that an organization cannot grow. The first growth period challenges existing policies and systems and provides the push for change. But why is it that some organizations spin out of control, and others hit warp speed and break through? What is the difference? Some of them crash and burn, some of them retreat to a slower pace that the organization can manage; and some charge ahead to meet the pace of growth. Why? It is more than a social mission and a large untapped market. It is more than access to capital. And it is more than the enabling environment. Although all these factors are pre-conditions for growth, they do not a recipe make. If these were the only ingredients, there would be many more MFIs capable of building their organizations to reach the market.

From the ACLEDA experience there are two answers to this time-honored question. The first answer is that the people who make up the organization matter. They did not block things – none of them did, from the staff to the technical advisors to the donors. They did not try to control, they tried to enable. Perhaps no one had a definite idea of the way microfinance would develop in Cambodia. They tried to support a direction – not because it was the right thing to do, but because they thought, "if we get the direction right, if we get the incentives

---

[79] Women's World Banking, *The Missing Links: Financial Systems that Work for the Majority* (New York: Women's World Banking, April 1995), 2.

right, it will come."[80] What is evident is that when someone did have a definite
idea of the way things should be done, from the early technical advisor who
insisted on a single entry bookkeeping system, through the quick foray into
neighborhood banks, to the quota system for women on the staff and board, the
efforts failed. When efforts succeeded it was because ACLEDA learned on its
own how best to structure and manage an organization that grew with the staff.
They did not re-invent the wheel, but experienced the well-worn track anew as
events unfolded in Cambodia. They considered and followed reasonable advice
of experts; they searched for the "diamond in the mud". And because they were
looking, they often found it.

The second answer is also the people. They care about what they are doing,
from the polite and knowledgeable receptionist who glues a telephone to each ear,
to In Channy who manages a growing institution with grace and honor. They are
not critical of others, as some ideologues who have an equal amount of passion
are. They are builders. The notion of building did not end with NGO transformation; they are still building. The answer may lie in management's drive for institutional innovation. People need something new, and if they are encouraged to develop new ideas for improving their jobs and their own performance, they often
do. Peter Kooi once commented on In Channy's drive for innovation, "He is concerned about staff's need to innovate, otherwise, he thinks, they will get bored."
ACLEDA discovered another management principle: it is more beneficial for the
organization to consider a great number of plans than to motivate staff to think
them up in the first place.

In the refugee camp, on the treeless Thai border, the director of UNHCR once
discussed ILO's recruitment of In Channy. "Don't take him," she said. "If you
recruit him he will be running an ILO project for the rest of his life, and he is
bound for bigger things." Well, she was wrong, and she was right.

In Channy is not the only motivating force in ACLEDA. Listen to the voices of
ACLEDA:

*"I always had the desire to improve. When we got knowledge from
abroad, I wanted Cambodia to improve as well. I wanted to be able to
talk about the good things, not the bad. You have to understand the
society and the country for change to really take place; people generally understand an organization in a very narrow manner. So much
knowledge from abroad was imported to Cambodia, but it really depends on the people to change, not just the technical aspects and the
new ideas themselves."* Chhay Soeun, Finance Department Manager

*"We studied in secret in those days. I got one dictionary, the 1963
Oxford English dictionary. I loved it so much."* Rath Yumeng, Chief
Accountant

---

[80] Peter Kooi. Author interview, 2003.

"We expect ACLEDA will become #1, not just the portfolio, or transfers and savings, but because of its transparency and its culture. It will set the example." Chea Sok, Chairman of the Board

"Competition makes you stronger. They attack your weaknesses. Why shouldn't we help the competition? You can be the market leader, but you don't have to take the whole market. If we help them become stronger, they improve and provide a better service to their customers. That is good for the Cambodian people." Terry Mach, IT Department Manager

"When you have no competitor you will sleep. If you see others do as you do, you will wake up and run. But if you fight, you must make peace with them. You do business with them, you are not a soldier." So Phonnary, Marketing Department Manager

"I am a mathematician. I like logic. Microfinance did not seem logical at first. But poor people are willing to pay for a good product, for access and convenience, like anyone else. Why do they come to us? We have a product they want to buy. We have a simple process. We treat them well. I trust this point. This is logic." Cheam Teang, Treasury Department Manager

"You will learn to treat people with such respect; even your parents will be surprised." Nay Soksamnang, Branch Manager, Phnom Penh

"We protect the organization, and its customers." Kim Sotheavy, Internal Audit Department

"I had a good stable job, but I did the same thing everyday. I left it to join ACLEDA. My family asked why, why leave the security? I wondered the same thing. I believed that ACLEDA would move forward, and because of that move forward, new things would come. I could contribute to that. Here I learn. I think. There is innovation. At the time, I wasn't clear about whether I made the right decision, but now I am." Rath Yumeng, Chief Accountant

What is common is that they are all motivated about what they do, and their faith in their evolving organization does not falter.

*   *   *

Marilou van Golstein Brouwers, the Senior Fund Manager of Triodos Bank, says, "One of the biggest mistakes donors make in the field of microfinance is to assume there is a recipe ... the "makeability" of society. If they just get the right pieces together and put the money in, there will be a successful institution. Donors want a good example of what to copy – the concepts, the money – the recipe. If you have these things, they think everything will work. That thinking is wrong. It's really about the people behind the institution, not the recipe. By following a recipe, donors lose out on the idea that it all starts with people with ideals."[81]

---

[81] Marilou van Golstein Brouwers. Author interview, 2004.

PART IV:

Odyssey

"The real difficulty in changing any enterprise lies not in developing new ideas, but in escaping from the old ones."

John Maynard Keynes

Prologue

The Formal Financial Sector in Cambodia 1993-2002

> *"Valued Customer: The bank is closed ... Please direct further inquiries to the National Bank of Cambodia."* Tales of Asia.

During the early 1990s many small local and foreign-owned banks leapt into Cambodia.[82] They offered limited services to the public. They operated mainly in the capital where they served their countrymen's trade finance and banking requirements. Others were opened for less patriotic reasons. If the banking sector was lopsided with a concentration of 31 banks in Phnom Penh, it was also focused on the new wave of gray market capitalism and commodities. Cambodia's porous borders, dollarized economy and newly found capitalist spirit made it an attractive locus and a haven for the trade in less socially acceptable products. Venerable banking institutions, such as Standard Chartered and May Bank, operated alongside banks with dubious origins and charters. The strong liquidity preferences of some of the more unsavory banking establishments would have made John Maynard Keynes blush. A noted reporter of the time commented, "Some banks spend more time laundering money than lending it."[83]

One by one, and later in groups, 23 commercial banks closed their doors. The Credit Bank of Cambodia, the Royal Cambodia Bank, the Municipal Bank, the P.T. Lippo Bank, and Siam City Bank were some of the first to cease operations. The Rich Nation Bank, the Emperor International Bank, the Cambodia Farmer's Bank as well as the Great International Bank soon followed suit. Many had simply ended operations; their closure was a matter of formality. After issuing the new law on Banking and Financial Institutions in late 1999, the NBC ordered all commercial banks to submit re-licensing applications within six months. The NBC's final decision on re-licensing would be made by November 2000. It is not unduly odd that in December of that same year 11 commercial banks closed their doors. Many of banks voluntarily liquidated; they were unwilling or unable to meet the

---

[82] From 1991 to 1996, seven foreign bank branches and 22 private banks began operations. By December 1997, five were in operation without renewal of a license. IMF Staff Country Report No. 98/54. (Washington, D.C.: IMF, June 1998), 40.

[83] Attributed to Nate Thayer, "Bankers' Bluff: Cambodia Starts to Clean up Its Banks" (Far Eastern Economic Review, June 1995) cited in "The New Aseans: Vietnam, Burma, Cambodia and Laos." (Department of Foreign Affairs and Trade. East Asia Analytical Unit. Commonwealth of Australia. 1997), 199.

meet the new minimum capital requirement, which rose from USD 5 million to USD 13 million. Others failed the new tests for solvency, prudential ratios, and professional qualifications for shareholders and.managers.[84]

Banks that were classified as non-viable banks followed compulsory liquidation orders. Residents of Phnom Penh saw the buildings along Monivong and Noro-dom Boulevards empty. Inside, hollow vaults closed and file cabinets locked as NBC administrators, who were appointed temporarily to prevent the unauthorized reduction of assets, oversaw their duties.

By September 2002 the crowd in the banking sector had dispersed; three-quarters of the banks operating in Cambodia in 1996 had their licenses revoked or left voluntarily. The twelve remaining private banks played by the rules of the game.

The sweep through the banking system was not as disastrous as some bankers predicted. Some lamented that the new law was "too strict for Cambodia, one of Asia's poorest countries, at this stage of its economic development."[85] *But it was difficult to prove that banks served Cambodia's people, either directly or through enterprise finance that would provide employment. Other bankers were supportive, saying the new law "would dispel suspicions that banks are using assets from money laundering."*[86]

The Cambodian government was adamant in its approach to reform, determined to shrink the sector. The law required background checks on directors and proof of the source of capital verified by outside audits and on-site inspections. According to Keat Chhon, Senior Minister of Economy and Finance, and Chea Chanto, Governor of the National Bank of Cambodia, "these measures are necessary to establish a sound banking system, promote savings, and increase the confidence of the public in the banking system."[87] *"Flight to quality represents the major motive for this action."*[88]

---

[84] The Law on Banking and Financial Institutions Article 18, (Phnom Penh: National Bank of Cambodia, 1999).

[85] Associated Press. Article cited in Asean Free Trade Area Online. Banking and Finance Archives, 2001). Accessed June 2004. Available from http://www.aftaonline.com.

[86] Susan Postlewaite, "Banking on Poor Borrowers" Businessweek, January 8, 2001. Available from http://www.businessweek.com/2001/01.

[87] Speech of Hon. Keat Chhon, Governor, at the 34th Annual Meeting of the Board of Governors of the Asian Development Bank. May 9, 2001. Available from http://www.adb.org.

[88] Statement of Hon. Chea Canto and Hon. Keat Chhon, IMF Board of Governors, 2000 Annual Meeting, Prague, Czech Republic, September, 2000. Available from http://www.adb.org.

CHAPTER 8

To Play by the Rules of the Game

A Member of the Club

It's hard to imagine that ACLEDA wanted to be a member of the club of licensed banking institutions in the Cambodia. The reputations of the banking industry were increasingly colored with voluntary liquidations, revoked licenses, and suspected money laundering, just as NGO microcredit operations were increasingly viewed as important agents of economic development and alternative banking organizations for the majority of Cambodia's poor and low-income population. Moreover, ACLEDA was directly affected by the hazardous behavior of formal-sector banking institutions; the loss of USD 267,932 of funds on account with the Cambodian Farmer's Bank still stung.[89]

Certainly reputation and prestige were not primary motivations for ACLEDA to establish its NGO credit operations as a commercial business. Nor was the idea that formalization by becoming a licensed financial intermediary was "the right thing to do", somehow implying a moral choice.[90] The "right thing" was hardly an example widely demonstrated by the Cambodian banking community of the time. ACLEDA's reasons for creating a bank had little to do with becoming a member of the club. Its motives were the practical reasons leading many NGOs to choose the same course.

This chapter discusses ACLEDA's rationale for transforming into a licensed financial intermediary, comparing and contrasting its reasons with those of other NGOs. The chapter highlights aspects of the legal and regulatory framework that proved valuable to building commercial microfinance in Cambodia as part of the formal financial system.

---

[89] ACLEDA maintained seven current accounts with the Cambodia Farmer's Bank, a bank whose license was suspended by the NBC. Unable to withdraw the amounts, ACLEDA provisioned for their loss in 1997 and 1998. In 1999 ACLEDA wrote off the remaining USD 152,761 of lost funds on deposit. ACLEDA, Audited financial statements, 1997-1999.

[90] For an excellent study on NGO transformation and NGO performance profiles prior to and after transformation see Nimal Fernando's *Micro Success Story? Transformation of Nongovernmental Organizations into Regulated Financial Institutions.* Manila: Asian Development Bank. June 2004. Available: www.adb.org/microfinance. Also see Fernando's Mibanco Peru: Profitable Microfinance Outreach, with lessons for Asia. ADB, Manila. June 2003, and von Stauffenberg, D. July 2001. *How Microfinance Evolves: What Bolivia Can Teach Us.* Microenterprise Development Review, Vol. 4 No. 1. Washington, D.C: Inter-American Development Bank.

What Is NGO Transformation?

NGO transformation is a somewhat romantic label for the rather dry, legalistic creation of a new financial company by an NGO that runs a credit operation. A financial institution is created, licensed, regulated and supervised under the banking laws of the country. The assets of the NGO are transferred in whole or in part in exchange for shares in the new company. What really transforms are the people; their horizons grow, their relationships expand and their perceptions about running the business evolve as they leave the donors' protective cocoon and formally enter the world of commerce.

As ACLEDA found, NGO transformation does not in itself spur growth; organizational depth, management expertise, technical know-how and profitability are pre-conditions for transformation. When a central bank grants a license conferring the legal status to operate as a formal banking institution, it recognizes the legitimacy that the customers have already bestowed on the organization. The NGO no longer operates at the pleasure of its donors; it operates according to the rules established to protect the financial system. ACLEDA clarifies a further misconception about transformation. Transparency is not conveyed with a banking license; it is rooted in the culture of the organization, the values of the people who run it, and the systems they design to protect it.

Peter Kooi recalls the day the ACLEDA staff voted to transform, opting to depend on themselves in the future, and not on donor funding. It was a difficult decision. There was no guarantee it would work. Yet 98% of the staff voted to establish a commercial company and set up the ACLEDA Staff Association (ASA) which would become ACLEDA Bank's first private investor. "Later, I had the courage to ask Channy, how did you manage to get all the hands up to vote for the transformation? He responded, 'Peter, we have transformed two times before. Each time we improved. Staff trusted management that this third transformation will again make ACLEDA stronger.'"

The vault attendant in the Kampong Cham branch makes the vote sound simple. For her, it was. "I voted yes," she says, "because it seemed to me that we could grow. Now as a bank, we did grow, we offer more products to more people."

"Microfinance as an industry can never reach its full potential until it is able to move into the sphere of prudentially regulated institutions, where it will have to be prudentially supervised," concludes CGAP's Microfinance Consensus Guidelines.[91] Yet the creation and operation of a regulated banking institution generate new demands, ones that must be met if the institution is to fulfill that potential. How the institution responds to those new challenges and opportunities depends on its history and prospects for the future.

---

[91] Robert Peck Christen, Timothy Lyman and Richard Rosenberg. "Microfinance Consensus Guidelines: Guiding Principles on Regulation and Supervision of Microfinance" (Washington, D.C.: CGAP/World Bank, 2003), 26.

Reasons to Transform

NGOs cite many reasons for transformation. Most of these reasons, given time, allow the organization to continue its growth trajectory, growth that NGO status inhibits. The reason that topped ACLEDA's list for transformation was the limited donor capital available for expansion to meet the huge demand for credit. By the end of 1999, ACLEDA's outstanding portfolio had grown to USD 13.7 million, an increase of 37% from the previous year. Given past trends and increasing demand, growth was expected to continue. As the business prospered, limited amounts of funding, coupled with concerns about reliability, pushed ACLEDA to seek independence from donors. Costs of maintaining separate reporting systems on target clients no longer matched the financial nature of the MIS. Calls for expensive impact studies and donor restrictions on the institution's own choice about how to place capital became burdensome.

Transformation could allow access to commercial sources of funding, yet Cambodia's banking sector posed special problems that were not apparent in Latin America where the bulk of NGO transformations had occurred before that time. In 1999 there were few commercial lenders in Cambodia that would consider lending to national enterprises, let alone to an NGO. Despite liquidity in the system, the absence of a strong commercial banking sector limited the availability of local sources of commercial borrowing. The measures and products so useful to the Latin American MFIs in the early stages of commercial entry, such as guarantees, were unavailable.

The Cambodian economy looked outward; each commercial bank that survived the capital rally of 2000 was funded largely from foreign or overseas capital. ACLEDA planned to seek loans from the Rural Development Bank, which by November 1999 was reconstituted as a wholesale lender to the MFI sector. The RDB was permitted to lend up to 20% of its capital to one institution. A prudent policy, no doubt, but one that would effectively limit the amount ACLEDA could borrow domestically. Unless the banking sector dramatically changed, or made way for new more stable and less innovative entrants, transformation would provide a legal standing for ACLEDA to increase borrowing from foreign, rather than domestic sources of funds. Deposits, of course, were another story.

ACLEDA planned to re-examine its approach to savings. Savings products, if properly designed, would provide Cambodian micro and small entrepreneurs with an important way to manage their finances and build assets. ACLEDA also looked to deposits as a source of funding for the organization. But savings products required extensive study. The sweep through the banking sector caused concern about the safety of deposits in the public's mind. Only later would confidence in banks, and the NBC's ability to supervise them, be restored. Legal status as an NGO prohibited savings other than compulsory savings tied to many group credit products. In 1999, the NBC estimated microfinance institutions held USD 1.6 million in forced savings from 134,350 clients, or an average deposit of USD 12.[92]

---

[92] National Bank of Cambodia. Rural Credit in Cambodia. 2000.

ACLEDA's own experience with savings figured in the determination to proceed cautiously. They experimented briefly with voluntary savings in 1997, based on demand from about half of their active borrowers. The product was later discontinued as concern grew about the legality of accepting deposits without a license.[93] There was really no experience in Cambodia about whether people would save in financial institutions, or had confidence in the system to properly guard their money. While the theory on savings was well known from Bank Rakyat Indonesia's successful model, which ACLEDA staff studied throughout 1997-1999, Cambodia's savers appeared more wary than their Indonesian counterparts. The total domestic savings rate in Cambodia was 4.4% of GDP in 1997, the lowest in Southeast Asia, compared with Indonesia's buoyant rate of 31% of GDP during the same period.[94]

Cambodia operated without money from 1975-1980, a further complication receiving the attention of savings experts. Afterwards, during a period of hyperinflation, goods held value whereas money, particularly savings in local currency, was collected at one's own peril. People saved in gold, rice, animals, gems, equipment, and inventory to the extent that it could be purchased. Those with more means saved in foreign currency, off-shore if they knew how to, but mostly in mattresses, suitcases and holes dug in the ground. During the bank restructuring period, from 1999-2002, many people congratulated themselves on their wise investments in mattress money when banks paid 34 cents on the dollar, if the depositor was lucky. Yet there was evidence, through ACLEDA's own limited experience with a very small and expensive product, that people would save. A study carried out in 1997 found that people did save in cash and would entrust ACLEDA with their money.[95]

The third reason for ACLEDA's transformation was a legal one. The impending regulation within the NBC would require ACLEDA to apply for a license, however limited, to continue to operate under the law. As we have seen, since 1995 the government was considering some type of regulation that would eventually determine the way microfinance developed in Cambodia. ACLEDA felt it prudent to support the direction, although not many of the earlier proposals. There was no idealistic push for formalization; it was really a matter of being ahead of the curve – a practical concern.

ACLEDA's expansion to 14 of Cambodia's 20 Provinces, and its growing operating profit prevented falling under the radar as an insignificant banking activity.

---

[93] An evaluation noted, "As a non-licensed financial intermediary, ACLEDA has not been able to actively promote savings and, consequently, savings collected amount only to $17,500 (one per cent of micro-loans outstanding, or an average $0.69 per account) at June 30 1997." David Lucock, "Project Evaluation Study of Alleviation of Poverty through ACLEDA's Financial Services" (CMB/95/010) (Phnom Penh: UNDP, August 1997), 25.

[94] Asian Development Bank, *Asian Development Outlook, 1999* (Manila: ADB, 1998), table A7.

[95] Lucock, Project Evaluation, 25.

Continued justification as a non-profit organization seemed equally unreasonable to the staff. In 1999, ACLEDA produced USD 1.3 million net profit from operations which enabled portfolio expansion to USD 14.8 million just prior to transformation.[96] ACLEDA management felt the organization had outgrown its non-profit status, and indeed it had.

Lastly, the uncertainty over the government's final decision about the ownership of accumulated donor capital encouraged ACLEDA to seek a legitimate ownership structure with clear claims on capital.

Why Not Transform?

Transformation is not an easy choice. Many NGOs that engaged in the policy dialogue with the NBC agonized over certain policies; some were critical of the overall concept as well. Their reasoning rested on financial considerations, and differences of opinion about banking activities. First, they would be subjected to tax, license fees and penalties for not following reporting schedules or prudential requirements. Second, they would have to give up donor funding. Although the regulatory discussions did not prohibit grants to legally incorporated private companies, there was an understanding that most donors would shy away from funding privately owned companies. Instead, new shareholders would accept the responsibility to raise additional capital. Third, many NGOs thought they should not be subjected to NBC regulation. They disagreed that they were engaged in banking activities, and advocated exemptions based on their social missions and poverty alleviation goals.

Oddly the opponents of transformation did not list several major concerns about NGO transformation that are often cited by practitioners and scholars. For the most part, they welcomed a more professional microfinance community, but failed to anticipate the host of prudential requirements and rigors imposed by the banking law, perhaps rigors their management could not meet. Further, wide-scale NGO transformation would bring on a plethora of organizational disruptions, the greatest of which would be staff attrition, management disaffection, a beleaguered leadership, and a perceived loss of control tied loosely to the concept of dilution of mission.

Even as late as mid-2002 some consultants questioned, "How it is possible that an MFI, which operates as a business, can serve the poor and operate commercially?" They claimed that microcredit operators "could end up marginalized by the requirement that they register as MFIs."[97] Such a questionable position must have shocked those who sat around the table in 1996, 1997 and 1998 when they carefully considered the future of their organizations and the impending regulation.

---

[96] ACLEDA Audited financial statements, December 1999 and August 2000.

[97] Caroline Green quotes Karen Rasmussen in "Micro-finance: who's helping whom?" Phnom Penh Post, June 2002.

The NBC Rules

From Prodem's pioneering effort in Bolivia, to the steppes of Mongolia, many NGOs have transformed within the context of an evolving regulatory framework. NGO transformations in Cambodia were no exception. Few NGOs have marked their transformations in the midst of massive bank restructuring efforts that would make even the most liberal banking authority over anxious about proliferation of under-capitalized institutions and suspicious of alternative banking structures.[98]

In January 2000 the law on MFIs and specialized banks was released. After two years of anticipation and considerable consultation with the NGO community, the law contained a tiered licensing system for microfinance institutions in Cambodia. The microfinance law was integrated into the Law on Banking and Financial Institutions, not set apart from it. It was viewed as a part of a comprehensive financial sector reform package in the transition from a mono-banking system to a two-tier banking system. Supporters of the new law, such as the Asian Development Bank, the IMF and the World Bank, emphasized the "importance of strengthening the supervisory and regulatory authority at an early stage to maximize the impact of subsequent reforms and to smooth the transition process. The law envisaged the development of a rural financial system by upgrading NGO operations to allow interaction with the banking sector in the long run."[99] It allowed for both prudential and non-prudential regulation and supervision.

The new legislation was revolutionary for the time. Some analysts attribute this to having the luxury of comprehensive financial sector restructuring, dodging the makeshift reviews and ad hoc laws passed to benefit microfinance in many other countries. Most importantly, the new law underpinned a very practical approach to banking in Cambodia. In December 1999 private-sector domestic credit stood at USD 202 million, mostly to finance trade and services, and denominated in foreign

---

[98] Bolivia and Mexico experienced financial sector crises in the mid-1980s and mid-1990s, respectively, more distant from the first NGO transformations in Bolivia in 1992, and Mexico in 1999. KREP in Kenya transformed in the context of bank failure. "In mid-1998, five small banks were placed under the Central Bank management due to lack of liquidity, followed by a run in December 1998 on the National Bank of Kenya, the country's fourth largest bank … Five years transpired between the K-Rep board's decision to transform the NGO's Financial Services Division into a regulated financial institution, and Central Bank of Kenya (CBK) issuance of a commercial banking license to K-Rep Bank." Jay Rosengard, et al., *Microfinance Development in Kenya: K-Rep's Transition From NGO to Diversified Holding Company and Commercial Bank*, HIID Discussion Paper No. 762. (Harvard Institute for International Development. Harvard University, June 2000), 13.

[99] Asian Development Bank. Report and Recommendation of the President to the Board of Directors on a Proposed Loan to the Kingdom of Cambodia for the Rural Credit and Savings Project (Manila: ADB, 2000), 10.

currency.[100] At the same time, 25 NGOs and projects which reported on a voluntary basis to the NBC had outstanding portfolios amounting to USD 22.8 million, roughly 11% of the banking sector's portfolio.[101]

The relatively narrow breadth of formal banking services further underscored the significant size and importance of NGO banking activity in Cambodia. Commercial bank branches operated in only nine of Cambodia's Provincial capitals. Rural residents relied on the more extensive reach of NGOs in 18 of Cambodia's 20 Provinces. Estimates of the day depict a Cambodia where less than 10% of the total population had reasonable access to formal banking services while NGOs and projects directly covered about 11% of rural households with semi-formal services.

"The Prakas"[102]

The Prakas on Licensing of Specialized Banks and the Prakas on Registration and Licensing of Microfinance Institutions anticipated three institutional categories: specialized banks, licensed microfinance institutions, and registered microfinance operations. These three categories differed substantially with respect to minimum capital and reserve requirements, license fees, and reporting data and intervals. The new law opted to distinguish among the types of charter, based on the size as well as the scope of the operation, with a scale of rights, responsibilities and limitations keyed to the type of license offered. Licensed MFIs and specialized banks fell under the prudential regulation and supervisory powers of the NBC. Registered MFIs followed non-prudential regulations, such as simple reporting requirements, disclosure of interest rates, and proof of a qualified governance and management structure.

Despite the worst fears of the MFIs in Cambodia, the new law did not restrict NGOs to the cooperative form of organization; it allowed organizations to incorporate as limited liability companies under commercial law, or as cooperatives or mutual noncommercial societies subject to special statute.[103] It allowed locally incorporated entities to operate as well as branches of foreign banks. Nor did the new law contain a mandate to affiliate with an APEX institution in which NGOs would become forced shareholders.

Finally the law did not include restrictions on interest rates. In fact, the law was quite clear, as were the banking authorities, that interest rates would be determined by the market. Like a recalcitrant phoenix rising from the ashes (but at shorter intervals), the subject of interest rate ceilings regularly flies into meetings, Senate

---

[100] IMF, Staff Country Report, 00/127. (Washington, D.C.: IMF, October 2000), Table 5.

[101] National Bank of Cambodia, "Rural Credit in Cambodia", 2000.

[102] A Prakas is a regulation issued by ministerial authority.

[103] As of 2004 there is no law on cooperatives or credit unions. See Torres, O. Rural Finance and microfinance Sector in Cambodia. World Bank. 2004.

and Parliamentary proceedings, and the press. The swift passage of the Prakas on MFI interest rates was quite prudent and far-sighted in this respect; it required an interest rate calculation on the outstanding loan balance and amortization tables for all loan agreements with customers. The banking authorities rallied around a truth in lending act, not an interest rate ceiling which would undermine the very market reforms they sought to implement.

Tal Nay Im, Director General of the NBC, notes the thinking about interest rates and government-imposed caps:

> *"It is the government's policy that the interest rate is determined by the market. If MFIs get a license and operate normally, the interest rate will go down, and the interest rate has decreased compared to five years ago. The government cannot fix the rate, and does not want to interfere. We want to influence the rate, by influencing the stability of MFIs, fostering competition and strengthening them. We did intervene in the method of calculation, by requiring a declining balance calculation. A flat rate is very heavy for the borrower, and the pricing is not transparent."*[104]

The law did require compulsory registration or licensing for NGOs depending on the size and scope of their lending and savings operations, as indicated in Table 8.1. Any microfinance operation with sizable banking services was required to submit an application for license by December 31 2002, or scale down its operations and operate as a registered MFI.

The banking authorities responded to Cambodia's weak financial sector, a proliferation of undercapitalized banks and the lack of a deposit guarantee facility, by

Table 8.1. Microfinance Institution Registration and Licensing

Compulsory Registration	*Loan Portfolio*: equal to or greater than KRH 100 million (USD 25,000), and/or
	Savings from the public: KRH 1 million (USD 250) or more than 100 depositors
Compulsory Licensing	*Loan Portfolio:* equal to or greater than KRH 1,000 million (USD 250,000) or 1,000 borrowers, and/or
	Savings from the public: KRH 100 million (USD 25,000 or 1,000 depositors)

Source: Prakas No. B 7-00-06 of 11 January 2000, amended by Prakas 7.02-49 of 25 February 2002

---

[104] Tal Nay Im, Author interview December 2003.

drafting the law with an influential shareholder clause. Influential shareholders own at least 20% of the share capital or voting rights. If warranted by the bank's financial position, they would be called on to increase capital contributions until solvency standards were met. And now the infamous Article 74, which would have made illegal any banking activity carried out by an institution that was not in compliance with the law, was softened by reasonable grace periods for MFIs to comply.[105]

The law and the series of Prakas that were released over time appeared strict to NGOs accustomed to following a self-regulatory regime whose only enforcement relied on the collective complaints of their peers. Meeting the new requirements for an MFI license or a specialized banking license appeared less daunting to ACLEDA and the other microcredit NGOs than a situation the earlier regulatory discourse might have produced. To them, the years of collective collaboration finally paid off.

The Specialized Banking License

ACLEDA's interest was in the Specialized Banking License. It was limited to specific banking activities permitted by the license, and it was valid for a three-year period. The specialized banking license differed substantially from a commercial banking license in its minimum capital and related reserve requirements, as Table 8.2 shows.

ACLEDA viewed the specialized banking license as a stepping-stone to a commercial license, not as a permanent institutional category. And while those stepping-stones may have lined up and disappeared somewhere in the future, ACLEDA determined to take them one at a time. For much of 1998 and 1999, ACLEDA focused on developing a plan to meet the NBC's criteria to qualify for the specialized bank license. In Channy recalls the most important areas "were to strengthen our capital base, diversify our ownership structure and reinforce management."[106]

If it were not for the more precipitous rulings of the NBC, ACLEDA Bank Ltd would have preferred to take more time undergoing its fourth transformation to become ACLEDA Bank Plc., a licensed commercial bank. Yet the greatest challenges surrounded ACLEDA's first entrance into the formal financial system, as we shall see.

---

[105] The initial grace period was December 2002. It was later extended to July 2003.

[106] In Channy, "Rural Financial Institutions: Start-Ups The Case Study of ACLEDA Bank" paper presented at Paving the Way Forward for Rural Finance, An International Conference on Best Practices, Washington, D.C. June 2-4 2003), 3.

Table 8.2. Key Provisions of the Microfinance Regulatory Framework

	Commercial Bank	Specialized Bank	Licensed MFI	Registered MFI
Minimum Capital	USD 13 million (KHR 50 billion)	USD 2.5 million (KHR 10 billion)	USD 70,000 (KHR 250 million)	n.a.
Guarantee with NBC (Article 16)	At least 5% of minimum capital, raised to 10%	5% minimum capital	5% minimum capital	n.a.
Reserve rate for deposits	5% of deposits	5% of deposits	5% of deposits (excluding compulsory savings)	n.a.
License	Valid 3 years	Valid 3 years	Valid 3 years	n.a.
Most demanding reporting interval	Daily	Daily	Monthly	Quarterly
Ownership	No restriction on number shareholders or the % of their shares, but a review for excessive concentration or wide dispersal (Article 25)			
Ownership	Influential shareholder, at least 20% of share capital or voting rights, will be enjoined to increase net worth until solvency standards are met. (Article 27)			
Services	Universal Banking	Restrictions on banking services, depending on license, e.g. wholesale or sector-specific lenders, and other activities, such as FOREX.	Restrictions on micro-finance defined as "the delivery of financial services such as loans and deposits, to the poor and low-income households, and to micro-enterprises."	Restrictions on amount of portfolio & deposits
Taxes	Commercial Rates	Commercial Rates	Commercial Rates	n.a

Sources: The Law on Banking and Financial Institutions, (Phnom Penh: National Bank of Cambodia, 1999). Prakas on the Licensing of Micro-Financing Institutions, (Phnom Penh: National Bank of Cambodia, 2000). Prakas on Licensing of Specialized Banks, (Phnom Penh: National Bank of Cambodia, 2000).

A Similar Pattern

Before transformation, ACLEDA was a growing and complex organization, an ant hive of activity, shoring up the architecture, developing the human infrastructure. Rapid growth during the three years prior to transformation positioned ACLEDA as a likely candidate for transformation into a licensed financial intermediary. The transformation process itself would become an all-consuming task over the next two years, culminating in the conveyance of a specialized bank license in October 2000.

At the time of transformation, ACLEDA's balance sheet probably looked similar to many other NGOs just prior to taking commercial vows.

- The operation had grown rapidly and substantially. The portfolio almost tripled during the three-year period prior to transformation; annual increments never dipped below a 35% increase.

- ACLEDA was profitable: retained earnings, excluding grants, amounted to ˙USD 1.8 million for the eight-month period prior to transformation.

- The operation had not only preserved donor capital, but had made up for accumulated operating losses since 1993 through retained earnings.

- At the time of transformation accumulated donor equity amounted to USD 11.2 million, or 58% of the asset base of USD 19.5 million.[107]

- The operation was under-leveraged with a debt/equity ratio of 0.44:1, compared with a typical bank debt/equity ratio of 10:1. The Latin American MFIs had typical debt/equity ratios of 1:1 prior to transformation.[108]

- It mobilized no deposits – time, term or demand deposits. ACLEDA borrowed from one 2nd tier lender, the Rural Development Bank, and two international donors, KfW and Catholic Relief Services.

In other important aspects ACLEDA's experience paralleled that of many NGOs whose ambitions drove them to become commercial operations. The legal and regulatory framework which would guide their development had not yet been established. The organization was driven by staff and management. The micro and small lending operation was the only business. ACLEDA was perceived as a leader in the field. And, it had no owners.

---

[107] Figures from ACLEDA Audited Financial statements, August 2000. Accumulated donor equity from 1993 calculated from audited financial statements 1993-August 2000.

[108] Tor Jansson, "Financing Microfinance: Exploring the Funding Side of Microfinance Institutions." Sustainable Development Department Technical Papers Series MSM-118. (Washington, D.C.: Inter-American Development Bank, 2003), 3.

CHAPTER 9

Inspiration: From the Andes to the Mekong

By the time ACLEDA began plans for transformation in 1997, there were seven NGO transformations world-wide; all of them were in Latin America.[109] Precedent, although distant, was important. Without the first experience in Bolivia and subsequent initiatives in Latin America and Kenya, it is unlikely that ACLEDA's plan would have carried the clout needed to convince the host of people who would ultimately make a difference — the NBC, the investors, and ACLEDA staff members themselves.

Three independent appraisals were conducted to assess the potential of ACLEDA to transform into a licensed microfinance institution. The appraisals, each with their own focus and each more comprehensive than the last, compared ACLEDA's performance, structure and environment with other notable institutions of the time that had transformed or were contemplating transformation – BancoSol and Prodem in Bolivia, ADOPEM in the Dominican Republic, CorpoSol in Colombia, KREP in Kenya, FINCA Costa Rica, ACEP in Senegal. The appraisals were positive; ACLEDA's performance could eventually match the others. But doubts lingered in the background. Just as early skeptics questioned the relevance of Bank Rakyat Indonesia's experience to Bolivia, citing the sparsely populated country as a limiting factor, skeptics now cited the level of poverty and the devastated physical and human infrastructure as constraints on the growth of commercial microfinance in Cambodia. To many experts in the field, Cambodia seemed to lie somewhere between perdition and the end of the earth.

It is difficult to say that the Bolivian model of NGO transformation was the sole inspiration for ACLEDA's own. It is easy to say that ACLEDA learned from BancoSol's experience. In 1998, ACLEDA senior management traveled to Bolivia to interview BancoSol and Prodem about the transformation that had taken place six years earlier. What they learned in the Andes had a powerful influence on the choices ACLEDA would make for its own transformation along the Mekong.

This chapter explores ACLEDA's lessons from Bolivia and how it applied them within its own organization.

---

[109] Fernando, N. Fernando, N. June 2004. *Micro Success Story? Transformation of Nongovernmental Organizations into Regulated Financial Institutions.* Manila: Asian Development Bank. P 31-39

The Prodem-BancoSol transformation, the first NGO transformation, occurred at a time when microfinance was just beginning to take off around the world. NGO transformation into a commercial entity was such a radical approach to development that it ushered in the entangled challenges of combining social objectives with the profitability of the business model. The four major issues in Bolivia were the transfer of donated funds to a commercial entity, the suitability of the interest rate, the profitability of the business model, and ensuring an ownership structure that was commercially oriented and developmentally sound.[110]

Many of the issues that defined critical choices for the first Prodem-BancoSol transformation were no longer as relevant to ACLEDA. Certainly the spotlight shining on this promising model for transition from the donor world to the commercial world had a great deal to do with the declining prominence of some of the earlier debates. Equally important was the Cambodian context. But what led ACLEDA's choice was its own organizational history.

Donated Money

Perhaps the most significant challenge for BancoSol's transformation was the decision to employ donor money to capitalize a private company. In Cambodia, after the tumultuous period devoted to relinquishing government claims on donated NGO capital, the propriety of using accumulated donor equity for the start-up of a microfinance bank stirred less debate. While other donor-supported projects and NGOs in Cambodia were not as fortunate, ACLEDA's grant agreements clearly designated donated equity as ACLEDA's own funds once they were loaned out and recovered. The new concern of ACLEDA and its technical advisors was how to ensure that donor capital did not subsidize the new investors in the commercial operation. This would occur if the NGO simply transferred its donated portfolio to the owners of the new venture, or if donors funded the share purchase for the new owners.

ACLEDA's investors would be coming to a going business with 27 branches, 330 staff, a portfolio of USD 13.7 million and 56,412 borrowers in 11 Provinces.[111] That seemed to be enough of a smart subsidy to jump-start a new commercial venture. A direct transfer of donated capital to the new company was not considered, nor was donor funding considered appropriate for share purchase by the new owners. The discussions instead centered on how to establish a commercial company that would limit the perpetual subsidy of the accumulated donor capital. The modest change in global attitude allowed ACLEDA to call for investment analysts; less time was devoted to arguing intractable principled positions.

---

[110] See Rhyne, *Mainstreaming Microfinance* for a detailed discussion of issues of Bolivian NGO transformation.

[111] Figures as of the December 1999.

High Interest Rates

The issue of high interest rates for microfinance featured prominently in the Ban-coSol transformation. Thinking at the time centered on the relatively high interest rates charged on micro loans as unacceptable for a commercial entity. The new bank's image might suffer if adverse public perception grew around lending to poor people at a price higher than that paid by mainstream, wealthier customers. The Cambodian authorities as well as the public had a new take on the relative interest rates charged by NGOs and banks. NGOs, they claimed, had development aims, access to donor money, and enjoyed tax-free status. From this perspective, the idea that NGOs charged high interest rates proved to be much more damaging. A bank established as a profit-making entity and paying taxes fared much better in the image contest.

Over time, experience supported the theory that interest rates decreased as MFIs expanded and competition increased. Yet there was a concern on the part of the government, including the NBC, that interest rates were too high. The NBC had already declared its adherence to a market economy. Interest rate ceilings would clearly be a violation of those tenets. Instead it chose to establish a truth in lending law, requiring all MFIs to calculate interest on a declining balance method and provide an amortization schedule to each borrower. The NBC anticipated gradually decreasing interest rates as organizations expanded, competition in-creased, and borrowers compared rates and the quality of services amongst many providers. Disillusioned with the quick-fix policies of the past and influenced by the IMF in the present, it determined to let the market work for the sector and the consumers within it.

Profitability of the Business Model

As strange as it seems today, the profitability of the business model was a key issue in BancoSol's transformation. By 1999, several microfinance NGOs in Cambodia were profitable or nearing profitability. Investment funds active in NGO transformations were not as skeptical of the profitability of the business model as they began to support NGO transformations in Kenya, Peru, Bolivia, and El Salvador. Yet one of ACLEDA's original investors doubted the profit-ability of the business model. Perhaps because of the amount of time spent on ensuring legal requirements were met on such a small investment of USD 490,000, the IFC was right to doubt that initial investment costs would not be recovered for quite some time to come.

Ownership Structure

ACLEDA's transition team was just as pre-occupied with the ownership structure as the BancoSol Co-Banco team was in 1991. The idea for ACLEDA Bank's ownership structure evolved from the early-1997 idea of 100% ownership by the

NGO to the late-1997 idea of creating a holding company with two subsidiaries – the NGO and the bank. In 1998 the, idea of attracting a group of outside investors emerged and won favor.[112]

The 100% NGO ownership plan, recommended in the first feasibility study, was seen as a way to speed up the process. It anticipated the NGO's sale of shares to interested investors over time. Later the plan was discarded as a structure that prohibited rather than encouraged the participation of investors. Yet one important concept in this plan remained — the idea that the parent NGO could gradually sell shares to the ACLEDA Staff Association, up to 19% of the total shares in the new bank. The discussion about ownership no longer centered on the desirability of attracting investors, or fretting about attracting private local investors as the Bolivia model had. The transition team determined to attract investors that shared the vision of the organization – those who would be valued just as much for their capital as for their expertise in microfinance, banking and governance.

The Plan

The architects of the BancoSol transformation anticipated the investment in time and money that such a transformation would require. BancoSol organized Co-Banco, a team that for two years and four months developed the business plan, worked with regulatory authorities and investors and planned the operational transition.[113] ACLEDA's own transformation followed a similar pattern. A three-year transformation project was established, recognizing the costs, technical assistance, training and feasibility studies that would be required to position ACLEDA as an institution meriting a banking license. And indeed, a three-year time frame was not excessive as the timeline in Table 9.1 reveals. Each step in the process took place in an atmosphere of political uncertainty, dogged determination, and what appeared to be an endless stream of consultants and appraisers paving the way from donor dependence to ACLEDA's new status as a member of the club.

A project to provide technical assistance to ACLEDA was financed in early 1999 by the UNDP, the U.S. Agency for International Development, and IFC's Mekong Project Development Facility (MPDF). The goals were to transform ACLEDA's governance structure, establish an ownership structure, and upgrade managerial and technical capacity. The project anticipated a new wave of corporate policies and strategy, changes in organizational structure, and improvements in management information systems. The transformation project allowed ACLEDA to dedicate time, resources and energy to increasing organizational strength and

---

[112] This evolution is shown in three feasibility studies: Prins Feb. 1997, Lucock August 1997, and Calmeadow Feb 1998.

[113] Amy Glosser, "The Creation of BancoSol in Bolivia" in *The New World*, 234.

profitability. The project financed a full-time technical advisor, several short-term specialists, and fellowships and training opportunities for ACLEDA staff.

According to Dennis Cengel, USAID's project officer at the time:

> *"The decision to support technical assistance and training instead of loan capital was a very good one. USAID's strategy for microfinance changed from an NGO focus to an economic growth strategy where support to microfinance as part of the financial sector was seen as vitally important. ACLEDA had a good understanding of what technical assistance and training it needed for the transformation process to take place. There was a common agreement that circumstances had changed and the best thing USAID could do was to collaborate with UNDP to provide technical assistance and training for that transition."*

ACLEDA's performance as an NGO was exceptional. If its plans to become the first NGO commercial transformation in Cambodia were fulfilled, it would make an important contribution to the development of an inclusive financial sector, one that embraced poor and low-income people, the majority of Cambodia's population, as worthy customers. The choice to support the dominant microfinance NGO to experiment with the new commercial status was intended to demonstrate the "show-how" that such a transition was possible in Cambodia. "ACLEDA was the leader, and everyone else was following," notes Cengel. "They inspired confidence with the banking authorities and among their colleagues." Paul Luchtenberg, regional technical advisor to World Relief, notes with the admiration of one such collegial competitor, "ACLEDA was always raising the bar, it affected everyone's performance."

As the feasibility studies of 1997-1998 translated into business plans and their subsequent revisions of 1998 and 1999, regulatory reform consultations with the Central Bank continued. Investor negotiations developed into models of ownership and operational plans to transfer assets and liabilities. New articles of association for the ACLEDA Bank, the NGO and ASA prompted legal advice, the scrutiny of three different Ministries and the eventual affixture of signatures that all the terms and conditions were fully and irrevocably binding.

When the microfinance law was finally passed in January 2000, ACLEDA and the IFC legal team carried on, dotting the "i's" and crossing the "t's" in the growing morass of inter-linked legal agreements. And all this time, ACLEDA's original local private investor group, the ACLEDA Staff Association, held the patient capital that many earlier NGO transformations had sought public investors to place. The valuation exercise was completed in August 2000, the subscription agreement and subordinated and senior debt agreements were ratified in September 2000.

On October 1, 2000, ACLEDA opened its doors as a Specialized Bank. A little over three-and-a-half years after the first transformation feasibility study, the flash bulbs popped.

Table 9.1. Transformation Timeline, 1997 – 2000

1997	Series of feasibility studies
1997-1998	Series of workshops with ACLEDA staff
Jan 1998	Transformation project begins, funded by USAID, UNDP and MPDF/IFC
June-Aug 1998	ACLEDA prepares business plan
June 1998	ACLEDA submits proposal for regulatory framework to National Bank of Cambodia
October 1998	Business plan submitted to four foreign investors IFC, DEG, FMO, and Triodos Doen
December 1998	National Bank of Cambodia reacts favorably to ACLEDA proposal
February 1999	ACLEDA General Assembly votes to become a bank, abolishes itself, and hands over governance to a transition team
February 1999	ACLEDA Staff Association, Inc (ASA) created.
Feb-March 1999	Investor institutional appraisal of ACLEDA
March 1999	Detailed negotiations with investors begin
November 1999	New law on Bank and Financial Institutions
December 1999	NBC gives "approval in principle" to ACLEDA to operate as a specialized bank
January 2000	MFI and Specialized Bank Law and regulations released
January 2000	NBC authorizes ACLEDA to conduct banking services as a specialized bank
April 2000	Ministry of Interior approves transformation of ACLEDA into ACLEDA NGO
April 2000	Ministry of Commerce approves statutes of ASA, Inc.
April 2000	Subscription and shareholder agreement signed.
August 2000	Valuation audit completed.
August 2000	NBC issues specialized banking license for ACLEDA Bank Ltd.
September 2000	Business purchase agreement signed between Bank and ACLEDA NGO
September 2000	Subordinated and senior debt agreements ratified
October 1 2000	ACLEDA Bank Ltd officially opens its doors as a licensed Specialized Bank

Innovation

Whether or not a commercial transition could occur without destroying the organization was open to conjecture. That risk provoked the imaginations of the architects of the transformation plan. Some idea of a mechanism for transformation evolved from the experience of the Latin American MFIs, but there was no one model for transformation. The mechanism of transferring an NGO's accumulated donor capital to a newly created private company, under the romantic label of NGO transformation, differed from institution to institution and country to country. What was known from the BancoSol experience was that the process could be long, expensive and tumultuous for the organization. The idea that a commercial company could better help the poor drew criticism from many quarters of the international development community. And within the organization, ACLEDA staff pondered their own fears of the unknown: the motives of international shareholders, the extent of government control, the essence of profit-making companies, and perhaps the harsher staff requirements and qualifications that a business would demand but an NGO might let slide.

Benefits, Risks and Costs

If the benefits of such a plan were tangible, the risks and the costs were just as easily catalogued. Risks emanated from the environment, and from within the institution. The questions seemed endless; they focused on sources of funds, the legal and regulatory framework, internal systems, staff capacity, and the objectives of the new owners:

- Would commercial sources of domestic borrowing be available? Why would a foreign bank lend to a fledgling institution in a country with Cambodia's high risk rating in international markets? Would the amount of commercial funding really ever exceed donor funding available?

- What would the legal and regulatory framework look like, and how would microfinance fit into it?

- Could ACLEDA's newly designed systems withstand the rigors of supporting a regulated institution?

- Would staff embrace yet another system change, or would they rebel? Could they upgrade their skills to match the growing sophistication of the organization? How many would stay, and who would go?

- Would shareholders' demands for increased value shift the organization away from microfinance customers?

Each risk translated into costs the organization would have to bear. The plan was to maximize the benefits, minimize the risks, and manage the costs as shown in Table 9.2.

Table 9.2. Benefits, Risks and Costs

Perceived Benefits	Perceived Risks	Perceived Costs
Access to commercial capital and deposits for expanded portfolio growth to serve more customers	Available sources of domestic commercial borrowing were limited. Foreign sources may not develop due to Cambodia's risk rating in international markets.	Increasing cost of funds as donor money is replaced by commercial sources; costs associated with identifying foreign lenders & subsequent appraisals; costs associated with mobilizing deposits.
Ability to offer a variety of new products important to customers, such as savings, transfers and other banking products that were unavailable in most of the country.	Newly established systems built for speed and accuracy, not security, were integrated and well understood by staff. Systems would need to be changed for security, deposit taking, and changing information requirements.	Upgrade systems to produce information required for prudent management of diverse products and security. Upgrade systems compliant with regulations, and reporting requirements.
Clear legal status conveys rights and responsibilities protected by the banking law.	The legal and regulatory framework for the entire banking system was still in draft form. Microfinance legislation was low on the list. Prior experience with banking authorities showed a preference for a high level of government control.	Subject to tax, license fees, reserve requirements. Raise minimum capital Rigor of reporting required dedicated staff. Training staff & management to meet requirements under the banking law. Costs of supervision.
Clear ownership structure & governance system enhances institutional stability & accountability	Shareholders may be less forgiving of organizational imperfections and more demanding of organizational growth	Organizational upheaval, resulting in staff turnover, high costs of training & replacement, loss of morale
Independence of donors removes uncertainty & restrictions; increases long-term institutional stability & business decision-making	Staff capacity: can a group of teachers become bankers? "Mission drift": will a drive for profitability pressure larger loan sizes and targeting more affluent, less risky clients?	Upgrade staff skills, conduct feasibility studies, market research, product pricing & costing, investor liaison, legal advice, management time devoted to institutional investment appraisals.
Plan: Maximize Benefits	**Plan: Minimize Risks**	**Plan: Manage Costs**

Uno, Dos, Tres

Three specific issues gained ACLEDA's attention from their BancoSol expedition. Each would have a lasting impact on ACLEDA's thinking about the basic structure of what was to become ACLEDA Bank. Employee ownership, competition and preservation of donor capital for its originally intended purposes figured prominently in the development of ACLEDA's own transformation model.

Owners and Workers

ACLEDA viewed the BancoSol transformation curious in its lack of provision for employee ownership. ACLEDA was a staff-owned organization, not in the traditional sense that profit accrued to staff, but in the real sense that ownership of the national development process had been successful. For ACLEDA it was imperative that staff, considered its greatest asset, should have a stake in the bank. First and foremost, the BancoSol transformation team sought access to capital for the growing organization. Perhaps they thought staff would not be in a position to match capital contributions in the timeframe investors could marshal the capital for a larger and more stably funded organization. There were doubts about profitability. The idea that staff would risk their own capital in such a fragile venture with no proven income stream as a regulated institution may have led the architects of BancoSol's plan to demur the issue of employee ownership of risk capital to other more pressing risks of the time.

ACLEDA management listened to Pancho Otero and the BancoSol and Prodem staff. Coming with a predisposition for employee ownership, they heard the stories of culture clash and plummeting morale as the bank no longer seemed to value the contributions of its NGO employees, and replaced them with more experienced banking professionals. While Channy and Soeun had no illusions about the power of an Employee Stock Ownership Plan (ESOP) to stem staff attrition, they did recognize the importance of the plan to employees. By inviting employees to participate as owners, the bank was making an important statement about how it valued them. The ESOP could ease the transition, creating support for the idea of a new company. In the long term ACLEDA thought an ESOP could enhance employee productivity, as well as provide a means to share in the productive capital of the organization. As ACLEDA's Human Resource Director, Chan Serey, notes, "as NGO employees we focused on the problems, later we focused on how to make the business grow."

By the time In Channy and Chhay Soeun visited Bolivia, BancoSol was a profitable institution. In fact, BancoSol was heralded as one of the top performers in Bolivia's banking sector, and was gaining world-wide recognition as proof that a commercial bank dedicated to the microenterprise market could be profitable.[114]

---

[114] Anita Campion and Victoria White, "Institutional Metamorphosis: Transformation of Microfinance NGOs into Regulated Financial Institutions," Occasional Paper No 4. (Washington, D.C.: Microfinance Network, 1999), 2.

Hindsight of what was considered an unpredictable experiment in the Andes in the early 90s encouraged the young Cambodians to pursue an employee stock ownership plan for their own transformation. Channy felt that creating a profitable enterprise without employee ownership would eventually lead to confusion and disappointment. At some point in the future the bank would make a profit. How would the employees understand exclusive shareholding by foreign agencies? If the profit exceeded expectations, why would the initial shareholders want to include others? What if shares for a microfinance bank developed from the sorry state of a thin secondary market into a more robust one? Even if the initial shareholders developed a well-executed exit strategy, why would they want to include staff? At some distant point in the future, the exercise of creating a means for employees to participate in the growth of the institution might be viewed as more burdensome than the simple transaction of one investor selling its shares to another.

"That's why we were determined to create ASA", recalls Soeun. "When ACLEDA became a profitable enterprise, perhaps the shareholders wouldn't want to include others, an exit strategy may not include employee shares." For ACLEDA's leadership, it seemed advisable to include employees from the beginning, just as they were included in 1993 as owners of the national development process. To ignore their history would be a mistake.

Yet ACLEDA's leaders were not the blind advocates for ESOPs that a comparison with shareholder structures of the Latin American transformation model would seem to indicate. At this point in time, ACLEDA's experiment with branch manager governance was beginning to go terribly wrong as the interests of some branch managers came directly into conflict with the interests of the organization. Four important lessons from this period guided ACLEDA's thinking about an ESOP.

First, ACLEDA's management thought ESOPs could be profitable for employees and healthy for the organization, but it was critical to balance the degree of ownership with concerns about conflict of interest. Second, it needed to prevent a widely dispersed ownership structure that might lead to an unstable capital base. Third, it was important that the shares should truly be owned by the employees, not subsidized from additional donor capital or transferred to individuals from the NGO as compensation for sweat equity. Otherwise, the management thought, how would the bank really operate on a commercial basis? And how would the new owners of the bank treat the ESOP as an investor with equal status if assets were simply transferred to employees and management? Lastly, they determined not to separate management from the rank and file, who contributed equally to how the organization evolved. The ESOP would be designed to treat all employees fairly.

These were some of the questions about employee ownership that the transformation plan later addressed. What became clear in the early discussions was that board-based employee ownership was not only a desirable outcome, but also a non-negotiable position for the future of ACLEDA Bank.

Competition

Consider the anatomy of an NGO transformation. The diagram shows two distinct organizational entities – the non-profit organization and the newly established commercial company. The first is already engaged in the business, and the other is about to start. The two organizations are tied to one another by a fluid organizational history, and a future financial relationship powered by the transfer of assets. Choices about the extent of the division between the two organizations shape how each will function in the future. Will the NGO transfer its entire operation to the new company, and become a holding company or trust, ceasing to exist as an NGO? Will the NGO continue, enjoying a positive financial relationship with the bank, as it earns dividends, fees, or as shares increase in value? And if the NGO does continue, will the NGO microfinance operation absorb the costs of developing new business for the bank, start its own microfinance operation, or focus on a new mission?

Each of these questions has been answered in different ways in the course of NGO transformations world-wide, and indeed the performance of Prodem, BancoSol's parent NGO, caught the eager attention of ACLEDA's management team.[115]

At the point of transformation in 1992 BancoSol bought the most mature and profitable branches from its parent NGO, Prodem. Initially the transformation plan relied on the NGO microcredit operation to feed new branches to the bank. Prodem absorbed the high branch start-up costs, nurtured the branches to the point of profitability and in the process, financed its own expansion with the sale of mature branches to BancoSol. The BancoSol plan proceeded to acquire a total of eight branches and a portfolio of USD 8.3 million from 1992 through 1994.[116] Meanwhile, Prodem's initial largess of unprofitable, mostly rural branches quickly developed into a bounty of new branches that operated efficiently and profitably.

In early 1998 when ACLEDA management visited Bolivia, Prodem was applying for a license as a regulated financial institution. It was already a profitable

---

[115] For example, Procredito the NGO exchanged its portfolio for deposits in the new commercial entity Los Andes, and ceased to exist as an NGO. It became a holding company for Los Andes, and became its largest shareholder, owning close to half of the equity. FIE NGO continued to own the portfolio and paid a fee to the regulated entity, the *fondo financiero privado* (FFP), to manage it. When customers repaid loans, the new loans were issued by the FFP. The NGO received cash which it put on deposit with the FFP. The NGO owns 60% of FIE FFP. The NGO is funded by dividends and interest from deposits and continues to deliver non-financial services. Prodem sold its profitable branches to BancoSol, and contributed $1.4 million of the initial capital becoming BancoSol's largest owner with a 41 percent share. See Rhyne, *Mainstreaming Microfinance*, 107-123. KREP designed a holding company that would operate the NGO, a professional advisory services company and the bank. See Campion and White, Institutional Metamorphosis, 49.

[116] Frankiewicz, The Story of Prodem, table 2.

organization with a client base that matched BancoSol's own.[117] From ACLEDA's perspective, Prodem would soon become BancoSol's biggest competitor.

ACLEDA also heard of the disruptive merger talks between BancoSol and Prodem, as shared visions cracked under the pressure of fierce organizational independence. At the time, ACLEDA staff prepared for their own organizational crisis as co-workers, dating back to the earliest days in Thailand's refugee camps, disagreed about the future of the organization. They were reluctant to undertake a model of operation that in a few years time might provoke similar unrest and calls for governance and ownership changes in Cambodia's unstable environment.

The value of competition in microfinance is rarely underestimated as a factor that brings down prices and improves the quality of the products on offer in the market. In fact, the driving rationale for BancoSol's commercial transition was to create a thriving competitive microfinance industry in Bolivia. The founders of BancoSol, its board and donor agency supporters, viewed fostering competition in the market for microfinance as a marker of a successful experiment.[118] ACLEDA's view of fostering competition in the Cambodian market was somewhat less ambitious; for competition to emerge, first there had to be strong organizations surviving on a commercial basis. Eventually they would compete on a level playing field. From the market perspective, Cambodia did not seem ripe for new actors, but for strong ones.

The experience of ACLEDA's early days in Kampong Cham figured in discussions about competition as well. As the small market became highly competitive, staff saw too many organizations courting too few customers, and all operations deteriorated predictably. Cambodia's national market, although far from saturated, called for a focused approach to building one bank where none yet operated. The more magnanimous purpose of fostering what appeared to be an abstract concept of competition in a marketplace that was dominated by subsidized government operations could wait.

In the end, the demanding work of establishing one bank, not of managing two organizations – one that they might be unwittingly boosting as their own competition, won out. ACLEDA's aspirations for a national network and the rising performance of its own rural branches prompted the decision to sell all of the NGO assets to the bank. If the NGO were to continue at all, it would continue in a way that was beneficial to the bank. The next challenge was to ensure how the NGO would support the bank without pouring subsidies into the newly created commercial venture.

---

[117] At the end of 1997, Prodem had 38,248 active borrowers and a portfolio outstanding of USD 18.2 million, and was operating profitability with a financial self-sufficiency ratio of 111%. Frankiewicz, The Story of Prodem, table 4.

[118] Rhyne, Mainstreaming Microfinance, 109.

Preservation of Donor Capital

The future of the NGO was the final lesson from the Andes. Having discarded the option of maintaining the NGO to feed profitable branches to the bank, ACLEDA decided the NGO would function as a trust, and become an investor and a lender to the bank. New articles of association were drafted to cage the NGO to the exclusive purpose of supporting the bank as a shareholder and lender. The NGO would discontinue any other operations. As the influential shareholder, the NGO's powers would be limited to a financial relationship with the bank.

The plan had several advantages. First, it allowed ACLEDA to preserve accumulated donor capital for its originally intended purpose, lending to micro borrowers and small enterprises. Second, it offered a stable source of commercial borrowing for the bank. In a country with a weak banking sector, this idea had extensive appeal. Third, the option had the added advantage of streamlining operations. They did not have to worry about running two operations; they could focus all of their resources on the growth of one. Fourth, as a trust established to optimize long-term shareholder value of ACLEDA Bank, the NGO operations did not conflict with the interests of the bank. It would not be possible for the NGO, the influential shareholder of the bank, to succumb to political pressure for pressing requests.

Finally, the plan attempted to address the issue of perpetual subsidy of the new commercial investors. The NGO established a commercial rate of lending to the bank. The NGO earnings would be re-lent to the bank at the same commercial rate, fostering the "virtuous spiral of commercial feeding of expanded outreach" that Pancho Otero originally envisioned for transformation in Bolivia.[119] The variant in Cambodia was that the architects of ACLEDA's transformation plan hoped this spiral would happen within the same institution.

Experiments often define the unknown. When they work well they do not blow up the laboratory. When they succeed, they contribute to a lasting body of knowledge; they prove a theory and shape more daring attempts that otherwise surrender to the perils of "learning by doing". The pioneers map out uncharted territory for others who are freed, with that knowledge, to follow a different path. As Soeun puts it, "we took ideas from everywhere and applied our own. From BancoSol we learned how we could preserve accumulated donor capital for its originally intended purposes, we learned the importance of incorporating an employee ownership plan, and we learned not to underestimate the competition."

And from others? "From BRI we learned about systems, products, and internal operations. We studied the microloan and the way BRI created district branches and posts in rural areas. We sent credit officers, tellers, audit staff, accountants, and IT staff in groups. We learned to weigh carefully the costs and benefits of every idea. We learned never to do anything that isn't profitable."

---

[119] Rhyne, Mainstreaming Microfinance, 131.

CHAPTER 10:

Invitation

"We had an assessment that was convinced that these people of ACLEDA, who built an NGO, and now had the wild idea of becoming a bank, just might be able to do it". Femke Bos, Triodos Bank

"Some staff couldn't convince themselves that experienced shareholders would believe that a group of teachers could become bankers." Chan Serey, ACLEDA

By 1998, ACLEDA's original plan to hold the company with 100% NGO ownership was discarded, although the banking law, issued in early 2000, eventually enabled this choice. ACLEDA began the process of identifying new international investors, as it increasingly realized the perils of an inappropriate governance structure and the importance of clear owners of capital.

ACLEDA's central preoccupation was to find investors, not for who they were, whether they represented local or foreign commercial capital, but for what they would bring to the table. And their list of investor qualifications was extensive. The investors ACLEDA had in mind would share the purpose of serving the lower end of the market. They would contribute banking expertise and a sound governance system to the new bank. They would bring strong commercial and financial discipline, enhance the bank's public image, have resources for future investment, and have a respectable amount of influence within Cambodia's financial sector and policy circles. ACLEDA sought investors who balanced its own expertise and added value in the highly uncertain Cambodian context. It was seeking investors who would bring stability and help the institution grow for the long-term.

The specialized bank license required USD 2.5 million in minimum capital, an amount ACLEDA could easily manage with its own equity. The law did not place restrictions on the minimum number of shareholders, or the level of each stake in the share capital.[120] The law was more concerned with wide dispersal of shareholdings than high concentration. While it was clear that the Central Bank would scrutinize ACLEDA's application for a license on many levels, including extreme concentration or excessively wide dispersal of shareholdings, it was also clear that the plan for ACLEDA Bank's ownership structure would be up to ACLEDA itself.

---

[120] Law on Banking Institutions and Financial Intermediaries, 1999. Article 25.

This chapter examines the steps toward a new commercial ownership structure. It explores the investor risk and reward profile that makes them substantially different from donors. The chapter shows how ACLEDA staff, management and technical advisors devised a plan to mitigate investor risk in a dynamic environment. It explores how ACLEDA built mechanisms within the organization that compensated for the absence of functioning financial markets in Cambodia. The chapter concludes with lessons from ACLEDA's transformation.

The Domino Theory

Throughout 1998, ACLEDA management and the technical advisors approached a small group of public and private institutional investors who would complement the organization's capital structure and provide expertise in governance. At the time, the list was a lot shorter than it is today. They approached Triodos Doen Foundation, the Netherlands Development Finance Company (FMO), Deutsche Investitions- und Entwicklungsgesellschaft (DEG), and the IFC. Triodos Doen, though small, was gaining recognition as one of the leaders in microfinance investment, having been instrumental in KREP's transformation in Kenya. It could operate with the alacrity of a private investor and bring banking expertise to the table. FMO, the Netherlands Development Finance Company, was a veteran investor in bank and non-bank financial institutions in emerging markets. DEG, the German Government's development finance institution for investments in the private sector, maintained a close relationship to KfW, ACLEDA's primary lender.[121] IFC's MPDF was involved with funding for technical support of the transformation project, a channel through which ACLEDA hoped IFC would take an equity stake in the bank.

It was thought at the time, that as FMO went, so would Triodos. As FMO and Triodos went, so would DEG. And if IFC joined, together they would have a stronger investor group that matched the institution as well as the environment. Officially or not, IFC was recognized early on as the lead investor, as the investor group acknowledged IFC's expertise and concern with legal perfection in the investment process. IFC was not the lead investor in the traditional sense of the concept; it was not the first of the investor group to make its decision to invest risk capital in the idea of ACLEDA Bank, but IFC did take the lead in structuring the deal as a precondition for its involvement, and devoted the staff resources to make it happen.

Triodos Bank pushed the lead domino, and FMO and DEG followed with the condition that IFC join the investor consortium. By mid-1999 each of the like-minded investors had made its decision to become an investor in the new bank. The lead investor struggled, as legal intricacies with over twenty cross-referenced

---

[121] DEG is now a 100% subsidiary of KfW. It has a similar function for German development policy as IFC has for the World Bank Group.

agreements mounted in Cambodia's uncertain regulatory and legal environment. A frustrating negotiating process ensued and led to an intense debate about whether the legal negotiations were protecting the investor group or simply holding things back. For eighteen months the IFC lawyers worked long and furiously through the night with ACLEDA management and its technical advisors to ensure that the last domino fell.

The dominos fell, but not as one expected — on their own, cascading by the sheer momentum. They were pushed by the invisible hand of ACLEDA's risk-mitigating strategists. Each perceived investor risk became a part of the transformation strategy that was hammered out and duly incorporated in a business plan. Finally, the business purchase agreement was structured to meet each investor's risk and reward profile.

What Investors Look For

Investors look at a microfinance institution using a common set of criteria viewed through the lens of their own risk and return perspective. The more farsighted perspective looks for a match between the company and investor, for an investment in a microfinance institution is a long-term proposition. The microfinance investor looks for appreciation of the value of shares or a flow of dividends as a profitable institution grows in the market. Investor interest in the growth of the institution also comes from an anticipated income stream through the placement of debt that only a stable, growing, profitable company is likely to require. Unlike the venture capitalists' aims to take a company public and get out quickly, the microfinance investor comes with the idea of building a commercial company of value to society. It wants a reasonable return on its investment, but it does not put short-term profit maximization above the objective of building long-term institutional strength.

Each of ACLEDA's potential international investors came to the table with a different risk and return profile based on their experiences, internal policies and perceptions about microfinance and Cambodia. Investor profiles influenced how their decisions were made and how the investment process took place. ACLEDA came to the table with three non-negotiable principles – the legacy of employee participation, the determination that all branches would be sold to the new operation, and a resolve that accumulated donor capital would not provide a perpetual subsidy to the new commercial venture. It also came with a business plan that offered high return in a high-risk environment. Now ACLEDA had to demonstrate how it could mitigate risks that might negatively influence profitability or open the investors to liabilities they would find hard to accept.

What makes the fascinating story of ACLEDA's transformation was how staff, management and the technical advisors developed a plan that attracted investors to a high-risk environment; a plan that was acceptable to potential shareholders. Few had intentions of investing in Cambodia, and all were mindful of the political uncertainties of the time. The investor group looked to IFC's expertise to perform the legal work that would protect shareholders in a volatile, changing environment. It also recognized that a legal agreement crafted outside the IFC would not satisfy the institution's requirements to make a sound investment. Just as investors viewed the added weight of IFC's involvement as crucial for the deal to succeed, ACLEDA looked to IFC's brand and connection to the World Bank Group to manage risk in a financial system that prepared for radical overhauls.

Let us consider how ACLEDA's plan mitigated investor risk, for the negotiations held throughout 1999-2000 and the subsequent licensing of ACLEDA Bank in October 2000 emerged from that plan. The plan recognized investors would be looking at an unconventional concept – an NGO operation proposing to transform into a commercial bank – in a high-risk environment. With these two unique characteristics in the forefront, the plan addressed concerns common to any investor: the expected return on investment, the anticipated ownership and governance structure, the management of the institution, the operating environment, and finally an exit plan.[122]

Return on Investment

Investors carefully scrutinize the prospects for profitability and study the risks that negatively influence them. The investor's risk/return assessment becomes the foundation of the investment decision. Reducing risk and increasing return favors a more successful outcome in attracting equity capital from private and public institutional investors. Investors compare the initial price of shares to the expected return; a view different to that of the central banker's competing preoccupation with capital adequacy to protect the bank in a crisis and prevent it from threatening the integrity of the financial system. Investors look at historical and projected earnings to ensure the bank is in a position of financial strength, one that will ward off a crisis that would prompt a capital call from the central bank.

ACLEDA's multi-year business plan grew from historical performance trends garnered from working in an environment that posed severe risks. Branch by branch projections and staff familiarity with risks proved advantageous from a business perspective. Over the years they had devised strategies to deal with credit and operational risk for the growing microcredit operation. For the most part, they could anticipate the financial consequences. The two main risks were delinquency or default that would lead to a reduction in portfolio earnings and asset erosion, and high unexpected operating costs. The business plan incorporated low, medium and high growth scenarios with an extremely conservative sensitivity analysis of key cost and pricing factors, such as inflation, increasing costs of capital, an operating cost

---

[122] This section relies heavily on Peter Kooi's "Raising Capital through Equity Investments in MFIs: Lessons from ACLEDA, Cambodia" a paper presented at the UNCDF/SUM and UNDP Africa Global Meeting on Young and Promising Microfinance Institutions, May 30 to June 1, 2001, New York.

increase of 50% above the projected increase, a write-off rate that exceeded historical performance, pricing scenarios based on the eventuality of competition driving
down the price, and a decrease in the projected increase in average loan size.

John Brinsden, the former Standard Chartered banker, viewed ACLEDA's
business plan together with Channy and Peter. "If half of these projections are
true, you can make this bank," he recalls his astonishment in the early-morning
meeting set up to recruit him as an advisor to the new venture. Channy and Peter
knew the projections were conservative, but at the time, the IFC was new to Cambodia, and to microfinance as a viable business model. Nor was it set up to support
an NGO transformation, as companies come to IFC already prepared for expansion. At the time questions centered on microfinance as a commercially viable
business model, and ACLEDA as a donor-supported NGO did not fit that model.
The initial skepticism about the viability of the business model overshadowed
some of the more protracted legal work and environmental requirements that later
became the bane of the equity negotiations.

Now microfinance occupies the work of a division within the IFC that boasts a
growing portfolio of investments in microfinance institutions and microfinance
funds. By the end of 2004, IFC had invested more than USD 256 million "to bring
microfinance into the mainstream of the banking industry."[123] But in 1998, like
many other commercially oriented investors, the IFC battled with the idea that microfinance could be a commercial proposition, and that an NGO could in fact transform into a commercial bank. According to Morgan Landy, "Over time, people
visited ACLEDA and saw how in such a poor country, microfinance could have a
large development impact in a very commercial way. The IFC was uniquely positioned to become a founding shareholder. It was the strength of ACLEDA itself that
changed attitudes; the hard part initially was getting an audience."[124]

The 1998 appraisal commissioned by IFC and the investor group noted, "Our
view is that ACLEDA has built an impressive organization and has become one
of the rare institutions worldwide which is well on the path to commercial viability. This achievement is reflected not only in the client and loan portfolio
growth and quality, but also in the culture of the lending operations, their focus
and objectives."[125]

A realistic business plan prepared by ACLEDA branches, a ruthless sensitivity
analysis and a careful appraisal by experts in the field of microfinance affirmed the
validity of a reasonable return on investment. Now investors sought ways to mitigate
the risk of ownership structure and Cambodia's high risk operating environment.

---

[123] IFC. Banking for the poor. 2004.

[124] Clark, H. Capacity Leads, Capital Follows: Donors and Investors Match Instruments to
ACLEDA's State of Development. CGAP Case Study in Donor Good Practices, No. 14.
June CGAP: Washington DC. 2004. p 3.

[125] Stephan Harpe and Barbara Calvin, *ACLEDA, Cambodia: Past Performance, Projected
Performance and Readiness to Transform into a Regulated Financial Institution* (Toronto:
Calmeadow, Feb 1998), 2.

Ownership Structure

Reputation risk lies deep in the hearts of institutional investors; they are concerned with potential liabilities lurking within the institution and those dealt to them in concert with other owners. Comfort levels increase when the proposed ownership structure favors like-minded institutions, for it is here that investors stake their reputations as well as their capital. The reputations of other investors and their shared interest in promoting the long-term value, stability and financial strength of the institution are keys to securing a microfinance investor group. Investors incur obligations under the law as owners of a financial institution; those obligations must be crystal clear. Just as investors seek to share the risk with others, shareholders with a minority stake seek policies that protect their positions. A slate of rights, particularly the right and authority granted by representation on the Board of Directors, is significant to minority shareholders.

An NGO owner often tips the investor risk/reward profile in unpredictable ways. Concern centers on the NGO as a dominant shareholder: will the NGO drive the company in ways that are in conflict with investors' expectations? For example, if the NGO continues its own microfinance operation, will it compete with the new bank? Will the actions of the NGO create conflicts that prove disruptive to the shareholding structure of the new commercial operation? For example, will the NGO as the perceived guardian of the social mission be reluctant to pursue policies that would lower costs or increase earnings to the detriment of the commercial operation? And, if there is a continuing financial relationship with the bank, are there safeguards built into the system that will ensure effective controls and transparent arm's-length transactions between the NGO and the new commercial entity?

ACLEDA's plan for the future of the NGO boosted shareholder confidence; it enhanced the financial strength of the bank. The plan called for the NGO to sell the entire operation to the new bank, and re-establish itself to act as a trust. The new NGO status, the structure of the sale, and a carefully designed mechanism to manage currency exposure mitigated investor risk.

The Trust

Cambodia's new law on banking and financial institutions called for influential shareholders; any shareholder with more than a 20% equity stake in the bank was required to respond to calls for capital to ensure the bank met capital adequacy ratios at all times. The transformation plan designated the NGO as the influential shareholder with a 44.91% equity stake in the new bank as seen in Table 10.1. On the one hand, the NGO's designation as the "influential shareholder" limited the liability of the shareholders to the amount of their capital, reducing the risk that mandatory calls for capital would unexpectedly reduce their coffers. On the other hand, the NGO as the majority shareholder presented an additional risk in the minds of investors. This risk was mitigated as the transformation plan called for the NGO to act as a trust with the sole purpose of investing and lending to the new bank.

Table 10.1. Shareholder Structure, 2000 – 2004

Shareholder	Initial structure: October 2000 Specialized Bank		Structure: December 2004 Commercial Bank	
	% holding	Amount (USD)	% holding	Amount (USD)
NGO	44.91	1,796,430	32.53	4,228,751
ASA	6.9	243,570	18.47	2,401,249
DEG	12.5	490,000	12.25	1,592,500
FMO	12.5	490,000	12.25	1,592,500
IFC	12.5	490,000	12.25	1,592,500
Triodos Doen	12.5	490,000	10.33	1,342,500
Triodos Fair Share Fund			1.92	50,000
Total	100	4,000,000	100	13,000,000

Source: ACLEDA Audited Financial Statements, 2000-2004.

When ACLEDA NGO sold its microfinance operation to the bank in exchange for shares and loans to the bank, it reconstituted itself to act as a trust with no operations of its own. The NGO board of directors was pulled from prime donors with long term interests in ACLEDA – the UNDP and KfW – and complemented by ACLEDA Bank management, serving ex-officio, and independent legal counsel. The NGO Board serves as trustees of the original donated capital with a mandate to preserve the capital for its originally intended purposes, providing access to financial services to micro and small entrepreneurs in Cambodia. As the majority shareholder and primary lender to the bank, the interests of the NGO to ensure the bank remained financially strong over the long-term aligned with the interests of the minority shareholders.

The Sale – Shares, Subordinated Debt, and Senior Debt

The transformation plan called for an ownership structure with total capital of USD 4 million to qualify for a license as a specialized bank. ACLEDA Bank purchased the NGO operation for USD 13,290,611 in exchange for USD 1,796,430 in shares and a subordinated loan in the amount of USD 11,494,181. All assets and liabilities, staff and equipment were transferred to the new bank. A special audit was undertaken for valuation of assets and liabilities prior to the sale.

Subordinate Debt. The subordinated loan to the bank, accounting for all the accumulated donor equity, carries an interest rate established at SIBOR + 2.5% for US dollars, as well as commercially established rates for the portion of the portfolio denominated in Cambodia riel and Thai baht.[126] Under the laws of Cambodia and the regulations of the NBC subordinated loans are treated as capital of the bank for purposes of calculating net worth and capital adequacy. The subordinated debt arrangement facilitated ACLEDA Bank's ability to borrow from commercial sources, offsetting the inherent weakness of the institution's inability to provide risk-free collateral. As most of ACLEDA's assets are used for on-lending, Cambodia's few commercial lenders rejected the loan portfolio as an acceptable form of collateral; they thought it would be difficult to seize assets in the hands of 90,000 borrowers.

Transfer of Liabilities. Prior to transformation, ACLEDA NGO had entered into two loan agreements with KfW. Under the terms of the business purchase agreement, the bank agreed to pay to the NGO the equivalent of amounts provided by KfW. These amounts are considered senior debt and lent to the bank at the same interest rate as the subordinated loan.

Currency Risk. Currency risk is a major risk for any lending operation in an environment where loans to the ultimate borrower are denominated in a currency other than the currency the microfinance operation borrows. ACLEDA's portfolio is made up of micro, small and medium-sized loans in riel, baht and US dollars, while its domestic and foreign borrowings are denominated for the most part in US dollars. A feature of the NGO's subordinated and senior loan agreements with the bank was dedicated to managing currency risk. For the sole purpose of managing exposure of the bank to permitted currencies, the bank is entitled to pre-pay part of the debt at any time in one currency and re-borrow the equivalent amount in another, using the prevailing exchange rates in effect at the time. The amount re-lent is automatically added to the subordinated debt and denominated in the permitted currency.

The Subordinated Debt arrangement is a unique mechanism that allows ACLEDA to quickly square off any currency position. The ACLEDA Bank's current policy is to maintain mismatches at less than 1% of net worth.[127] It is important to note that this mechanism is not a currency hedge fund as the bor-

---

[126] SIBOR is the Singapore Inter-bank Offered Rate. The interest rate for subordinate debt denominated in Thai Baht is determined by the Baht Corporate Customer Rate. The interest rate for subordinate debt denominated in Cambodian Riel is the Riel Refinance Rate.

[127] The foreign currency exposure ratio is defined as the adjusted net position divided by net worth. Adjusted net position is defined as assets in foreign currency minus liabilities in foreign currency minus provision for foreign exchange losses. According to regulation B795.001 RGT of 16 January 1995 on the monitoring of banks' or financial institutions' open foreign exchange position: "a bank shall at all times observe a limit on the long or short position in each currency not exceeding 5% of the bank's net worth and a limit on the aggregate short position (including riel when appropriate) not exceeding 15% of the bank's net worth."

rowed and re-lent amounts are transacted at the prevailing exchange rates and the transactions occur simultaneously. The mechanism does shift the risk of the currency gain or loss to the NGO as the NGO absorbs the currency loss or the gain when it matches its own liabilities and assets. The mechanism allows the bank to maintain an efficient non-cash currency swap mechanism, maintaining appropriate currency matches for assets and liabilities held in each currency. As Soeun notes, "ACLEDA cannot control currency exchange loss or gain, but it can plan to manage the risk".[128]

Dominant NGO ownership, the one risk that could have heightened ownership risk, was structured to make the deal more attractive to commercial investors. In the eyes of the potential investors the NGO became a sound partner and decision maker about prudent policies and actions that contributed to the financial strength of the bank.

The ESOP: ACLEDA Staff Association, Inc.

Just as a dominant NGO owner makes commercial investors hesitate, an employee group with a dominant share poses similar qualms. A poorly designed ESOP creates conflicts of interest in decision making, blurring the check and balance system between the board, management and employees. NGOs with majority shares or ESOP investment companies often appoint NGO management or staff to board positions, creating a structural conflict of interest that is difficult to resolve. An ESOP that owns a majority share in the company also increases the risk of bankruptcy, as the pooled resources of employees may be inadequate to meet additional calls for capital. Generally an investor looks at ESOPs as positive for the productivity of the company, but a weaker financial ally in times of company distress or in poor market conditions that affect the overall industry.

Broad-based employee ownership was a non-negotiable position for ACLEDA's transformation. The ACLEDA ESOP is a unique feature of ACLEDA's transformation that other NGO transformations have by-passed. As such, its creation deserves a little extra attention in the discussion of transformations and their proposed ownership structures.

ACLEDA Staff Association, Inc. (ASA) was born during ACLEDA's stormy governance period. It was not conceived as an exclusive executive compensation program, nor was ASA's creation necessary to meet the minimum capital requirements for ACLEDA Bank. It was principally conceived to allow all employees to share in the ownership of the bank along with the new foreign investors and to enhance the bank's performance. If many architects of previous NGO transformations thought employee ownership would obscure the link between profit and

---

[128] Over the three years the subordinate debt currency swap mechanism was in use (2001-2003) the NGO absorbed both foreign exchange losses and gains depending on the prevailing rates of three different currencies – the riel, Thai baht and US dollars. Over the three-year period the NGO absorbed USD 6,869 of currency losses. (Source: ACLEDA NGO audited financial statements for the years 2001-2003).

development, the architects of ACLEDA's plan were convinced that employee ownership of even a minority stake in the bank would help broaden local capital participation in Cambodian development efforts.

ASA Inc. is a corporation established under Cambodia's commercial law. ASA's board of directors is voted into office by all ACLEDA employees. It has the right to appoint two directors to the ACLEDA Bank board. ASA serves as a holding company, a vehicle that allows employees to participate in the long-term growth and increase in value of the stock of ACLEDA Bank. The employees are stockholders of ASA, and ASA beneficially owns the stock in ACLEDA Bank that is held in trust for them. As a trust-based model, combined employee ownership allows efficiencies in management and lower costs in acquiring blocks of shares.

The ACLEDA ESOP is substantially different from other ESOPs that were created during MFI transformation. Many ESOPs were created with new donor funding or assigned from accumulated donor funding as employee benefits or awards for sweat equity.[129] ASA is a commercial investor that has the rights to purchase shares on behalf of its membership. It is a profit-sharing plan where employees purchase stock at the same price offered to other investors and participate in the same dividend earnings and share appreciation benefits. It features broad-based employee ownership as ASA has voting rights and board representation in the new bank; it limits conflicts of interest as ASA is entitled to appoint outside directors, and assign proxies to other bank directors. ASA does not limit individual risk; ASA assumes the same risks, rights and responsibilities that the other minority shareholders assume.

ASA has the right to purchase block shares from the ACLEDA NGO up to 19% of the share capital of the bank. ASA also has the right to sell shares back to the NGO, thus providing the liquidity mechanism that allows employees to acquire an ownership stake in ACLEDA Bank. Provisions were made to allow ASA to retain dividends to establish a reserve to fund the repurchase of ASA membership certificates from employees who leave the employment of ACLEDA Bank or retire. ASA also has provisions to become a leveraged ESOP, although this mechanism has not been used to date. "Leveraged ESOPs provide employees with access to

---

[129] In three of seven NGO transformation cases, reviewed by Campion and White in "NGO Transformation" (Bethesda Md.: Development Alternatives Inc., June 2001), p. 20-23, an "employee stock ownership program was designed to reward and acknowledge the contribution of staff and management's service to the organization ....non-voting shares were made available to staff based on a combination of seniority and professional status. Campion and White also note, "In a number of NGO transformations, donor funds have been used to capitalize individual shareholdings. While in some cases, shares in the new financial institution were sold to private individuals, in others the shares were simply transferred to board members, managers or staff of the former NGO. This raises ethical questions as to the fairness of transferring share capital partly accumulated with taxpayer money to a few well-placed individuals. Donors that have supported the subsidized transfer of shares to private individuals argue that funding individual share ownership helps foster enhanced levels of governance and accountability."

credit – backed by the sponsoring corporation's guarantee – to acquire an owner-ship stake."[130]

With the formation of ASA Inc. ACLEDA's staff became the first true private local commercial investors in the new bank. The limit on total share purchase to 19% of the new institution mitigated ASA's risks with respect to the NBC's influ-ential shareholder ruling. Creating a trust-based ESOP which featured a block of shares also mitigated the risk of a diluted ownership structure. Finally, ASA estab-lished safeguards to ensure that the ESOP would not be vulnerable to the buy-out of a large block of equity that could concentrate ESOP ownership and ultimately ACLEDA Bank's stock in the hands of a small group of people. ASA defends the plan's broad-based ownership structure by limiting the percentage of indirect em-ployee ownership to at most 5% of the stock in ACLEDA Bank and by prohibiting the formation of investment groups within ASA.

The foreign investor group looked favorably on ASA as a commercial owner of the institution, and indeed over time ASA has served the dual purpose of enhanc-ing the bank's performance and allowing all employees to share in the ownership of the bank along with the foreign investors. At the end of 2004 each staff member held on average 1,200 shares of ACLEDA bank stock; an 18.47% equity stake in ACLEDA Bank.

Governance

Simply put, corporate governance is the system by which companies succeed or fail. With corporate objectives at the core, good corporate governance provides for a system of checks and balances between the board and management. Just as good corporate governance is the backbone for accountability structures throughout the organization, integrity and transparency of the board, management and systems are the neural fibers.

ACLEDA's investors saw a governance structure in line with sound banking principles and a board of experienced directors to safeguard the interests of the shareholders. Their requirements extended to a clearly defined management struc-ture at the central and branch levels. ACLEDA's management, never remiss to upgrade organizational infrastructure, established a code of conduct policy, and refined operational and financial management policies, loan loss reserve and write-off policy, dividend policy, product policies, and policies and procedures in line with regulatory requirements.[131] Investors assessed the systems that backed management decisions, the software, financial administration and organizational structure, ensuring checks and balances in working order.

---

[130] For an enlightening paper on the value of ESOPs in the restructuring or privatization of financial institutions see David M. Binns and Ronald J. Gilbert, "The Role of Employee Stock Ownership Plans in the Restructuring and Privatization of State-Owned Financial Institutions", a paper presented to a World Bank Conference on: "The Role of State-Owned Financial Institutions: Policy and Practice" April 26-27, 2004.Washington, D.C.

[131] Kooi, Raising Capital, 11.

ACLEDA Bank's governance system reflects its ownership structure. Each of the initial shareholders had the right to appoint directors to the board. The bank is governed by nine non-executive directors, elected by the shareholders. The ACLEDA NGO selected three board members. ASA has the rights to two board seats, while DEG, FMO, IFC, and Triodos Bank each have the right to select one board member. Each share carries one vote, and each share participates equally in all dividends and other distributions of the bank. ACLEDA's transition team rejected golden shares, preferred shares or grandfather clauses that would allow initial shareholders to retain board seats once their shares were sold.

The governance structure was one of the major roadblocks to a swift investor negotiation during the transformation period. There were two issues on the table. First, investors differed in their points of view about the extent of management decision-making and board oversight. The foreign investors preferred to maximize the number of management decisions for which a super majority vote was required in order to protect their minority rights. ACLEDA management wanted to minimize the management decisions for which such a vote was required.[132] They anticipated changes in Cambodia's dynamic environment. Apprehension grew about an allegiance to a system of micro-management that would limit quick and decisive decisions in an environment that required both.

An agreement was reached on decision-making. Decisions by the board require a 51% majority vote of the shareholders except in critical matters of governance, which require 75% of the votes of the shareholders. The super majority vote clause, designed to protect the rights of minority shareholders, swings into effect on critical policy areas that would affect the viability or structure of the bank. Some of these areas are amendments to the articles of association, changes to the policy guidelines, business objectives, banking license, or registered share capital. Merger or consolidation which would require a substantial part of the assets of the bank to be transferred to some other entity, or voluntary dissolution or liquidation of the bank require a super majority vote of the board. Major operational decisions, such as the general dividend policy, changes to annual budget, appointment or removal of the General Manager, and additional meetings of the Board of Directors also fall under the super majority vote clause.

ACLEDA's governance structure anticipated four board committees, each headed by a board member. The audit committee, the credit committee, the assets and liabilities committee and the compliance committee were designed for board members to play an active role in oversight of the institution. A division of four board committees among nine board seats further guaranteed minority shareholder participation.

---

[132] Kooi. Raising Capital, 22.

CEO and Chairman of the Board?

The second critical issue in a proposed governance structure for ACLEDA Bank was whether the board would include executive directors, particularly whether the general manager would serve as the Chairman of the Board or hold any board seat at all. Several technical advisors actively advocated that the General Manager take the Chairman slot; it was thought that this arrangement would allow for quick decisions in a changing context. Yet ACLEDA management had recently experienced a bad dose of conflict of interest that nearly led the organization to destruction.

A host of reasons were advocated for non-executive directors. In the early 1999 General Assembly meeting the branch managers, all of whom were executive directors of ACLEDA at the time, voted to relinquish their board seats to non-executive directors appointed by shareholders. ACLEDA management were also schooled in the European model of corporate governance which holds dear the separation of the CEO from the Chair, to avoid the inherent conflict of interest of a cross-hierarchical relationship. At the time of the proposal for the new governance structure, Vann Saroeun, the prior board chair and manager of the Siem Reap branch, had recently attended a conference on governance sponsored by the MicroFinance Network. He returned convinced that, "What we practice is bad governance." Now positions were put forward that argued otherwise. How could this be?

Peter Kooi and In Channy discussed this issue long and hard with the advisors. While the offer of a director's seat on the board may have seemed like an honor to Channy, he was determined to build a governance structure for ACLEDA's new commercial operation that would avoid the conflicts of interest of the past and establish a clear relationship between management and the board. As the small group bantered about the changing hats of the General Manager and the Chair, particularly in relation to compensation, a drama unfolded for the benefit of the advisory team, to put the issues in perspective:

> *"What they are proposing is that you become GM and Chair. How will you deal with this when it comes time to ask for a raise?" Peter asked. "You will put on your GM hat, and say, 'Mr. Chairman, I have achieved the business plan, increasing the bank's profitability and expanding our operation. I request a raise.'"*
>
> *"Then you take off this hat, and don the hat of the Chair, crossing, if you like, to the other side of the table," Peter continued. "You will state, 'Yes, Mr. GM, you have achieved great progress and merit a raise.' You will abandon the Chair hat, cross to the other side of the table, don your GM hat, and say, 'Thank you Mr. Chairman.'"*
>
> *"Cross the table one more time, and don the Chair hat. You will respond, 'You are welcome Mr. GM. You have achieved spectacular results.'"*
>
> *Channy looked concerned. "Companies in the US are run this way?" "Oh," he said, "you cannot do this in Cambodia."*

To the relief of Vann Saroeun and In Channy, the advisors conceded that the style of governance practiced by many US companies, often to the chagrin of their shareholders, is perhaps not the most accountable. In Channy and Vann Saroeun are confident of their positions on good corporate governance. Their beliefs are backed by D. Quinn Mills, a professor of business administration at Harvard Business School, who states, "CEOs in large American publicly held corporations have too much power; that's the core of the abuses that have been going on." As corporate governance slips from the boardroom to the public limelight, opinions begin to change about conflict of interest. The Corporate Board Member, a trade publication for large US companies, notes, "Many corporate governance experts have long argued that having a non-executive chairman makes sense, saying that executives who hold both posts can't be expected to monitor their own performance effectively. The recent rash of accounting scandals has injected new vigor into that argument."[133]

Opponents of the European model of corporate governance often cite enhanced company responsiveness to changing conditions as a key reason for combining the two positions. ACLEDA management also felt that investors were requiring too much micromanagement, and feared a sluggish board response to a rapidly changing environment. An executive seat on the board, especially uniting the GM and the board chair, would have provided a solution to this impasse. Yet ACLEDA was also particularly honed to good governance practices, and the difficulties bad governance could create. In assessing the trade-off, they opted to choose gains in the accountability of the corporate governance structure. They would negotiate the conditions under which management alone would respond to changes in the environment and market conditions, resolving to consult regularly with the board on matters that appeared to cross the line.

Strong Institution; Risky Environment

The presence of the NGO and ASA assured investors of reasonably sound partners whose interests in preserving the financial strength of the bank coincided with their own. The NGO played an active role in risk mitigation in an environment that favored a more high-risk tolerance than any of the foreign investors would face alone. In anticipation of future developments, the transformation plan built a support structure that did not yet exist in Cambodia's financial sector or legal framework. ACLEDA's strategy was to mimic as far as possible within the institution a functioning financial market that was yet to develop in Cambodia. How else could a strong institution just at the beginning of its growth

---

[133] D. Quinn Mills as cited in the Corporate Board Member, March/April 2003 in a feature story by Randy Myers, "Chairman + CEO: Two Jobs, Two People". Accessed October 2004. Available from http://www.boardmember.com.

path expect to attract outside investors in an environment that makes the noblest of investors shy away?

In the meantime, turning the plan into action enabled the institution to function reasonably well, as Cambodia's policy makers pulled together reforms and passed laws little by little, reflecting priorities at the top of a long list of legal and structural reforms.

The transformation plan designed mechanisms and systems that mimicked a well functioning financial market in three important ways. The NGO acted as a trust where no trust law existed in Cambodia. The main functions were to preserve accumulated donor capital for its originally intended purposes without subsidizing new shareholders. The subordinate debt agreement established a mechanism that acted as an inter-bank lending market in an environment where commercial borrowing on the domestic market was limited, and no recognized interbank or capital markets existed.[134] The arrangement ensured the availability of a source of funds that would grow, multiplying the original donor capital, as the bank paid interest on subordinated debt.

Secondly, the currency swap mechanism mimicked an exchange market that enabled the bank to manage its exposure to currency risk. As a non-cash swap mechanism it lowered transaction costs. It also limited the risk of physically transporting large amounts of cash to authorized FOREX agencies in an environment where security concerns prevailed.

Finally, the provision that the parent NGO could sell shares to the ACLEDA Staff Association and re-purchase them imitated a capital market that does not exist in Cambodia. Without such a liquidity mechanism available externally, employees would be unable to sell and purchase shares, leading to a less than desirable dead-end transaction.

Stability?

Cambodia's high risk rating in international markets was easily the major risk each investor weighed with careful precision. The group was not unanimous in its approach. Each investor, some more than others, agonized over whether to choose ACLEDA and the return it offered, or let considerable speculation about the environment hold sway. The investor group scrutinized the legal and regulatory environment, the business and macroeconomic environment for signs of stability and growth.

---

[134] For additional information on the financial sector in Cambodia, see Cambodia Financial Sector Blueprint for 2001-2010. Ministry of Economy and Finance, National Bank of Cambodia and ADB. Phnom Penh. 2001. The blueprint is a result of the Financial Sector Steering Committee, its Working Group and technical assistance by the Asian Development Bank.

The Macroeconomic Environment

The operating environment posed a number of risks, particularly as the new banking legislation was still in flux. At the same time, the macroeconomic environment
showed tentative signs of improvement. Inflation ranged from 14% to 4% from
1996 through 1999, down from the historical high of 104% in 1990-1992.[135] The
government showed a credible commitment to market reforms, including a policy
that rejected the idea of interfering with interest rates or setting interest rate caps.
The Cambodian riel was also stabilizing. The "extensive dollarization of the Cambodian economy enabled a weathering of exchange rate disruptions and inflationary pressures so prevalent in other countries in Southeast Asia during the financial
crisis of 1997."[136] ACLEDA's currency risk mechanism further produced an atmosphere of stability.

The Business Environment

While the IFC focused on the perplexing and evolving legal environment, Triodos
looked to the business environment and the prospects for market growth. Demand
studies for microcredit and other microfinance products are tricky endeavors. They
are always overly optimistic; they often confuse need for small amounts of money
with financial services people are prepared to purchase. Triodos assessed the market,
not based on need, but on ACLEDA's current and potential customers who were
willing to pay the price for its financial products. "The possibilities in the market
were strong points," recalls Marilou van Golstein Brouwers, Senior Fund Manager
of Triodos Bank. "We looked at a commercial assessment rather than a legal one."

Demand estimates for micro and small business credit in Cambodia ranged
from USD 70-125 million. But savings products were virtually untested. While
analysts were encouraged by anticipated demand for savings, there was little evidence that depositor confidence was on the rise. A money transfer system held
immense possibility. Banks lacked a presence in most Provincial capitals and all
rural areas; there was no reliable electronic means of communication. Individuals

---

[135] Inflation showed a downward trend from 10% in 1996 to 4% in 1999, with a spike of
14% in 1998 due to the political crisis of mid-1997. IMF, International Financial Statistics,
line 64 X, various years.

[136] "Real growth in Cambodia averaged about 6% over 1993-1996 and inflation which had
averaged 140% a year during 1990-92 was reduced to single digits during 1995-1997. The
Cambodian riel initially fell less precipitously than other Asian currencies because of the
extensive dollarization of the Cambodian economy. Cambodia was insulated from the sharp
credit crunches and rapid flight of portfolio investment observed elsewhere in the region
because it was not well integrated into global financial markets and received virtually no
volatile shorter-term capital inflows. The extensive dollarization of Cambodia's economy—
as much as 70–90 percent of all transactions are carried out in dollars, and commercial bank
assets and liabilities are denominated almost exclusively in foreign currencies. This has
helped limit the exchange rate impact of the external shock and inflationary pressures."
Ngozi Okonjo – Iweala, "Impact of Asia's Financial Crisis on Cambodia and the Lao
PDR". Finance & Development. September 1999, 48-49.

and institutions relied on friends, taxis and employees carrying great amounts of cash over the rough and dangerous terrain of the countryside and pock-marked by-ways that led to Provincial capitals. Surely, a more efficient, less perilous system of cash transfer would receive a warm welcome in Cambodia.

On the demand side the business environment appeared encouraging. On the supply side, microcredit operations were gaining in size, strength and better practices, as they quickly moved to fill the gap in credit services to poor and low-income people in the rural and urban areas. Even with the growing operations of the top ten microfinance operations, the market for micro and small enterprise credit was far from saturated. It appeared that a bank with the strength to enter the savings and transfer market and the skills and capital to expand in the small enterprise credit market would gain the lead. That strength would be found within the institution, not in the legal environment.

The Legal and Regulatory Environment

The legal environment in Cambodia had little to recommend it. In 2003, as in 1999, the environment offered little protection to investors, and did not adequately protect lenders. Even today, the legal environment is notable for the absence of several prominent features of importance to lenders. The absence of a secured transactions law, an unclear land law, and an outdated contracts law subject to interpretation by many different local courts, are some of the more striking features of Cambodia's legal environment. The absence of a company law that sets out rules of corporate governance and regulations governing the relationship between shareholders, directors, managers and third parties tends to muddy the waters as well.[137] Contracts are not backed by credible guarantees or fair treatment in the courts. Judicial rulings are often arbitrary, as the courts and local authorities are just as likely to be swayed by personal relationships and monetary enhancements as they are to side with the letter of the law.

Political risk weighed heavily on each investor. Jutta Wagenseil, DEG's representative on the board, notes "that the development impact outscored the political risk, which was considerable. ACLEDA offered a way to pursue development objectives together with a return on investment. This is what DEG likes to see. But, using our established country risk ratings, the return that we normally expect did not clearly outweigh the risk."

The one factor ACLEDA could influence through dialogue, but was in no position to determine, was the regulatory and legal framework for its own microfinance bank. Nor was ACLEDA in a position to determine the timing of the new law as it passed between the NBC and parliament for over a year. From the for-

---

[137] "Important gaps in Cambodia's legal system relating to bank lending arise from the Land Law (2001), Contract Law (1988), an absence of a company law, and to a lesser degree, the absence of a bankruptcy law." Stephen Harner, Financing SMEs in Cambodia: Why do Banks Find it so Difficult? Mekong Project Development Facility (MPDF) Private Sector Discussions Paper Number 14. April 2003), 22.

eign investor perspective, the deal would depend on an established legal and regulatory framework for microfinance. The ACLEDA transition team preferred to continue transformation plans even while the framework was in flux.

ACLEDA encountered a supportive central bank eager to buoy the microfinance community. But the NBC was also keen to ensure that microfinance banks, as institutions engaged in banking activities, would fall under the letter of the law. A cautious optimism presided over the entrance of MFIs into a system where only one quarter of the banks were expected to survive the "two-year purge on capital adequacy and management competence"[138]. In the meantime, ACLEDA's investor group reserved capital subscriptions until the legal and regulatory framework for the transition was in place. At least this framework would offer some clarity in the otherwise chaotic legal and judicial environment.

Early on the NBC expressed willingness to work with a large number of NGOs in crafting a new regulatory framework. Their receptiveness yielded results in early 2000 and signaled a promise of further openness as experience was gained with implementation. The five-year dialogue, detailed in its nature and occasionally derailed by ideology, finally produced the Law on the Licensing of Microfinance Institutions and a Law on the Licensing of Specialized Banks. Tal Nay Im explains the rationale for a specialized banking license. "Overall we felt MFIs would benefit from licensing, enabling them to take deposits and to access financing from foreign shareholders, commercial institutions and the Rural Development Bank," she recalls. "ACLEDA originally requested a commercial bank license, but the first step for them was a specialized bank. They had to gain experience with a commercial operation and deposit mobilization."

The impasse between ACLEDA management and the foreign investor group on tying transformation to the publication of the new regulation came to end. "The issue solved itself," says Peter Kooi, "because the regulation was in place before the internal legal documentation on transformation was finalized."[139]

Management …

MFIs the world over have sought international investors with an attractive business plan. The credibility to implement that plan comes from past performance of management and staff, the values they hold and the decisions they make.

In its commercial assessment, Triodos focused on the management of the institution. Recent experience from an investment gone sour in Georgia pointed to weighing ACLEDA's management above all other factors. "When the legal framework is uncertain, you need to have 100% trust in management," notes Femke Bos, Triodos Bank's Senior Investment Officer. Marilou van Golstein Brouwers underscores the point. "Our decision was based on the strength of the team in place. They were very committed, professional and knew what they were

---

[138] John Brinsden's description of bank restructuring.

[139] Kooi, Raising Capital, 23.

doing. They wanted to make the transformation work and they had the qualities to make it work. We looked at the process of decision-making. As a shareholder and board member, Triodos would be supervising management. We wanted to know how they came to certain decisions, and what systems backed them up."

"The legal environment is important, but not the most important factor in an investment," says van Golstein Brouwers. When discussing the difference between Triodos' approach and that of other investors active in microfinance, she notes that "the legal environment is never as important as the people that can make it work; the other way around, it never works. When an issue arises in an uncertain and unpredictable legal environment, what do you have to fall back on? You fall back on your work with a management you can trust."

Each investor looked to the strength of the institution – its systems, the business appeal in a growing market, and, most importantly the people who ran the organization and those who advised it. ACLEDA's management came from a unique perspective, a history of guarding the institution as carefully as the bird with golden feathers, but with a great deal more foresight than the owners of the bird in Cambodian lore.[140]

The transformation project enabled management and staff to study, improve skills and learn from more experienced organizations. The 6,187 training days in the two-year period prior to transformation paled in comparison with what was found in during the transformation period. As their experience grew, skills improved, and new subjects found their way onto the Human Development Department's roster. A middle-level management capacity emerged:

Technical advisors also found their roles changing. Just as Roel Hakemulder handed his position in 1995 to a technical advisor who would take the organization to commercial breakthrough, so did Peter Kooi when the time came in 2000. What ACLEDA needed at this point in time was a banker, someone who could mold the commercially oriented micro-credit NGO into a bank of stature. Peter recalls:

> *"I imagined someone like John Brinsden before I ever met him, He was a banker who understood the culture deeply, an advisor who would build a strong trust relationship with the ACLEDA team, and provide new roles and banking services for them to explore. He would promote investor confidence; he had set up several banks in Asia before and knew about the technical intricacies of banking departments and how they should function. He could advise ACLEDA on good international banking practices and standards. When I got to know John from 1999, I came to realize that he was the perfect fit to support ACLEDA's management and staff in their compelling commitment to build an inclusive financial sector in Cambodia."*

John Brinsden would later remark, "These are the best banking days of my life."

---

[140] Cambodian lore features a bird with golden feathers, similar to the Western lore of the goose that lays the golden eggs.

... And Staff

There came a time of doubt for every staff member as they pondered the transformation over the course of two years. Would it be best for them to hand the institution to foreign investors, relinquishing their ownership and direction of the NGO? Would they become driven by the bottom line to neglect and consequently reject their original customers? Could they meet the more rigorous demands set for them by a private enterprise? Would they be replaced by banking professionals? As Sar Roth, the branch manager from Kampong Cham, recalls, everyone asked themselves, "Will I be the one to fall off the cart as it makes a sharp turn at a break neck speed?"

Much has been made about the clash of culture in an NGO's transition to a commercial entity. Some NGOs made the transition more easily than others. ACLEDA did not experience the massive disruption or staff desertion rates that some NGOs underwent during transformation, nor was it immune.[141] In fact 1998 and 1999, the years marking the initial planning for transformation and the dramatic shake-up in governance, rank first and third respectively for the highest staff retention. The year of transformation, 2000, is remarkable only in its average performance for staff attrition, one that equaled the average over ACLEDA's ten-year history.

ACLEDA's staff attrition rates must also be seen in light of the Cambodian context, where the pool of qualified people was much smaller than the demand for their service. Active, even somewhat ruthless poaching led to high attrition rates among organizations with generous staff training programs. There were simply too many offers in the burgeoning NGO and international development community. But in 1998, after reaching all-time lows, staff attrition began to climb; it accelerated in 1999 and 2000 with each step closer to transformation, as shown in Table 10.2. Unlike the spike in 1993 during the first transition from a highly prestigious international donor project to the more mundane local NGO, the increments in staff attrition were barely perceptible, but stable and persistent. Finally in 2001 staff attrition would hit its peak, but that is a different story told in the next chapter, and only indirectly linked to ACLEDA's new commercial status.

Reasons for staff departure around the time of transformation varied. Some let their apprehension about the banking law confuse regulation with a carefully designed trap for government control. Some preferred to work with an NGO because they did not trust the motives of a private company to work effectively with poor customers. Others were more concerned about falling short of performance targets. They worried that their contracts would be more vulnerable to termination; that would not happen in an NGO. And certainly poor performance figured high on the list.

---

[141] In 1998, the year ACP transformed to MiBanco, staff attrition was 21%. Campion, et al., The Transformation of Acción Communitaria del Perú (ACP) to Mibanco (Bethesda, Md.: Development Alternatives, Inc., October 2001), 13. The Prodem FFP transformation in 2000 saw a staff turnover rate of 32%, prior to that Prodem NGO held staff turnover consistently at 14%. Frankiewicz, The Story of Prodem, 68.

Table 10.2. Staff Attrition and Recruitment Rates

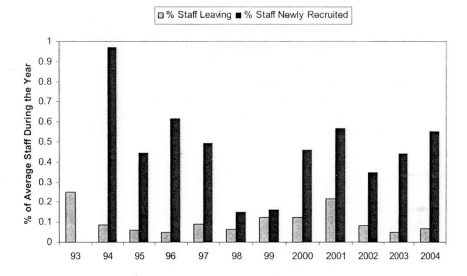

Note: The method of calculation is described in the Technical Note.
Source: ACLEDA Human Resource Department Records and Reports, 1993 – 2004.

An organization pays a high price for staff attrition, particularly an organization such as ACLEDA that invested heavily in staff training. Increasing numbers of staff leaving within a two-year timeframe exacted a high emotional price as well as a sizable dent in the budget. We will never know whether earlier and more intensive training programs might have deflected the upward trend in staff attrition. But four factors encouraged staff to stay during the transformation, and prepared them for new roles as commercial bankers. Those who stayed fared far better, in the long run, than those who let their fears conquer their "trust in themselves to do a good job", as So Phonnary puts it.

Ironically the first factor, articulated by Chan Serey as one of ACLEDA staff's greatest fears about courting investors, was "the group of teachers turned bankers". ACLEDA's group of teachers stressed the importance of training and capacity development from the very beginning of the organization. They saw investment in staff as a key to success. Everyone, from the vault attendants to the branch managers, was encouraged to develop skills through intensive in-house training and a generous staff education program. ACLEDA's management committed to bring all staff skills up to commercial banking standards through heavy investments in human resource development, no radical departure from the values of the past, but one that saw costs climb.

Secondly, the assurance that all staff would be transferred to the new company was a credible one; it was backed by extensive staff opportunities to increase skills.

Moreover, the environment favored staff perceptions about retention. There were few others in Cambodia who knew more about the micro-banking business than ACLEDA's current staff, and there were no traditional bankers on the horizon eager to replace them.

Perhaps the two greatest factors in keeping experienced staff were the way the transformation was communicated and the creation of ASA Inc. Two years of workshops allowed all staff in each branch to air concerns and raise questions. Together they developed a consensus around the transformation plan. The most tangible incentive was ASA. The ESOP guaranteed ownership – not just a perception of owning the process; ASA offered the power and the challenge of real ownership of the institution.

When discussing the Bolivian transformation model Rhyne notes, "... the obvious lesson that it is much easier to create a financial institution if you plan to do so from the very beginning. Changes in organizational vision are among the most difficult changes to implement."[142] ACLEDA's experience with transformation suggests another obvious lesson: it is much easier to transform if vision and core values are not lost in the process. Changes in organizational strategy or legal form are not as disruptive for an organization when vision and core values are not at stake. The challenge for ACLEDA was to link the business vision, "customers not donors are the future", with an organizational strategy that made sense. The second challenge was to yet again back the consistent organizational practice of considering staff the greatest asset with a credible plan.

ACLEDA management and staff were up to the challenge. Cheam Teang, the Director of Treasury, recalls that every time ACLEDA made a transition, it grew, and the organization improved. "A bank could help a lot more people than an NGO ever could," he says. "The doubters said we could not grow, but we did. Then we grew again." ACLEDA found a magic formula: continuity and change.

"They seem to have no ceiling," says Peter Kooi. While the foreign investor group looked to a management they could trust, the group of staff investors looked to a leadership they could believe in and follow. Trust.

The Exit

It seems appropriate to give the initial words on exit to Emile Groot of FMO, the investor who was first invited to the kitchen:

> *"Initially, we were concerned about an NGO sponsored by donors. Our reference point was banks and non-bank financial institutions, not NGOs. But there were a lot of factors that mitigated the risk in*

---

[142] Rhyne, *Mainstreaming Microfinance*, 120.

Cambodia and the NGO status. The reputation and actions that supported transparency within the institution were attractive, the presence of a former Standard Chartered banker as an outside director was attractive, the continuity of technical advisors who knew the institution was attractive, the IFC with access to policy levels through the World Bank was attractive, and the consortium of investors was attractive. We were impressed with the local participation and commitment through the NGO and ASA. All of these factors mitigated risk.

With a special fund that guaranteed the investment, we initially were softer on the prospects for exit. In five to seven years, perhaps there will be shares available to private parties or to other strategic investors. With ACLEDA's performance, attracting shareholders should not be a problem. We are not pressing for exit, but of course, the ultimate test is the exit."

Other investors share Groot's perspective on an exit strategy. None are pressing for an exit; although each one recognizes that an exit strategy was important in their initial assessment. For a purely private investor, ACLEDA's proposed exit strategy was perhaps a bit remote, but the plan fit the investor groups' profile and interests.

A strategy discussed, and quickly dismissed was a put option with the NGO majority shareholder. This was not a realistic plan for ACLEDA NGO that was more interested in devolving ownership over time than increasing it. It was not the development the investors were looking for in broadening the bank's capital base and creating a strong financial institution that would invite local capital participation.

The second exit strategy – to require high dividend yields to offset the risk of the limited market for shares and as a repayment for the initial paid up capital – was also rejected. Again, this strategy fell short of investor expectations for the growth of the asset base of the institution.

The last strategy, one that optimized a longer-term exit matched to a reasonable annual return, opted to pay dividends on shares up to 30% of net profit, as well as to actively pursue listing on a regional stock exchange. This strategy fit the interests and the profiles of each investor. Investors were comfortable that their exit strategy would appear in time, but none has yet become overly anxious about exit.

"ACLEDA Bank is one of our top performers – one of the first to start paying dividends and increase book value of shares," says van Golstein Brouwers. "At first we thought we would exit in five years. Now we're changing our minds. The shares perform and have yielded an annual return. As a shareholder, we contribute to institution's governance. At first, a put option with majority shareholder

(NGO) was discussed, but this is not a realistic plan with ACLEDA; it is not the development we are looking for. We're not in a hurry to exit. We can become a more strategic investor in the country. Local investors will come with listing on a stock exchange, and then we will have a mission change. In the meantime, we like the idea of having our bank in Cambodia," says van Golstein Brouwers.

The IFC is also pleased. In 2003, IFC, along with the other initial investors, increased its paid-up capital to USD 1,592,500 for the transformation into a commercial bank. In 2004, IFC made available to ACLEDA Bank a USD 6 million line of credit. IFC's investment in ACLEDA Bank is now more in line with their traditional investment profile, and soon the initial costs of the investment in staff time and legal work may make up for the high costs of placing such a small amount of money in the first transformation.

A Plan to Mitigate Risk

The plan that painstakingly sought to mitigate each possible investor risk eventually led to a more robust outlook. Indeed there are high hopes for ACLEDA as Cambodia's leading retail branch network. In 2003, shortly before ACLEDA's transformation to commercial bank, Tal Nay Im mused about ACLEDA's future. "Very soon ACLEDA will be a commercial bank and the biggest bank for the people in Cambodia because of the national network," she said, with a sense of pride and caution that only a director of a central bank can summon.

If Tal Nay Im initially hoped that a proper regulatory framework for microfinance would attract additional long-term investment to Cambodia's microfinance institutions, she would not be disappointed in the investor capital that has followed. Since IFC's first investment in ACLEDA in 2000, the institution has placed over USD 18 million in equity and loans to enterprises in Cambodia. Triodos has become a strategic investor and lender to the Cambodian microfinance sector by making loans to AMRET and Cambodian Entrepreneur Building, Ltd., two other growing MFIs in Cambodia. An array of private and public investment funds are active in Cambodia, investing in MFIs and complementing or replacing their NGO owners.

"It's hard to imagine ever exiting from ACLEDA Bank or Cambodia," says FMO's Emile Groot. "You have to believe in the development of both."

Interlude: The Third Transformation

As the chapter on ACLEDA's third transformation comes to a close, we examine to what extent the transformation fulfilled its original aims and what lessons come from the process.

The transformation process was certainly costly. The transition plan itself had a price tag of USD 500,000, similar to other transformations in Latin America.[143] The costs, shared by investors, place that figure much higher. But the real question is whether the benefits of a commercial transformation are worth the initial investment of donor money. Does the institution operate profitably without continued subsidy? Does it meet the objectives of adding value to society?

Traditional performance ratios, such as return on equity, efficiency measures and those that decipher asset quality, assess these benefits of commercialization. The link to the broader financial system shows through leverage of commercial sources of funds, such as deposits and commercial borrowing. The microfinance community has begun to examine ownership structures more closely, searching for commercial investors with their own risk capital at stake and anticipating gains in improved governance. Most often these financial and ownership measures combine with measuring outreach to answer the big "so what" of commercial microfinance: does the institution offer a broader range of services to more customers, and does it continue or increase service to poor and low income clients?

The next chapter discusses ACLEDA's challenges of running a commercial bank, the evolving customer base and contribution to society. We return to analyze some of the figures presented here that show interesting trends to the technically adept eye. For the present we look at the big picture.

Performance

ACLEDA's post-transformation experience shows increased asset growth and profitability as well as improvement in efficiency and risk management (see Table 10.3.) The last piece of grant funding trailed into the organization in early 2000. In transforming, ACLEDA parlayed accumulated donor capital into a source of funding for the bank that carries commercial terms. The new loan agreements with the NGO required the bank to pay a cost of funds in excess of the deposit rate, the common measure used to determine the extent of subsidized funds in the institution.[144]

---

[143] Kooi, Raising Capital, 22. Banco Sol's transition planning was estimated to cost US$560,000. Glosser, Transformation of Banco Sol, 242.

[144] The accumulated donor capital which belongs to the NGO is lent to the bank at SIBOR +2.5. The standard measurement used by MIX Market for subsidized cost of funds is the IMF published deposit rate. Data for shadow interest rates are obtained from line 601 of the International Financial Statistics, IMF, various years. That rate is used here to establish a subsidized cost of funds. SIBOR +2.5% ranged from 4.44% to 3.615% in 2003 and 4.3% to 4.4% in 2002. The IMF deposit rate for 2003 and 2002 was 2.017% and 2.492%, respectively.

Table 10.3. ACLEDA Performance: Pre- and Post Transformation

	Pre-Transformation	Transformation Specialized Bank			Transformation Commercial Bank	
	1999	2000	2001	2002	2003	2004
Total Assets (USD million)	15.94	22.29	27.34	30.97	48.24	83.97
Loan Portfolio (USD million)	13.71	16.66	20.98	27.54	40.57	65.98
Portfolio to Total Assets	86%	75%	77%	89%	84%	79%
Debt/Equity	0.41	3.96	4.46	4.69	1.90	3.74
Deposits (USD million)	–	–	1.95	5.68	13.16	31.59
Deposit/Loans			9.29%	20.61%	32.44%	47.87%
Administrative Cost / Total Average Assets	22.28%	24.00%	20.92%	19.92%	19.29%	17.84%
PAR > 30 days	3.56%	4.62%	4.46%	1.71%	0.76%	0.39%
Write-off	4.96%	3.49%	5.84%	4.00%	1.16%	0.47%
Equity (USD million)	11.21	4.31	4.69	5.14	15.93	17.19
ROAE	14%	10%	11%	12%	19%	12.49%

Notes: See Technical note for method of calculation. All ratios use end of year audited figures.
Source: ACLEDA Audited Financial Statements, 1999 – 2004.

Cambodia's high risk rating in international markets tends to increase the commercial bank lending rate. These two factors pushed ACLEDA's more aggressive deposit mobilization much earlier than other transformed NGOs that initially relied on comparatively less expensive borrowing from commercial banks.

The figures in Table 10.3 show a dramatic increase in assets, funded by the new shareholders, depositors and debt financed by the NGO and loans from other sources. Most of these assets are placed in an expanding loan portfolio. A transformed institution is expected to gain efficiencies of scale, and indeed administrative costs to total assets have fallen, even as transformation required significant costs to meet new standards and build the future deposit business.[145] In commercial terms, the result of the transformation is an efficiently run, growing, profitable banking institution, one that complies with safety and soundness standards of capital adequacy, liquidity and solvency, cherished by central banks the world over.

Customers

Who has benefited from transformation? ACLEDA Bank's national branch network brought the formal financial system to the majority of its customers for the first time in the history of Cambodia. Certainly the micro and small entrepreneurs who borrow to support their enterprises are at the top of the benefits list as shown in Table 10.4. By the end of 2004, ACLEDA Bank managed a gross loan portfolio of USD 65.98 million and guarded the safety of USD 31.59 million in voluntary deposits; 91,566 micro-loan clients borrowed amounts from USD 5 to 500. The average outstanding balance in the microcredit portfolio was USD 128, or on average 41% of GDP per capita. The bank's principal products – small and micro loans – are complemented by an array of financial services, including international and domestic transfers, payroll services, company overdrafts and a variety of deposit account options. Large firms and international institutions use payroll services and cash management services. Village Development Committees that receive and manage funds for social infrastructure now access bank accounts backed by transfer services. Factory workers send salaries home to their families in the village, who open bank accounts to accommodate them. Small enterprises transfer payments to suppliers; and farmers dig up badly worn Cambodian riel, travel to ACLEDA's branch and deposit them.

What did they do before ACLEDA's services became available? They borrowed from informal lenders who offered interest rates in excess of 10% per month, they kept the funds for community infrastructure investments in the house of the treasurer of the development fund, and they moved millions of dollars across Cambodia in taxis and in the pockets of friends. They kept their deposits in the backyard and in off-shore accounts; deposits that are attracted out of the ground or back into the country to finance Cambodia's micro and small entrepreneurs.

---

[145] For a banking institution that has a range of products, such as deposits, transfers and other cash management services, as well as the traditional lending product, it is more appropriate to use the administrative costs to total assets as a measure of efficiency. Using a more common measure in microfinance, administrative costs to portfolio outstanding will provide a distorted view of efficiencies as total costs are related only to portfolio management, which is only a part of what the institution does.

Table 10.4. History of ACLEDA's Banking Services and Customers, 1993 – 2004

Sources: ACLEDA Portfolio Reports, 1993 – 2004, Audited Financial Statements, 1993 – 2004. Annual Reports, 2001 – 2003, and Financial Records for Transfer History, 2001 – 2004.

Lessons

It is not surprising that the four big lessons from ACLEDA's transformation mine the experience of organizational history, the new ownership structure, the innovative mechanisms of the transformation and the regulatory environment.

Trust

Many years ago, a learned scholar of financial systems wrote, that credit is essentially about trust. It is based on "the borrower's promise to repay the loan at some date in the future; and that future is uncertain."[146] The simple word "trust" sums up ACLEDA's greatest lesson of transformation. Change offers numerous and unfathomable risks, ones not normally countered by automated financial projection spreadsheets or meticulous legal preparation in a volatile environment.

To be sure, business risk and legal risk are important factors for mitigation in any business plan. But management and leadership determine whether an organization succeeds or fails. Credibility turns managers into leaders, giving them the standing to make changes. That factor alone is not rapidly constructed in a business plan or injected as a point for negotiation. Credibility flows from a history of transparent decision-making; it does not appear overnight as the new share capital arrives on account.

---

[146] J.D. von Pischke, *Finance at the Frontier: Debt Capacity and the Role of Credit in the Private Economy* (Washington, D.C.: World Bank, 1991).

As the central banker knows, transparency does not convey with a banking license. It is rooted in the culture of the organization, the values of the people who run it, and the systems they design to protect it. From its earliest days, ACLEDA staff trusted each other; it was a hard-won trust. Gradually that trust led to other values they incorporated along the way — meritocracy, accountability, transparency, professionalism and team building. In constructing the transformation plan, ACLEDA left behind its old legal status, but pulled its core values into the future together with a stronger organization.

Ownership

New owners with deep pockets play a desirable role in transformation, especially as NGOs feel the very tangible push of portfolio expansion and often daunting requirements to meet minimum capital and capital adequacy standards. Perhaps this is one reason why ESOPs have not been so prevalent in the NGO transformation model, although they have been effective in restructuring and privatizing other companies in many parts of the world. Microfinance institutions have taken a curious approach to ESOPs. Many of them are structured as rewards for past service or convenient ways to dispose of accumulated donor capital to broaden the ownership structure of a transforming MFI. When ESOPs are structured as stock purchase plans, their members are the local private investors so sought after in commercial microfinance. As the search for the ideal ownership structure continues, the MFI community might take another look at trust-based, commercially-oriented ESOPs as a way to broaden local capital participation in microfinance and development efforts.

Financial Markets

The absence of financial markets did not prohibit managing currency risk, providing liquidity for the ESOP, or establishing a mechanism that acted as an inter-bank lending market. ACLEDA's transformation plan mimicked elements of a financial market by structuring the NGO to perform some of the functions that are normally the province of financial markets in more developed economies. In anticipation of a time when Cambodia's financial market progresses beyond its current limitations – replete with stock markets, currency swap mechanisms, deposit guarantee facilities and inter-bank lending – the functions of the NGO will be taken over by the market. In the meantime, the NGO preserves donor capital for its originally intended purpose – lending to Cambodia's micro and small entrepreneurs.

Legislation

The NBC's vision and willingness to experiment with a specialized banking license was auspicious for ACLEDA and the growing microfinance institutions in Cambodia. Doomed to a quiet extinction as neither fish nor fowl, the specialized banking license for microfinance eventually succumbed to complaints about unfair competition from the commercial banking sector. Concerns about abuse of the specialized license for microfinance mounted as more cunning operations saw a way to avoid minimum capital requirements. Yet the NBC's early support for ACLEDA's transformation under a specialized banking license was critical for the future transformation into a commercial bank.

While it lasted, the specialized banking license created possibilities such as ACLEDA had never known. The age of the commercial venture had arrived and ACLEDA Bank Ltd had become an associate member of the club.

PART V:

Momentum

"ACLEDA Bank's vision is to be Cambodia's leading commercial bank providing superior financial services to all segments of the community. Our mission is to provide micro, small and medium entrepreneurs with the wherewithal to manage their financial resources efficiently and by doing so to improve the quality of their lives. By achieving these goals we will ensure a sustainable and growing benefit to our shareholders, our staff and the community at large. We will at all times observe the highest principles of ethical behaviour, respect for society, the law and the environment."

ACLEDA Bank Vision and Mission Statement

CHAPTER 11:

The Bank You Can Trust

Inside ACLEDA Bank

Inside ACLEDA Bank's branches customers arrive to make loan payments, savings deposits and wire transfers. They arrive on foot, by motorcycle, and in vehicles bearing logos of international agencies and private companies. They wear suits and sarongs; they carry briefcases and baskets for hauling goods to market.

Upstairs, posted on the wall, a running tally of staff performance is found. The loan portfolios of each credit officer and the risk rate their portfolio carries are viewed by a bevy of credit officers. The portfolio status is updated weekly. The branch's monthly performance is posted as well. There is a keen interest by all staff in seeing solid performance. At the end of the year, the top three branches will reward their staff with bonuses tied to the branch's net profit. The head office is filled with new recruits undergoing orientation training and staff taking refresher courses. Information spews from computers tracking daily balances of each branch, deposit transactions and liquidity ratios. ACLEDA Bank feels like a well-oiled machine.

In December 2003, ten years since its founding as an NGO, ACLEDA Bank Ltd went through its fourth transformation from a specialized bank to a commercial bank. The occasion saw the original shareholders increase their capital subscriptions to meet the USD 13 million capital requirements for a commercial bank license. Modest growth projections for the next five years prompted the increase in capital. As a quality portfolio grew, new products were added. Three years of building the market, managing risk, and getting the incentives right for a commercial operation began to show acceptable returns.

Transition to a commercial bank did not bring with it the drama associated with ACLEDA's first entrance into the formal financial system. By March 2004, on the occasion of ACLEDA Bank's inauguration as a commercial bank, they had an eleven-year history of managing an evolving business in a changing environment. Since 1993, ACLEDA had disbursed 896,599 loans totaling over USD 261 million.[147] The deposit base outpaces commercial borrowing. Money transfers surpassed even the most robust expectations. When mounting pressure in the NBC prompted a request for ACLEDA to submit an application for a commercial license, ACLEDA was ready.

---

[147] In Channy. Speech on the Occasion of the Grand Opening and Licensing of ACLEDA Bank Plc. on March 1, 2004.

Table 11.1. Current Performance for Four Commercial Banks Transformed from NGOs (Dec 2003 & Dec 2004)

	ACLEDA		BancoSol		KREP		MiBanco	
Year Project-NGO Established	1992		1985		1984		1969	
Year of Transformation	2000		1992		1999		1998	
Country	Cambodia		Bolivia		Kenya		Peru	
	2003	2004	2003	2004	2003	2004	2003	2004
Offices	97	119	32	34	27	28	29	33
Gross Portfolio (USD million)	40.6	65.98	91.2	108.6	21	26.7	114.1	128.4
Active Borrowers	98,905	122,173	42,831	51,996	45,379	55,441	120,830	114,809
Deposits (USD million)	13.2	31.59	73.2	82.6	15.5	20.4	69.2	90.7
Savers	35,054	57,091	n.a.	58,622	62,648	71,796	42,345	53,294
Assets (USD million)	48.2	83.97	114.3	138.2	28.6	34.6	139.2	162.7
Equity (USD million)	15.9	17.19	16.8	18.6	9.0	9.8	31.9	37.1
Portfolio/Total Assets	84%	79%	80%	79%	71%	77%	82%	79%
Deposits/Loans	32%	48%	80%	76%	39%	76%	61%	71%
PAR >30 days	0.76%	0.39%	8.96%	5.15%	6.7%	7.5%	3.8%	3.7%
Write-off as a % of average portfolio	1.16%	0.47%	2.16%	2.64%	0.13%	0.41%	3.28%	3.85%
ROAA	4.1%	3.05%	2.09%	3.11%	2.3%	2.0%	5.9%	5.03%
ROAE	18.7%	12.49%	14.5%	22.2%	8.9%	5.6%	26.1%	21.9%

Notes: Performance data for all institutions as of December 31, 2003 and 2004, based on audited financial statements. The calculation of ROAE does not include subordinated debt. Sources: ACLEDA's 2003 and 2004 audited financial statements. KREP 2003 and 2004 audited financial statements and information provided by KREP. For Mibanco and BancoSol, information provided by Accion International.

From humble beginnings and speculation about whether or not it could meet international benchmarks of best practice, ACLEDA Bank has arrived. The bank's performance sets it well among the ranks of the handful of commercial banks that transformed from local NGOs as shown in Table 11.1. These four commercial banks are significant in the banking systems of their own countries. BancoSol in Bolivia, K-REP Bank in Kenya, and Mibanco in Peru match profitability with continued service to micro and small enterprises, showing a commitment to the market and staying power within it.

ACLEDA's prominence does not translate into complacency. As experience has taught, there are simply too many risks in their chosen business. A commercial license offers many advantages, but it is neither static nor a pinnacle of achievement. The status is an accomplishment that calls for increased vigilance and innovation. Nor does ACLEDA's status translate into arrogance. There is something very modest there; a sense that knowledge and learning from others find no compromise in tackling Cambodia's isolation for the rest of the world. Now ACLEDA turns to banking networks for that connection; the Asian Bankers Summit, the Cambodia Bankers Association and the Risk Management Association provide benchmark learning tools and a bridge to international best practices in banking. They seek to share their experience by providing internships to students and staff from domestic and international microfinance organizations as well as local academic institutions.

ACLEDA Bank keeps deep roots in microfinance as it expands its retail branch network with a decidedly commercial orientation. The chapters in Part V examine several misconceptions about microfinance and the commercial approach. The series starts with an examination of how ACLEDA Bank and its customers dealt with new opportunities and risks associated with commercial banking. The following chapter moves on to explore the topical notion of "mission drift", a concept that causes considerable consternation in the donor world. The thesis of this chapter is that a commercial approach to microfinance can enhance an organization's outreach and depth of outreach rather than limit it. The chapter takes the opportunity to summarize ACLEDA's history of serving Cambodia's micro and small entrepreneurs with appropriate products. The concluding chapter pulls experience from ACLEDA Bank's history and microfinance as it has developed in Cambodia. Both offer lessons to the rest of the world.

The Great Delinquency Crisis of 2001

By mid-2001, shortly after the euphoria created by the specialized banking license, the regular and steady warning signals that all was not right turned into a full-scale alarm. Creeping delinquency in four branches, that were never stellar performers, began to rise. The pattern was a familiar one. A high portfolio at risk one year turned into a higher write-off the next year. But something else was happening. Compared with 1999 the portfolio at risk for the entire portfolio increased only one percentage point, and the write-off rate reached all time lows; it went from 4.96% in 1999 to 3.49% in 2000 as shown in Table 11.2.

Table 11.2. Portfolio at Risk and Write-off, 1999 – 2004

	1999	2000	2001	2002	2003	2004
Portfolio @ Risk > 30 days						
In Micro Loan Portfolio	2.59%	3.95%	4.00%	1.68%	1.01%	0.14%
In Small Loan Portfolio	3.94%	4.9%	2.24%	1.73%	0.67%	0.36%
Total Loan Portfolio	3.56%	4.62%	4.46%	1.71%	0.76%	0.39%
Eleven Mature Branches with:						
Micro Portfolio PAR 30 > 5%	2	5	5	0	0	0
Small Portfolio PAR 30 > 5%	3	4	3	0	0	0
Write-Off						
% Micro Loan Portfolio	8.69%	4.02%	10.21%	4.11%	1.87%	0.25%
% Small Loan Portfolio	1.56%	2.52%	5.54%	2.66%	0.92%	0.13%
% Total Loan Portfolio	4.96%	3.49%	5.84%	4.00%	1.16%	.47%
Eleven Mature Branches with:						
Micro Portfolio Write-off > 2%	9	6	9	9	0	0
Small Portfolio Write-off > 2%	4	4	7	5	0	0

Notes: All figures as of December 31. For definitions and methods of calculation see the Technical Note.
Source: ACLEDA Credit Control Reports 1999-2004.

By mid 2001 other branches joined a disquieting trend. Those branches that had maintained respectable portfolio at risk and write-off rates, below 5% and 2% respectively, now found their place on an increasingly troubled roster, (see Table 11.2.) And while the total portfolio grew incrementally in 2000, by 2001 it had increased 53% from its 1999 level.

Perhaps most disturbing of all, the four branches that always experienced a higher level of delinquency and default saw both skyrocket. In Banteay Meanchey, Battambang, Kampong Thom and Pursat either the portfolio at risk or the write-off rates in the micro lending portfolio exceeded 10%; in two branches both exceeded 20%. The quality of the small business portfolio in these same branches fared better, yet it too began to erode quickly. Was the organizational chaos, so favored in the theory of NGO transformation, playing its hand?

For much of 2001, buoyant financial projections aside, ACLEDA was preoccupied with the mounting delinquency and default in the portfolio. They reined in plans for deposit mobilization and shelved plans for portfolio expansion. Redoubled credit officer and branch manager training paralleled the unavoidable resignations and contract terminations. Even as ACLEDA scrambled to stem the frightful trend, another urgent request came from unexpected quarters.

ACLEDA's delinquency crisis and the Prime Minister's speech on public sector reform could not have collided at a more precarious moment in ACLEDA's short history as a licensed specialized bank. In a puzzling digression from a speech on public sector reform, the Prime Minister expressed concern about rumors that ACLEDA had jailed 100 borrowers:

> ... I would like to speak a few words about ACLEDA of an incident that I have yet to find out if it is true or false. But I have my number here of people arrested and jailed for being unable to pay debt to ACLEDA. The court has ordered to arrest the loan takers from ACLEDA and imprisoned them. At this moment I have limited information on that. Please collect more information... I would like to suggest the following solution.
>
> ACLEDA has filed the case to court to get the people to pay back their overdue debts. They do not pay back the debts because they do not have money. If they had money to pay back the debts, they would probably be set free. So I suggest to all provincial governors to collect data for me on the number of people who have been jailed for failing to pay back the loans. I would pay back the debts for these 100 or so people ...
>
> May HE Chea Chanto inspect this case to see if there were a need to strip off the operating license from ACLEDA for we would not accept any micro-finance organization to force our people to fall into such condition.[148]

The press had a field day as if taking great satisfaction in the comeuppance of one of Cambodia's most successful home-grown development efforts, reflecting a much earlier sentiment that "Cambodia was not ready for microfinance." Apprehensively, Cambodia's first licensed micro and small business lender watched as its new commercial status tumbled into political jeopardy. DEG's premonition of political risk rose to the fore.

---

[148] Closing Address to the Forum for Dissemination of the Governance Action Plan and the Public Administration Reform. Cambodia New Vision, Issue 47, December 2001. Available from http://www.cnv.org.kh.

Tracing the Origins of the Crisis

Every year the Mekong overflows its banks to the delight of small farmers who live in bamboo thatched houses perched precariously on stilts. The floods deposit fertile silt on rice paddies and renew wetlands and the great Tonle Sap Lake, before the big muddy stream empties into the South China Sea. In some years the flooding is called a blessing; in others, a disaster. In 2000 and 2001, the waters of the Mekong and its tributaries rose to historical heights, and the floods lasted for an unprecedented amount of time. In 2000, Cambodia's National Committee on Disaster Management struggled to reach an estimated 1.9 million people with assistance. The Asian Development Bank estimated over USD 100 million in damage to crops, livestock, and infrastructure.[149]

One key to solving a delinquency crisis is to determine how it started. It was easy to blame the floods. The floods had a devastating affect on the livelihoods of many of Cambodia's rural people sweeping away houses and livestock, making the next planting season impossible, and imposing greater vulnerability, long after the waters receded. And indeed the floods were a contributing factor in each of the four branches with the highest delinquency. But again, as ACLEDA found during 1997, an external crisis exposes internal weaknesses in the organization that may otherwise go undetected.

The Big Balloon Inflates

The origin of the balloon loan for agricultural is murky, nevertheless, balloon loans had been a long-time feature of the Cambodian microcredit environment. First designed as a reasonable product for agriculture, balloon loans were rapidly incorporated into the portfolios of many microcredit operators. The balloon loans held an alluring promise of prosperity for the rural areas. The defining feature of the loan is that principal is paid at the end of the loan term, not at regular intervals throughout the loan term. ACLEDA's balloon loans required regular interest payments throughout the term; other organizations required payment of principal and interest only at the end of the loan term. While the first method is relatively less risky than the second, both products tend to be a greater gamble for the customer and the lending institution.

Unlike a working capital loan with regular installments of principal and interest, a repayment schedule of a balloon loan does little to predict the likelihood of the borrower's ability to repay the loan at some point in the future. Even diligent monitoring during the loan period may not reveal any but the most obvious problems, as the ability to repay is generally pegged to a future lump-sum return on investment, such as a harvest. A balloon loan also requires careful timing.

---

[149] Asian Development Bank, Country Economic Review – Cambodia (Manila: Asian Development Bank, December 2000), 3.

Repayment must match the harvest, not a week too early before the sale, subverting the very idea of a balloon loan, or a week too late when other senior debts have already been claimed.

· Balloon loans are designed for agriculture, based on the practical cycle of the agricultural business: an up-front investment and a long growing season ending in a harvest, when the loan is expected to be repaid in full. Yet traditional agriculture is a risky business at the best of times. In fact, that is one fairly predictable pattern that makes lenders shy away from crop production. Combining the cyclical nature of risk in traditional agricultural with a balloon loan diminishes the ambiguity of default; the unpredictable "if" becomes the certainty of "when". That certain destiny arrived in four ACLEDA branches that were heavily invested in agricultural loans.

ACLEDA's focus on small business lending through Provincial and district branches has been held up as evidence that it shunned agriculture lending to the micro borrower. Lending to agricultural customers was not a new venture for ACLEDA. In 1996, as a part of a rural financial service, ACLEDA developed a balloon loan product to serve the unique investment return patterns of agriculture. While trade, services and manufacturing maintained the dominant share of the portfolio, by the end of 1997, 25% of ACLEDA's microcredit customers borrowed for agriculture. They sought the increasingly popular balloon product to finance their enterprises. By 2001, 14% of ACLEDA's micro credit portfolio was dedicated exclusively to agriculture. Several rural branches, such as Pursat and Kampong Cham, invested over half of their portfolios in crop loans. Battambang followed with 29% of its portfolio in crop loans. Eighty-five percent of the loan portfolio in the Pursat branch was concentrated in balloon loans.

When the Balloon Bursts

In late 2000, the portfolio quality began to deteriorate and then plummeted throughout 2001. With each new report spun out of the sophisticated MIS, the figures turned more shocking. If ACLEDA seemed to take the delinquency crisis in stride, only the surface was calm. Below, a strong rip-tide pulled under branch after branch. Pursat, Battambang, Kampong Cham, and Kampong Thom each held contaminated portfolios bobbing above 20%, and each had sizable portfolios concentrated in balloon loans. The evidence was piling high, and it served as an indictment of a very popular, but risky, product designed to help struggling Cambodian farmers earn a meager living. And now as loan losses mounted, borrowers plunged into debt, and a small but vocal band of experts became highly critical of microcredit.

During the first delinquency crisis, ACLEDA had the luxury of moving into untapped markets. This was different. As an NGO in 1996, ACLEDA could work quietly to solve problems, out of the limelight, alone or with its donors. Now as a commercial operation, regulated and supervised by the NBC, the rapidly deteriorating portfolio attracted attention. In the eyes of the supervisors ACLEDA Bank's size had the potential to threaten the financial system. Two years of research on deposit mobilization resulted in the roll-out of savings products in 2001, adding to the NBC's uneasiness about ACLEDA's growing delinquency.

The announcement by Hun Sen bounced the dilemma into the public arena. Before any more fall out occurred, ACLEDA dispatched staff to each Provincial Governor's office to discuss the rumor and make clear their intent to verify it, or refute it with the tally of borrowers in jail. They scoured the provincial jails, they reviewed court dockets; they matched their own records with those of the local authorities and wardens. They submitted preliminary reports and final reports to Provincial Governors and the National Bank of Cambodia. The age of defending the commercial operation had begun.

Heart

The most sobering duty of managing a delinquency crisis, besides watching it mount, is the search to uncover all the factors that caused it. The resolve to do something about it immediately follows. ACLEDA's analysis revealed three saving graces. First, ACLEDA was adequately provisioned. The loan loss reserve was equivalent to 80% of the outstanding balances of all loans with installment payments overdue 30 days or more. The aggressive provisioning policy of the past provided a safety net, but one that already strained under the continuing trend. Secondly, while some branches plummeted into default, others barely blinked. Records of the period also show several branches where delinquency spiked and portfolios were quickly brought under control. Others, chronically ill, worsened. The total portfolio of the branches in crisis represented about one third of ACLEDA's overall portfolio for the period. Hardly encouraging, yet the geographic diversity of a national network left some glimmer of hope that the crisis could be contained.

The last saving grace was a mixed blessing; the most serious default was in the micro portfolio, which represented 30% of the total portfolio, but 80% of the number of borrowers. Counting meager blessings, this could easily have led to hasty conclusions – to close branches in areas deemed unsuitable for lending, or to wind up the micro lending business, chalking it up as a venture too risky for a commercial operation to continue. The crisis required a more ruthless analysis of the causes, and a cure that would avoid punishing the customer.

In their efforts to detect origins of the crisis, other factors besides the balloon loan emerged from the shadows. In 2000, ACLEDA hired 182 new staff, most of them credit officers. The next year, 320 new staff joined ACLEDA. In 2001, for each staff member who had worked more than one year for the organization, there were two who had worked less than one year for the organization. The number of new staff increased to an all time high, at a time that called for more experienced staff to support the growing business. Perspectives about the level of performance new staff could muster in a short amount of time contradicted a harsher reality.

Expectations for growth figured high on the list of contributing culprits. The pressure to fulfill the potential of the new commercial status increased. With prospects for growth aglow, ACLEDA tied incentives to expanding portfolios, numbers of clients and portfolio quality. Several branch managers blundered in emphasizing growth first; they could worry about quality later. As the real or imagined competition among branches for portfolio expansion ensued, branches found disbursement targets unsuited to the deteriorating portfolio quality. Unfortunately, they did little to correct the plans. Business development continued unabated.

Despite hopes to the contrary, the evidence was in. The cherished balloon loan for agriculture, developed out of ACLEDA's virtue for putting its customers first, caused massive delinquency. Just over half of the startling write-off rate of 10% in the micro loan portfolio was attributed to balloon loans. By the end of 2001, the write-offs for balloon loans were almost seven times greater than the entire outstanding balloon loan portfolio at the end of the year.

Now the ultimate test came for high-flying ACLEDA — could it balance its commercial orientation of pleasing the customer with the risk management necessary to protect the institution, and ultimately the assets of the borrower? The 2003 figures attest to ACLEDA's determination to reach that balance. Within two years, the application of these dual business concepts would create a position of institutional strength without sacrificing absolute loyalty to its customers.

Resolving the Crisis

The drama and virulent energy associated with rampaging delinquency never match the slower more painstaking efforts to get it under control. ACLEDA management and the credit committee of the Board of Directors spent a great deal of time analyzing the portfolio – by branch, by credit officer, by product, by sector, by sub-sector – cross-matched with the prevalence of balloon loans.

What appeared to be borderline performance, a steady, predictable and ultimately manageable problem, was masked by rapid portfolio growth that concealed underlying weaknesses. Standard indicators of portfolio quality, deemed reliable in a steady state of growth were fallible measures in the context of rapid portfolio expansion. ACLEDA's analysis called for unconventional adjustments to reveal just how bad the crisis was.

The MIS adeptly produced a new set of data. First the portfolio at risk (PAR > 30 days) was determined at the mid year point, then an adjustment was made to add the write-off for the period back into the PAR. Finally, an adjustment was made for growth, discounting increments over the past six months. The results were dramatic. What looked like a barely acceptable PAR of 10% in one branch when combined with the write-off for the period, and adjusting for portfolio growth, became an astonishing 35% portfolio at risk.

On the theory that the old portfolio was not the only problem, an analysis began to closely examine all new loans made since the beginning of the year. In one branch, the figures showed a PAR of 89% in loans disbursed only three months earlier. ACLEDA generally found that loans nearing the end of the term were more likely to experience delinquency than newly disbursed loans. Another frightening trend was revealed.

The analysis quickly focused on four branches that were responsible for 72 % of the total delinquency in the microcredit portfolio. Five branches were responsible for the majority of the small lending portfolio delinquency, but four branches were on both lists confirming that the deteriorating portfolio quality was primarily a management issue; one that was exacerbated by agricultural lending and the balloon loan. Emergency measures to stem the tide of delinquency and default included suspending new lending for both crop production and the balloon loan, pending an investigation into the extent of the problem, and an analysis of how risks could be managed at acceptable levels.

Preventing Another

Old axioms of microfinance fall out of favor from time to time, when new ideas or methods appear to offer greater advice for those eager to listen. As ACLEDA began to get the delinquency crisis under control, it deepened its belief in one such axiom to explain the present: the level of delinquency in a credit operation depends on the organization, not the borrower. Another old axiom guided the future: it is easier to prevent delinquency than to manage a crisis. For most of 2001 and 2002, ACLEDA put new policies and practices into place to manage risk without abandoning its clients.

- The first action established new policies and rigorous monitoring. A new policy regulates the balloon loan, a product ACLEDA was reluctant to abandon. It limits the balloon loan to 10% of the total branch portfolio, unless the branch history proves superior portfolio quality. Only then are those limits expanded on a sliding scale that ties increases in the product offering to the amount of portfolio at risk. There is more cautious lending to agriculture, particularly when combined with the balloon loan. The MIS tracks loans by sector, cross-referenced to crop loans and the balloon product; it ticks off warnings when those levels are exceeded. Newly established branches with high growth rates, as well as mature branches are monitored closely, adjusting performance for growth.

- Secondly, the incentive system was revised to tie year-end bonuses to return on equity and portfolio quality at the branch level. ACLEDA always favored a group-based incentive program tied to branch performance. Past incentives that included the number of clients and portfolio outstanding in the mix were now identified as factors that led to pressure to expand rapidly. The new incentive plan included two main performance measures – return on equity at the branch level and the portfolio at risk adjusted for write-off. Combining these two measures allowed a clearer focus on a return and portfolio quality.

- As management requested and accepted resignations of branch managers and credit officers, it redoubled credit management training. Business plan training for branch managers landed high on the list of priorities. A policy was established to require all branch managers to regularly update their cash flow analysis and loan disbursements. The effort was designed to avoid the past situation, where branch managers felt compelled to disburse loans in an attempt to reach projected targets even as the portfolio worsened and the business environment changed. Credit officers receive three months of on the job training with experienced credit officers. In the short term this shows up in lower productivity ratios, but in the long term, it was expected to yield higher benefits to the institution and better service to the borrower.

- Strengthening branch management received priority. A new post of chief credit officer at branch level was created to strengthen management and overseeing of the increasing number of credit officers. A loan recovery officer, who works in tandem with other loan officers to recover bad debt, was added to the roster. At the central level, the credit department forms an expert team complemented by experienced managers from other branches. The team can be assembled quickly to respond to emerging problems in any branch in ACLEDA's network.

While ACLEDA shored up credit management, political risk receded to a quiet corner. The time and energy branch management spent visiting every official in every district yielded results. ACLEDA found seven debtors in jail, but only one ACLEDA borrower. In retrospect, the announcement that ACLEDA carted defaulting borrowers off to jail may have helped the beleaguered organization. Many delinquent borrowers who heard the announcement quickly paid up. Those who found encouragement to default with the generous offer of government to pay their debts questioned the reasonableness of repayment. Yet, it gradually dawned on them that they would have to go to jail first to collect on the promise. The sophisticated consumer chose the better deal.

By mid-2002 the delinquency crisis abated. By year-end 2003 it appeared to have never happened at all. All eleven mature branches reported portfolio at risk and write-offs well below the limit ACLEDA had established for each, 5% and 2% respectively. The overall portfolio quality would be the envy of any of any microfinance institution, or commercial bank. The recovery of bad debt continues. Table 11.3 shows the remarkable improvement in bad debt collection over time.

Table 11.3. Percentage of Write-off Recovered: Trends, 1999 – 2004

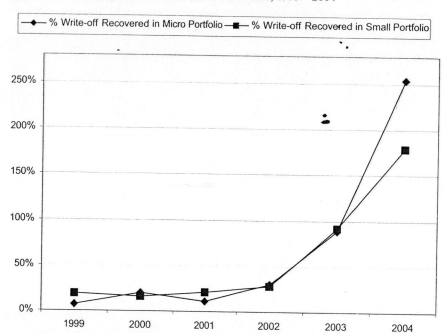

Notes: The percentage of write-off recovered is: the amount of previously written off principal that was recovered during the year divided by the total principal written off during the same year. Percentages over 100% show bad debt recovered from previous years.
Source: ACLEDA Credit Control Reports, 1999 – 2004.

Lessons

One of the most famous delinquency crises in microfinance is the Bolivia crisis in 1999 and the borrower revolt that followed. The Bolivia crisis is attributed to over-lending in a declining economy and a competitive market for microfinance that turned cutthroat with the arrival of the consumer lender. ACLEDA's crisis emerged from a broader combination of internal and external factors. A risky product, untracked by the MIS, and a rapidly expanding loan portfolio that masked the true levels of delinquency and the most important trends were the two factors that figured high on the list. Certainly the number of new staff and the high expectations for growth pushed a burden on recent recruits that they were unable to handle. The incentive system that had worked so well in the past suddenly backfired in this new era of growth. When the floods came in 2000 and 2001, just as the consumer lenders swept into Bolivia in 1998, they became the surge for the volatile delinquency crisis that is legendary in microfinance.

In ACLEDA Bank today there is a general atmosphere of confidence as the well-oiled machine, applies new rigor to retail banking. Staff turn-over rates are among the lowest in ACLEDA's eleven-year history; investment in human resources is at the highest of all previous years. The portfolio at risk and the write-off rates in both the small and micro portfolios (as well as the total amount) are at historic lows as well. ACLEDA is expanding in the traditional line of business – the micro and small-scale credit market. The bank makes tiny loans, as low as 1% of GDP per capita. The on-line IT system enables a new range of products and services that are safe, convenient and valued by poor and low-income customers in provincial towns and rural areas. The financial health of the institution inspires the confidence of the National Bank and depositors alike.

But "the great delinquency crisis of 2001" is not forgotten. It is lodged in the collective memory as a time when events conspired to produce a chaos that led Cambodia's rising star to question one fundamental value. Did the commercial orientation of putting the customer first weaken risk management that would ensure both the institution and the customer survived?

Despite events that could have led the staunchest microfinance organization to question commitment to the rural microcredit customer, ACLEDA has not become the distant, risk-fearing commercial bank of the ilk that provoked microfinance organizations around the world to enter the market in the first place. True to their history ACLEDA staff came away from the experience with new lessons, and an improved operation that roots them more firmly in the market they are determined to serve. There is still USD 1 million of ACLEDA's 2001-2002 portfolio floating about the Cambodian countryside. Eventually ACLEDA hopes to recover most of it; in the meantime the concrete plan is never to let it happen again.

CHAPTER 12:

Commercial Microfinance and Poverty

Dogma and Business

Business and development goals make for the uneasy alliance of microfinance. One of the major concerns of the early 1990s centered on the profitability of the business model. After years of trying to prove that reaching poor and low-income people with financial services on a profitable basis was possible – indeed a whole industry emerged to pursue the debate on both sides of the question – the modest success in doing so prompted a new question. Does the drive for a respectable rate of return push an institution, away from its original clients, poor and low-income customers? This philosophical question tends to obscure the business dynamics of markets and how they work. The far better question becomes, *how* does the drive for a respectable rate of return push an institution closer to its original clients, poor and low-income customers?

The Push for a Respectable Rate of Return

A popular mathematical proof is offered to explain how a drive for a respectable rate of return pushes an institution away from small borrowers. Higher profits are derived from the lower costs and lower risks associated with larger borrowers. They are easier to reach and work with because their businesses are more established, their literacy rates are higher, and they have a more equal footing in the unequal power relationships in their communities. Microcredit is famous for its high costs of reaching the poor, often isolated borrower, with a very small loan. For example, a 10% interest rate on a loan of USD 10,000 is USD 1000. For an institution to make the same amount of money, it would have to disburse, and collect, 100 USD 100 loans. The cost of administering loans for 100 borrowers is much higher than the administrative costs for one loan.[150] The same is true for the relative costs of small and large savings accounts. Simply put, the costs associated with small accounts are higher and the profit, at the same unit price, is lower.

Basic microeconomics teaches that price differentiation, increasing efficiency and reaching economies of scale, when pursued in concert, are solutions to this

---

[150] See CGAP, Interest Rate Ceilings and Microfinance: The Story So Far. Occasional Paper No. 9. (Washington, D.C.: CGAP, September 2004).

dilemma. The most successful market-oriented microfinance organizations around the world learned that just as one loan size doesn't fit all, one price forces a cross-subsidy of the less profitable small accounts. It is the cross-subsidy, or the pricing of products, not necessarily the products themselves or the customers, that weighs heavily in the profit-making venture's choice to continue a product line or leave it.

During the earliest days of working in the market, as we saw in Chapter 2, ACLEDA staff learned this basic principle of pricing and how the market responds. If they were to pursue the microcredit customer, as well as the small business customer, they had to design products appropriate for each market segment and price products so that neither subsidized the other.

As we saw, in the early days ACLEDA staff feared a price increase, as their development philosophy hindered a customer-oriented response. How could they justify a higher price on a smaller loan size? When they changed their pricing and products, this move was not based on pressure from increasing competition; it was based on the vision of becoming the market leader. The vision sprang from the concept that customers, not donors were the future; if there were no customers, there would be no future. They wanted to please the customer and if the price was to increase, then the quality of the service had to match it. To maintain the vision of market leader, as we have seen in Chapter 3, ACLEDA dedicated resources to technological innovation, and shoring up systems which later enabled the organization to reach higher levels of efficiency, expand new service points and increase outreach, reaching economies of scale. These efficiencies have been passed on to the customer in terms of lower interest rates on loans, better service and a variety of new products. When ACLEDA developed the organizational capacity to respond to the customer, it did so. And the customer responded.

Risk is the flip side of price. Risk translates into costs in a higher loan loss reserve and ultimately in the loss of the income-generating asset, the portfolio. In Channy maintains the micro credit customer is less risky overall than the small business customer. He draws this conclusion from the evidence of portfolio at risk trends in the microcredit portfolio over time and the small absolute amounts the percentage write-offs in the micro portfolio contribute to the total portfolio write-off. Yet as we have seen, the microcredit portfolio overall is much more vulnerable to sudden shocks because its customers live more closely to the margin and have fewer resources to rely on in times of crisis.

ACLEDA found risk can be managed; not eliminated, but managed. Its strategy argued for more sector and geographic diversification, well-established procedures and policies designed to mitigate risk, and systems that tracked specific risk for each product and market segment. ACLEDA's analysis of the great delinquency crisis of 2001 revealed that risk is a central part of its business. And just as a commercial orientation enabled ACLEDA to respond to a greater number of customers with a greater number of appealing products, risk management enabled protection of the institution's assets and the assets of the customers.

Mission Drift: Why Continue to Serve the Original Market?

No matter what the view, the costs are higher for microcredit than for small business lending. In a steady state risk in the microcredit portfolio is generally less, however the portfolio overall is more vulnerable to sudden shocks. This is the theory that stimulates the jump to the next question. Why would an MFI that has transformed into a commercial bank continue to serve their original market when it has other more attractive options? The costs are higher, the risks more unpredictable. It is against the backdrop of the dynamics of business growth that the concept of "mission drift" surfaces along with attempts to measure it.

Inadequate Measures for a Fuzzy Concept

"Mission drift" is an unfortunate term that implies no one is at the helm. The term is used as a euphemism for leaving behind the original clients, poor and low-income borrowers, once a new commercial status is gained. In microfinance, mission, or organizational purpose, is often confused with operational strategy, quite a different thing. If the mission is to serve the lower end of the market with financial services, or to provide sustainable microfinance for very poor people as a pathway out of poverty, an operational strategy is to develop and deliver products and services that suit that purpose. Jim Collins, the guru of organizational change in corporate America, notes "enduring great companies preserve their core values and purpose while their business strategies and operating practices endlessly adapt to a changing world."[151] Oddly, the concept of "mission drift" in microfinance focuses on the changes in business strategy and practices, not purpose.

Generally, the MFI turned commercial bank comes to that new legal status with several credit products that have stood the test of time in appropriately serving a large number of customers. And it is on these original products that an analysis of "mission drift" tends to focus. Unfortunately, this leads to an uneven view of both "mission" and "drift". Perhaps one of the main failings of attempts to detect "mission drift" is to treat microfinance organizations as static credit-only development projects, not the businesses they are, or strive to be. While there tends to be acceptance of a non-profit organization's mission to reach the poor, there is skepticism about a for-profit business's ability to reach the poor on any basis other than a predatory one. The values of a business are called into question following the apparent choice between "profit or purpose", when there is a more obvious choice – "profit and purpose".[152]

The most commonly used measure of "mission drift" traces the increase in average loan size over time. This curious measure of "loan creep", while simple, is

---

[151] Collins, *Good to Great*, 195.

[152] Collins and Porras, *Built to Last*, 48-55.

inadequate on many counts. On the most obvious account, measuring "mission drift" using average loan size focuses on only one product that is valuable to poor people. The common use of the measure shows the advocate's fascination with credit rather than the range of products that are useful to poor and low-income people. The measure ignores the value of savings and transfers that are of equal value to poor and vulnerable households in maintaining or building assets and reducing costs on income transfers. Indeed, transfers are the sole source of income for many of the poorest households in rural areas.

On a less obvious account, using increasing average loan size to verify mission drift assumes a one-dimensional financial institution, the one-size-fits-all micro-credit operation of yesterday. The use of average loan size presents a lopsided picture of the borrowers, and ignores a very likely trend toward providing a greater variety of credit products to a broader range of customers, even while the organization expands outreach to its microcredit borrowers.[153]

A more relevant framework that allows the analyst to determine how an MFI turned commercial bank may be leaving one market segment in pursuit of another is one that reveals an understanding of business growth and market dynamics. Admittedly this is a more complex task than rooting out one simple measure. But it is more useful in understanding the dynamics of business growth and pressures that may lead the commercial institution away from its original customers, or closer to them.

H. Igor Ansoff Frames the Choices for Market Expansion

The Ansoff product-market matrix frames the choices all businesses face in managing growth.[154] The first choice is market penetration, expanding in the existing market with the same products. The second is product development, expansion in the existing market with new products. The third is market development, reaching new markets with existing products. And the fourth is diversification, developing new markets with new products. Each of these business growth strategies carries with it a range of costs and risks that are determined by the competency of the business, the market and the competition.

---

[153] Even when compared with GNP per capita the same effect occurs, since the problematic numerator, average loan size, does not change. For a discussion of mission drift and trends towards providing comprehensive banking services see Fernando (2004) and von Stauffenberg (2001).

[154] Dr. Igor H. Ansoff is known as the "father of strategic management". His classic product/market matrix, one that is widely used today, was published in "Strategies for Diversification", Harvard Business Review, 1957.

Table 12.1. The Ansoff Product/Market Growth Matrix – ACLEDA's Markets & Products

	Current Products	New Products
Current Markets	*Market Penetration* Micro & small business credit in rural and urban areas	*Product Development* Transfers & savings services in existing branches for micro, small & medium sized businesses
New Markets	*Market Development* Extending micro & small business credit to additional rural districts and unserved Provinces.	*Product Diversification* Cash management, payroll services for organizations, large companies. Transfers & savings for urban salaried workers & general public. Personal loans for salaried workers

The reason businesses stay in a market, or leave one, is because it makes business sense to stay there, or exit. Why would a business abandon a thriving market that it has developed at considerable cost, effort, systems, and investment in the human and physical infrastructure? It wouldn't make sense to leave that market unless the business were forced out by competition, changes in the broader economy, or changes in customer preferences. Perhaps the business has other more attractive options well within the reach of its own competence to respond, and this might lead it to abandon its existing market, chalking up the considerable investments as serving a by-gone era. Most microfinance organizations know their existing customer base – a customer base that continues to grow, and they have developed products to reach them. Just as penetrating the existing market with existing products is the least costly growth scenario, diversification – developing new products in new markets – is the most costly and risky business growth strategy.

The Market of Last Resort?

Cloudy questions now emerge. Well, if microfinance is such a good business opportunity, why weren't the traditional commercial banks in that market to begin with? And why do many of them retreat from the market for microfinance, once they are convinced they should enter it?[155] Consider the reasons why a commercial bank does not serve the microfinance client. The option is not perceived as an

---

[155] "The commercial downscaler experience is mixed, and includes cases of bank exits as well as many sluggish programs. There are a few banks that have been able to reach large numbers of people with a well-defined, well-integrated product." Lisa Valenzuela, "Getting the Recipe Right" in the Commercialization of Microfinance (Bloomfield, Conn: Kumarian Press, 2002), 72.

advantageous one that fits easily with its existing business strategies; it is neither the existing market nor the existing product. The corporate culture, technologies, locations, and internal incentives are based on serving the bank's own established customer base. An unclear regulatory framework or one that requires loan documentation or collateral requirements that would be prohibitive for microcredit makes serving that market a more risky or more costly endeavor. High on the list of constraints is the expense involved in developing a new product to reach a different segment of customers, particularly customers that are generally viewed as higher cost and higher risk. Why compete in a new market when the current one yields acceptable returns? Commercial banks have an established customer base, and the true-blue banker courts these customers and their loyalty with an increasing array of products and services. Why leave them?

These are some of the reasons why commercial banks do not leave established markets in search of the microfinance customer. They are equally compelling reasons for transformed MFIs to stay in their own developed market segment.

Inherent in the lack of reasoning about markets and established players, is the assumption that the high-end market is the most desirable one; the market for microfinance is the market of last resort. Discount retailers of all sorts know that this is not necessarily the case. The high end of the market is just another segment; one that is generally well served. The low end of the market is generally far from saturated. There is no mystery in microfinance. The early leaders discovered a large unserved market segment, one where the only competition was a high-cost, small provider of credit who had inadequate capital and little means to expand beyond the village. MFIs discovered the magic of the mass-market discounter in nations full of boutique shops.

Mission Drift in a World of Options

ACLEDA's case is unique in the list of MFIs turned banks, just because the financial sector in Cambodia is underdeveloped. The new frontiers for ACLEDA Bank are products, geographical areas and customers who are not so far from the mainstream. In many countries where microfinance has advanced, MFIs do not have these options; these competitive market segments are under the command of established commercial banks. Ironically, in just such a case the ultimate test of "mission drift" emerges. In a country where there are options for an NGO MFI turned commercial bank to enter mainstream banking, does it leave its original customers behind?

Let us look more closely at ACLEDA Bank's performance in maintaining its outreach to poor borrowers – the microcredit customer. Has the bank adopted a market penetration strategy? The absolute number of customers in the traditional market segment is revealing, as well as loan size, but adjusted for averages. Second, it is also relevant to determine the expansion of products and who uses them. Has the organization seriously explored developing new products for the existing customer base? Third, what new markets have been tapped and where they are? What is the extent of outreach to rural areas, the poorest segment of Cambodia's market? And finally, let us look at diversification, new markets and new products.

Existing Markets, Existing Products

From its earliest days ACLEDA moved from directly targeting specific groups of people through a variety of means tests to a broad-based approach following market principles. ACLEDA staff found that customers tended to appreciate an approach that respected their privacy and treated them like the customers they were, not beneficiaries of development aid. Since its inception, ACLEDA's portfolio has been divided between small businesses and micro businesses. Chapter 3 explored the dramatic growth of the late 1990s; when ACLEDA traded in a public assistance mentality for a market-led approach, growth boomed.

A more sound way to detect a drift away from the original micro borrowers is to look at the extent to which the organization continues to penetrate existing markets with existing products. Is the microcredit customer base expanding? At the end of 1999, the year before transformation, ACLEDA served a total of 56,412 loan clients. There were 48,024 microcredit customers, and 8,257 small business customers. By December 2004 there were a total of 122,171 active loan customers; 91,566 micro clients, and 27,311 small business clients. Table 12.2 shows that as a commercial bank, ACLEDA has almost doubled the number of micro clients

Table 12.2. Pre- and Post Transformation Number of Active Borrowers

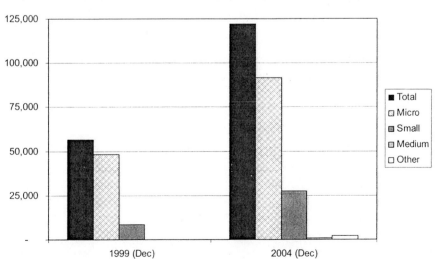

Source: ACLEDA Credit Control Reports, 1999 and 2004.

Table 12.3. Micro, Small and Medium Loan Customers as a Percentage of Total Customers for Existing Loan Products, 1999 and 2004

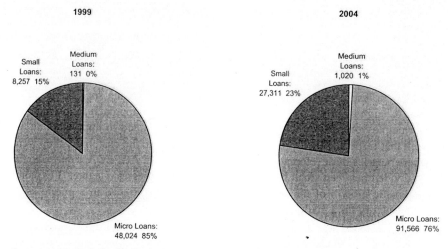

Source: *ACLEDA Credit Control Reports, 1999 and 2004.*

served within a three-year period, from a reasonable starting base in 1999. The number of small business credit customers has almost tripled, from a more modest starting base during the same period.

The relative percentage of the number of total customers in each category of micro, small and medium-sized loan customers has remained stable, as shown in Table 12.3, indicating a greater market penetration for the existing micro credit market, rather than a "drift" away from it.

Are Tiny Loans Lost?

A quick look at average loan sizes may indicate that tiny loans have been lost, that the micro borrower has been left behind. But beneath the mystique of average loan size, another picture emerges.

Table 12.4. Average Loan Size 1999 – 2003 (in USD)

	1999	2000	2001	2002	2003
Average Loan Size	243	274	257	330	409
Average Micro	81	91	83	98	110
Average Small	1,054	956	903	1,001	1,092
Average Medium	8,498	7,929	8,673	12,595	15,660

Source: *ACLEDA Credit Control Reports, 1999 and 2003.*

Table 12.5. Commercial Bank: Number of Loans and Loan Sized in the Microcredit Portfolio

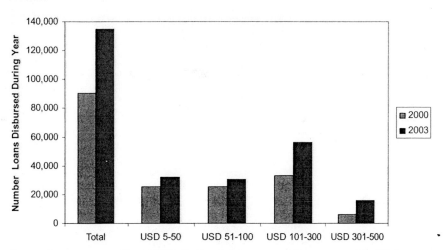

Source: Report prepared by ACLEDA's Credit Management Department, July 2004.

As we see in Table 12.4, average loan sizes mask the depth of outreach when a financial institution serves micro, small and medium-sized businesses with credit products. What is not obvious from the above figures is that ACLEDA Bank increased the number of micro loans disbursed in the range of USD 5 to 50 by 25% from 2000 to 2003. In 2003, ACLEDA disbursed 32,300 micro loans in the USD 5 to 50 range (see Table 12.5.) When we take a look at the differential loan size, we see that the number of tiny loans in the micro portfolio has increased over time, a trend that is concealed by using average loan balances. The make-up of ACLEDA Bank's micro portfolio shows a continued and increasing presence in all loan categories in the micro portfolio.

Even as advocates continue to reach for more sophisticated measurements for poverty targeting, the value of small loans to poor customers cannot be underestimated. Eighty percent of Cambodia's labor force is self-employed or unpaid family labor in small and micro enterprises. That percentage rises to 87% in the rural areas. Sixty percent of the national household income is derived from self-employment, and this percentage rises to 71% in the poorer rural areas. In 2003, ACLEDA Bank disbursed 119,153 loans under USD 300, that time-honored but inexplicable benchmark for a poverty lending focus.[156] In 2003, the total amount of disbursed loans under USD 300, totaled USD 13.8 million, eclipsing ACLEDA's entire portfolio outstanding at the end of 1999.

---

[156] The USD 300 loan size to indicate poverty measures is falling out of use, as attention focuses on more sophisticated methods of poverty measurement. However, that information is still requested by the MIX Market, as a measure of depth of outreach, reflecting the state of the microfinance industry and what it wants to know.

Table 12.6. ACLEDA Bank Network and Coverage 1999 and 2004

ACLEDA Branch Network		
	1999 (Dec)	**2004 (Dec)**
Total Branches	27	119
Provincial Branches	11	18
District Branches & Posts	16	106
COVERAGE		
	Total Cambodia (Census 1998)	**ACLEDA operations (Dec 2004)**
Provinces*	24 (21 Provinces and 3 Municipalities)	21 (18 Provinces and 3 Municipalities)
Districts	183	154
Communes	1609	1342
Villages	13406	8181

Notes: There are 24 Provinces in Cambodia, which include the municipality of Phnom Penh and the "Krong" or "Towns" of Sihanoukville, Kaeb and Pailin.
Source: NBC Network Information. December 2002.

Whatever "mission drift" or loan creep, might be found in ACLEDA's portfolio, two points are clear. First, the portfolio represents a trend to provide credit services to a wider spectrum of loan clients. The larger average loan size reflects that just as the number of micro credit customers continues to increase, so too do the numbers of small and medium-sized enterprises. Secondly, the micro loan portfolio now reaches a larger number of borrowers – nearly double the number of micro customers financed at the end of 1999 and double the amount of portfolio. The statistics show penetration, if not entrenchment, in the micro credit market, not a drift from it.

New Markets, Existing Products

Entry into new markets with existing products is a second way to expand. Since its conversion as a specialized bank, ACLEDA has sought out new markets for its existing products, attracting both the micro credit and the small business borrower. In 1999, ACLEDA served eleven Provinces with Provincial branches, district offices and rural posts. By the end of 2004, ACLEDA Bank established 15 Provincial branches that serve 21 of Cambodia's 24 Provinces and major cities and towns. The number of offices reached 136 by June 2005. Expansion reached to the

Pailin, Koh Kong, Preah Vhear, Otdar Meanchey and Kratie, long isolated by lack of communications, impassable roads and heightened security. Expansion of district branches and rural posts increased six-fold, covering 61% of Cambodia's villages as shown in Table 12.6. While there is great diversity in the poverty level of villages within districts and individuals within those villages, ACLEDA Bank locates district offices and rural posts in 23 districts mapped by World Food Programme as having 50% or greater incidence of poverty.[157]

Existing Markets, New Products

Establishing district offices and rural posts enabled ACLEDA's extensive outreach in a cost-effective way, as we saw in Chapter 3. Branch locations are important for people who use the new products as well. New products, such as savings and transfers, are now available to the existing customer base because of ACLEDA's license as a regulated financial institution; but these products are available to an increasing number of Cambodia's rural people because of ACLEDA's mission.

As many MFIs that have transformed into regulated financial institutions have found there can be a considerable time lag for savings services to take off. This is due to a number of factors. Key among them is institutional prudence, not institutional passivity, as some analysts of NGO transformations would suggest. As discussed in Chapter 4, the absence of commercially available borrowing advanced ACLEDA's business development strategy to mobilize deposits earlier than in many financial institutions that had this option available. ACLEDA's savings products and the support systems to manage them in 119 offices took almost two years to develop. The time lag paid off in products that are appropriately developed for the market, as well as the safety of the institution that collects them. Time deposits and demand deposits are available for the small saver, as well as for the large saver. By the end of 2004, ACLEDA Bank's deposit to loan ratio reached 47.88%, a 50% increase over the previous year. While there are large institutional depositors, the average balance on 32,270 accounts, or 98% of the accounts was USD 214 (2003).[158]

As ACLEDA's district offices come on-line, deposits in the rural areas have begun to grow. By June 2005, ACLEDA's deposit to loan ratio reached 65.8%; deposits reached USD 52.4 million and the loan portfolio USD 79.6 million. In Channy sees a decisive trend; the district offices are attracting savings into the system for the first time, not taking business from other banks. Those deposits are

---

[157] See Tomoki Fujii, "Commune-Level Estimation of Poverty Measures and Its Application in Cambodia" (Berkley: University of California, 2003), 19. The paper was prepared for the World Food Programme.

[158] Deposit to loan ratio at the end of December 2004. Figures on savings balances reflect status at the end December 2003.

used by micro and small enterprises in rural and urban areas of Cambodia, reaffirming the "virtuous spiral" ACLEDA hoped to achieve with the transformation in 1999.

Who uses demand deposits? Given the lumpy nature of investment in agriculture and its lumpy return, demand deposits are attractive to the farmer. Traders transfer cash from savings accounts in one city to an ACLEDA branch located in a rural area or another city in a distant Province. Manufacturers too used savings accounts linked to transfers to pay suppliers, and customers to pay manufacturers. The on-line system makes electronic transfers from one account to another easy, convenient, reliable and less costly for the small enterprise.

New Markets, New Products

In Cambodia, 85% of the population, as well as 90% of Cambodia's poor people live in rural areas. Generally household income exceeds expenditures by a slim margin. The 1999 Cambodia Socio Economic Survey concluded that household expenditure exceeded household income up to and including the 3rd decile for the whole country. The study noted that "about 40% of households in the rural areas and possibly about 60% of households in Phnom Penh had household income lower than their household expenditure. The gap is often met by consumption borrowing and sale of assets."[159]

Just as the income demographics of Cambodia boosted the popularity of microcredit for consumption smoothing and enterprise investment, they influenced the development and market appeal of new products. This is particularly true for the popularity of local transfers, a new product serving a new market. Certainly a broad range of international organizations and large businesses use transfers, but so do very poor people in rural areas, as they increasingly depend on transfers from family members working in urban factories. The Economics Institute of Cambodia estimates that about 75% of Cambodia's 240,000 garment workers send about 50% of their income home each month, supporting about 1 million rural people in their home villages.[160] The traditional system to transfer funds to rural areas relies on friends, taxis and third parties. The system is expensive, hazardous and unreliable; there are few opportunities for recourse if the transfer goes astray. While savings services are just beginning to attract a greater number of poor people in rural areas, transfers from the urban to the rural areas are services they have already found of value.

---

[159] In Phnom Penh household expenditure exceeded household income up to the 6th income decile. In the rural areas, household expenditure exceeded household income up to the 4th decile group. Cambodia Socio-Economic Survey. A Poverty Profile of Cambodia, Ministry of Planning, 1999, 59.

[160] Economics Institute of Cambodia, *Cambodia Economic Watch* (Phnom Penh: Economics Institute of Cambodia, 2004), 38.

Not all banking is glamorous loan disbursement. Many of ACLEDA Bank's new products were developed to serve Cambodia's development efforts. Some of the direct services are described above, but there is also value in providing indirect services to poor people, even the most vulnerable, food deficit populations, those who have no excess to save and no economic opportunities for which to borrow. Consider the commune level development committee that does not have access to a bank account for village infrastructure projects. The cash is vulnerable to theft in transit or in hand. While a bank account does not prevent theft, it eliminates the risk of robbery in transit, and reduces the cost of physical transport: a safe way of sending cash, and a safe place to keep it until it used. New products were also developed for medium and large-scale enterprises. Payroll services and cash management services such as overdrafts are used by these new ACLEDA Bank customers.

Mission Evolution

> *"What if you were told you were too rich to borrow from an institution because you made $2 a day?"* Microfinance Matters, UNCDF

ACLEDA's mission has evolved since its birth as a rehabilitation project. One could hardly argue that the mission has evolved away from the micro credit customer. The sheer numbers are too compelling to maintain that position. Rather, we see an ACLEDA whose mission has evolved in a changing Cambodian context. From its earliest days as a project, the mission was to provide services – both business development services and credit to micro and small businesses in a post-conflict environment. The original target group became more inclusive over time. No longer focused on demobilized soldiers or victims of war, the target group evolved to include the rural and urban small and micro entrepreneur. As the economy provided more opportunities and the organization's capacity to respond to them developed, so did ACLEDA's offerings. The organizational structure and business strategy evolved to reach more people with financial services.

Even as ACLEDA continues to reach the unbanked, others find their services attractive as well, including the average Cambodian. The average Cambodian earns less than USD 2 day.

But what of the future? In Channy affirms that microfinance and small-scale credit is and will remain the bank's core business. In Siphann, ACLEDA Bank's credit department manager, avows ACLEDA will never leave the micro credit market, as do many of ACLEDA's old guard. They are philosophically and historically bound to it; they are even somewhat mystified by the question. "We would be crazy to leave a successful market," explains Siphann. "Why would we throw away the micro loans? We have a national outreach. Who else will serve them?"

But what of the new generation? One thing is certain, new staff do not join ACLEDA because they want to work in development. They join for professional and philosophical reasons. The new generation wants to be a part of ACLEDA's ethical code in Cambodia's sea of corruption. ACLEDA's early values influenced the way the mission evolved, from a service provider for small and micro entrepreneurs to the aim of becoming Cambodia's leading bank for the people. What both generations know is that Cambodia's leading bank for the people requires strong governance, transparent systems, and high ethical standards.

They also know that 80% of Cambodia's people are small and micro entrepreneurs.

CHAPTER 13

Yesterday, Today and Tomorrow

Microfinance in Cambodia evolved along with the development of the financial sector. Today the financial sector in Cambodia is led by the banking sector. With the passage of banking laws during the late 1990s and their vigorous enforcement by the National Bank of Cambodia, the banking system emerged from a period of chaos to a "flight to quality."[161]

As the discussion turns to an inclusive financial sector, we trace the history of microfinance in Cambodia. This chapter summarizes three sets of lessons about re-building the banking sector in Cambodia, and the attempts to make it an inclusive one. The shape of the financial sector depends on many aspects of the economic and political environment, including the customers and the financial institutions that serve them. The first group of lessons centers on the customers. The second group of lessons focuses on the MFIs, their interaction with one another, and how that changed over time. Finally, the mind-set of banking authorities, the regulatory frameworks they chose and the reforms they put in place set the course for Cambodia's evolving financial sector.

Affinities among customers, retail financial institutions, policy makers and policy implementers shape an inclusive financial sector as it develops, turning it from a nebulous concept into one that concretely serves the people, their enterprises and their goals for the future.

Yesterday – The Nebulous Concept

Microfinance in Cambodia emerged from practical ideas and moral ideals about the reconstruction of society in post-conflict upheaval. Long excluded from the meager benefits Cambodia could offer to its citizens, a fragile peace brought a flood of foreign assistance to a war rocked country and a disenfranchised population. Microcredit took a back seat to the pressing priorities of establishing a truce, de-mining the countryside, repatriating refugees, settling internally displaced people, and ensuring free and fair elections and some semblance of the rule of law in a country reduced to absolute poverty.

---

[161] Statement of Hon. Chea Chanto and Hon. Keat Chhon, IMF Board of Governors, 2000 Annual Meeting, Prague, Czech Republic, September, 2000. Available from http://www.adb.org.

The Customers

The first attempts of the early providers of microcredit centered on targeting groups of people in more accessible urban and rural areas. Microcredit projects targeted women, demobilized soldiers, returnees, farmers, all of whom were victims of war. Credit was supplemented by other services – health services, business services, and agricultural extension. The early projects, supported by foreign donors, found that despite best efforts to target, others who were less poor had no access to financial services either. It became difficult to deny those who earned 20 cents a day and those who earned 60 cents a day. Likewise, small enterprises that earned USD 1.23 day had no other options to borrow.

Common perceptions about Cambodia's borrowers changed as tiny informal businesses began to benefit from microcredit. As Cambodians shared in the most basic benefits offered by peace, their abundant responsibilities for keeping their families alive extended to new responsibilities as credit customers. They readily accepted those obligations, quickly shedding the designation as beneficiaries of donor charity. Poor and low-income families became customers, participants in the economy. The benefits of donor-financed microcredit projects contributed to making poor people marginally better off. With access to small amounts of capital, but usefully large sums, their tiny firms grew.[162] Some did not grow at all, but their owners maintained a means to survive, and survival was important. This accomplishment, often overlooked by theorists of economic development, was championed by the NGO microcredit organizations as the major accomplishment if was.

Poor people invested in their futures, even if they didn't grow their firms. Families invested in their children; they diversified their economic activities, and managed risks that could drop them back into the poverty pit from which they climbed. Now they had choices. They became discerning customers who were willing to purchase services they perceived to be valuable. Even if those initial products were inferior and costly, they were much better than those they had before, which is only saying a little, not a lot.

With the liberating view of borrowers as customers, the concept of economic justice gradually merged to the quest for lasting financial justice. The microfinance operations became the bridge between hundreds of thousands of poor and low-income people and the small amounts of money required to support their enterprises. Continued sharing in society's benefits for the majority of Cambodia's population depended on the permanence of the microfinance operations. Cambodia's microfinance organizations joined together to enter into a dialogue with government and their donors about the future. The debates were long and heated, but from those encounters emerged a framework that would allow a variety of microfinance institutions to become a permanent part of the financial system.

---

[162] For a discussion about the importance of usefully large sums of money to poor entrepreneurs see Stuart Rutherford, *The Poor and Their Money* (New Delhi: Oxford University Press, 2000).

The Microfinance Institutions

The noble aims of microfinance progressed along with practical concerns. Institutional permanence would require more than break-even; it would require profitable institutions that did not depend on donor funding. In Cambodia, MFIs had fewer choices than their counterparts in more developed economies. They had two choices: they could wait *until* the financial system developed, or they could become a part of the financial system *as* it developed. Private-sector options appeared more limited in Cambodia during the early years. Yet the practical concerns were the same as elsewhere; no donor could ever muster the amount of funding required to reach the numbers of people who did not have access to formal financial services. And one day, the donors would leave.

The concept of market leaders developed; institutions that had the strength, the vision and the capacity to prove the effectiveness of the microfinance experiment in their own context. No one considered it an easy road; the "show-how" proved to be a lonely road for the innovators. They confronted the practical hardships of uncharted waters. They questioned their progress, their practices, and their beliefs about the role of business in development and as a means to reduce poverty. They gained the critics' spotlight, and attracted the advocates' misplaced enthusiasm.

The early innovators learned from outsiders, just as they learned from each other. As development workers and teachers, they found great strength and the skill to work with a population that was not literate and had little experience with institutional credit products or the benefits and the risks of using them. Some of these lessons were learned the hard way.

They each brought unique experience as they experimented with different products to serve different segments of the market. They also experienced the weighty issues of governance and management, and shared those with each other through the common bond of working as collegial competitors. Amret, formerly EMT, focused on rural and agricultural lending through community banks. Originally a project of the international NGO, GRET, it was the first to transform into a licensed MFI, showing robust performance and serving nearly 105,000 borrowers[163]. Thaneakea Phum Cambodia (TPC) centered its approach on lending to women in rural areas through local NGOs; it was the first to experiment with mergers among its NGO partners.[164] Hattha Kaksekar Ltd was the first with the vision to provide province-wide services, locating its headquarters in Pursat Province and providing individual loans for agricultural and rural enterprise.[165] Cambodia Community Building (CCB), a project of the international NGO World Relief, centered its approach on urban-based community banks targeting women

---

[163] Figures cited as of December 2004 from the MixMarket.

[164] Abrera E, Spingler M, McCarter E (2002) Case study 2: Thaneakea Phum Cambodia (TPC). In: McCarter E (ed) Mergers in Microfinance: Twelve Case Studies. Catholic Relief Services, Baltimore, pp 11–18.

[165] For a brief history see Hattha Kaksekar Ltd Annual Report 2003, Phnom Penh, pp 8.

and focusing on the importance of education; it was the first to foster an independent, local organization through an "institutional coup".[166] The new local NGO has transformed into Cambodian Entrepreneur Building Limited (CEB), a licensed MFI that serves over 9,400 borrowers and raises equity and borrows from international funds.[167] CCB has transformed as well; CREDIT MFI received a license in 2004 and now serves 10,900 borrowers.[168]

Through sheer perseverance they survived the experts' advice; and listened to gems of wisdom that came from distant countries, their own small rice fields, and the back streets of Cambodia's cities and towns. The discipline of microfinance enabled them to develop a broader range of products and enter the brave new world of commercial microfinance. And with the leaders, new actors came to the fore. Microfinance operations merged, finding strength in numbers; some split from their parent NGOs, finding strength in choosing their own path; others disappeared, victims of donor policy shifts and managerial weaknesses.

As the first innovators gained experience, competition in the marketplace appeared largely as predicted. New products emerged, interest rates declined, the quality and diversity of the services improved. The inferior products of the past found their place on dusty shelves as footnotes in donor evaluation reports. The MFIs were rapidly proving that microcredit was not a public sector good; the benefits clearly accrued to individuals, they did not accrue equally and all customers did not pay the same price. Microfinance was a private sector good that found its place in a long-ignored market segment. As MFIs grew their businesses, providing services to a capital-starved market, they gradually began to counter theories of market failure, eliminating the justification for direct government subsidies for the provision of retail services.

In their new commercial incarnation, the MFIs expanded, building their own capacity to respond to a large under-served market. By 2004, ACLEDA Bank and nine licensed MFIs established as commercial companies with shareholder structures provided the bulk of financial services to Cambodia's poor and low-income populations. Together they serve over 400,000 active borrowers, representing about 17% of Cambodia's 2.4 million households. They provide 24% of the total outstanding private sector domestic credit in Cambodia.[169] The leaders are NGO microfinance organizations that transformed into commercial companies as Table 13.1 shows.

---

[166] Larson D, Pierce M, Graber K, Doyle K, Halty M (2002) Developing a post-conflict microfinance industry: the case of Cambodia. In: Larson D (ed) Microfinance Following Conflict Technical Briefs. USAID, Washington, D.C., pp 3–4.

[167] Triodos-Doen Foundation (2004) Annual Report. Zeist, The Netherlands, pp 13.

[168] Data from the MixMarket, and CREDIT MFI Audited Financial Statements, 2004.

[169] Credit to the private sector in Cambodia as of December 2003 was USD 338 million. IMF (2004) Cambodia: statistical appendix: IMF country report No. 04/330. IMF, Washington, D.C., Table 16.

Table 13.1. Retail Microfinance in Cambodia, June 2004

	ACLEDA	2 Specialized Banks (a)	9 Licensed MFIs	28 registered NGOs (b)	Total
Portfolio (USD)	49,711,076	4,930,189	19,564,570	8,165,082	82,370,917
Active Borrowers	109,094	524	295,915	77,563	483,096
Deposits (USD) (c)	21,603,048	424,055	1,124,438	138,915	23,290,456
Savings Accounts	45,340	29	94,098	15,539	155,006

Notes: a) There are 3 specialized banks; two lend directly to small and medium enterprises. The other is the Rural Development Bank, a wholesale lender, which is not included here as much of its portfolio is lent to retail MFIs. b) PRASAC is included in the registered NGO column, representing 69% of the NGO active borrowers and 78% of the NGO outstanding portfolio. PRASAC received its license as a regulated MFI in December 2004. c) NGO savings are generally compulsory savings. About 60% of the deposits listed for licensed MFIs are compulsory savings.
Sources: Network Information: Specialized Banks, MFIs and NGOs. NBC: June 2004; Information on ACLEDA Bank's status as of June 2004, provided by ACLEDA.

The Policy Makers

The first MFIs that served Cambodia's people were largely left to their own devices. The financial sector policy to include microfinance evolved slowly. Many were anxious to quickly draw up guidelines and regulations that would limit the legal charters of retail providers. They were also eager to establish one directive about the ownership of donated capital, despite the variety of agreements in force between donors and the microfinance institutions. They discussed the benefits of a system of neatly organized community-owned cooperatives, affiliated as shareholders to a rural development bank. That model may have been appealing in another market, or at another time, but it was unrealistic for Cambodia at the stage of development of the rural economy. The policy makers were wise enough to see that. In hindsight, the gradual development of the policy and the regulatory framework were great strengths.

The first set of microfinance policy makers was drawn from social sectors and rural development departments. While they shared the same goal as the microfinance institutions, they often advocated different means of achieving it. The National Bank of Cambodia was not directly involved until 1997. Banking authorities rightly focused attention on writing a banking law, restructuring the formal banking sector, and implementing re-licensing requirements. Each of these would later become the foundation for including microfinance in the formal financial system.

In the interim the central bank gained experience with the new market reforms that were taking place in Cambodia's transitional economy, and with its role as regulator and supervisor under a two-tiered banking system. From 1998-2002 the NBC focused on supervision and regulation, applying prudential rules to the existing formal financial sector. It classified many banks as non-viable; it revoked licenses and established new requirements for re-licensing, dramatically reducing the number of banks operating in the sector. As the NBC strengthened its supervisory capacity, the stability and soundness of the formal financial sector improved.

During that time the NBC brought about regulatory changes that enabled NGOs to transform to licensed financial institutions. And behind those changes policy champions – those who led with vision – emerged. The mindset of policy makers was firm in three areas. First, they came up with an answer to the question that still puzzles many – is microfinance charity or banking? Second, they debated government control of the interest rate. They analyzed the effects of an interest rate ceiling and determined to let market forces hold sway. They were often called on to defend this choice in national political circles. By opting for a truth in lending law instead of an interest rate ceiling, they provided the space for microfinance operations to continue and established a framework that honored MFI efficiency, transparency and competition. Third, the NBC was determined to present two clear options to microfinance providers – become professional or opt to focus on other development activities in Cambodia.

While initially the formal licensing requirements were seen as high hurdles by many NGOs, again, in hindsight, these policies created incentives for MFIs to strengthen their operations and become sustainable. Many are now sound enough to attract savings. Others are developing the systems that will ensure safety of customers' deposits – a new responsibility that weighs heavily on many MFIs. Over the next five years it is not unreasonable to expect an increase in financial intermediation, especially in the rural areas, due solely to the increased strength and outreach of licensed MFIs.

One of the key lessons from Cambodia is the importance of an open dialogue among MFIs, national policy makers and their international counterparts in allowing a free flow of ideas about how to proceed in uncharted territory. They explored many options, analyzing the feasibility of the proposals and their consequences. They compared and contrasted experiences from the region and from around the world. They called on technical advice from the Asian Development Bank, particularly in rural finance, the AFD, the ILO, the World Bank, and the IMF. They commissioned studies and sector reviews of rural areas and analyses of the small and microenterprises in Cambodia. They reviewed the potential of small and microenterprises to grow and contribute to the real sector, and how the growth of the financial sector would support that potential. Just as these studies were important for establishing the size and breadth of the lending market, so were the experiences of MFIs in establishing the level of risk found there.

It was not an easy process, but they owned it. The dialogue was often diverted by politics, advocacy of models favored by one donor or another, and above all the understandable wish for a government-owned rural development bank that would serve Cambodia's farmers. Yet these too were fair game for the dialogue. Policy makers saw the trends of the growing microfinance organizations; they were concerned about stifling the competition that was just beginning to emerge. The Asian Development Bank relied on their experience in the region and argued that a government-owned retail bank in Cambodia would be subjected to some of the same vulnerabilities that hastened the failure of state-owned banks in other countries. Cambodia could not afford that failure; nor could it afford the budget allocations that would be required to support such a bank to meet the estimated demand of USD 100-120 million for credit in the rural areas alone.

Dialogue between the ADB and the Ministry of Economy and Finance resulted in one of the first steps to build financial infrastructure in the country, a wholesale lender. That too was a risky choice. At the time there were no licensed MFIs that would be the clients of the RDB, and the list of NGOs that could qualify for a license was slow to develop. Delays in licensing, the developing capacity of NGOs to manage higher requirements and standards, as well as bureaucratic encumbrances and philosophical differences, further pushed the horizon into the future. But by 2004 many of the licensed MFIs had borrowed from the RDB to expand their rapidly growing portfolios. RDB became a source of capital where none other existed in the local market; and the track record of borrowing at commercial rates contributed to the transition of NGOs into commercial operations.

This first step to create a government-owned wholesale lender supported MFIs that were now in a position to grow. As experience is gained in the wholesale market, there is every reason to expect increasing private-sector competition within it, as international banks, socially responsible investment funds and private domestic banks have begun to lend to retail microfinance operations.

Today – Building an Inclusive Financial Sector

The subtle shift in terminology from donor-driven microcredit to market-driven microfinance is not a matter of semantics. It poses grand philosophical difficulties, and additional practical problems for each microcredit operation that grew up nurtured by the donor dollar. The most obvious one is a reluctance to let the donor go, and the donor's reluctance to depart. Today, in Cambodia's world of microfinance, despite significant advances of the leaders as commercial players in an evolving financial sector, three approaches co-exist.

The first approach is business as usual. Twenty-eight registered NGOs continue with the support of donors. Their operations are small and focus on specific target groups or geographical areas. Removing PRASAC from the mix, the average customer base of the registered NGOs is around 800 borrowers, with a borrower base ranging from 30 to 6,300.[170] As many as 60 unregistered NGOs are reportedly active in microfinance. Their performance is unknown.

The second approach is business as usual under the guise of a commercial legal status. The majority of MFIs in this category only recently transformed to licensed microfinance institutions from projects or project credit components. The previous donors continue as majority shareholders in some cases, grant-funding operating losses. Attempts to operate as commercial entities have been slow to materialize, although there are efforts to increase business-like operations, enhance management and improve transparency by publishing audited statements. It is too early to tell whether all of these operations will survive new commercial rigors, as they have yet to fully test the fundamental organizational and ownership transformations that the conveyance of the license would imply. Some are committed to staying in the market. They are well-managed operations and show robust performance. In others, donors have simply found convenient mechanisms to continue grant-funded operations while abiding by the law. Just as their donors traded names and have become shareholders, the projects have transformed into wholly owned subsidiaries. They will continue as long as their donor shareholders deem it appropriate. In the meantime, together they will provide loans to about 10% of the microcredit market.

The third approach is the commercial approach. These organizations strive to become lasting leaders in the market. They search for strategic shareholders that would bring new discipline and rigor to their operations. They borrow from foreign sources and domestically on commercial terms. Their governance and transparency are admirable. They seek to expand in the market, offering quality services to their customers. They have chosen to join the financial system, not to fulfill a legal requirement, but because their horizons are not limited by the past; they imagine the future.

Today, there is no recognized inter-bank lending market and levels of financial intermediation, particularly in the rural areas, are still limited. There is no credit bureau or deposit guarantee facility. Capital markets that support trade in securities, bond issues and mortgage markets, insurance, leasing and a pension system are elements of Cambodia's financial sector that await the attention of policy makers in the Financial Sector Blueprint for 2001-2010.[171] Attention will shift as

---

[170] The NBC issued a license to PRASAC in December, 2004 to operate as an MFI under the 2000 Prakas on Registration and Licensing of Microfinance Institutions. As of June 2004, PRASAC reported 53,253 active borrowers and a portfolio outstanding of USD 6.3 million. National Bank of Cambodia, Network Information, June 2004.

[171] See, Chun B, Zhang X, Sharma A (2001) Cambodia: financial sector blueprint for 2001-2010. ADB, Manila. The Blueprint was adopted by the Ministry of Economy and Finance and the National Bank of Cambodia in 2001. It outlines the progress to date and the future vision for Cambodia's financial sector development. The Blueprint was a product of a multi-stake holder dialogue and built on the long-term technical assistance relationship at the policy level between the Royal Government of Cambodia and the Asian Development Bank.

well to property law, protections for lenders, and an administrative and judicial system that guarantees fair treatment.

Building a sustainable and competitive banking system at the lower end of the market is a long-term proposition. Building an enabling environment that begins with macroeconomic policy and extends to the local courts and village councils will perhaps take longer. There are no quick-fix policies; and those that are implemented with the intent of bringing about quick change, are likely to backfire or have little lasting impact. A key lesson of the ACLEDA story is that "It really depends on the people to change, not just the technical aspects and the new ideas themselves."[172]

And Tomorrow

The challenge for microfinance in Cambodia, now that it has grasped both the benefits and costs of joining the formal financial system, is to sort out the kinds of efforts that are most likely to support Cambodia's evolving inclusive financial sector. The commercial microfinance institutions are often considered the most dynamic part of the financial system, as well as the most transparent. The course towards full integration into the financial system will eventually lead to further consolidation. New actors will appear, old players will disappear, and some will remain small and insignificant.

Microfinance in Cambodia grew as the financial system developed; the financial system is still developing. Cambodia is a small market, but a relatively dynamic one. Changes can be dramatic and difficult, and predictions are – well, predictions. One thing that is certain is the deliberate course charted for microfinance institutions propels them to become part of the financial system. In that sense, what is healthy for the financial system is healthy for microfinance and its customers. Often donors and their advocates emphasize the uniqueness of microfinance. In doing so, they force a separation between microfinance and the formal financial system, creating a "separate but equal" industry, seemingly ignoring a trend that is generally viewed as positive for customers and the financial system at large.

There is no longer a justification for grant-funding individual organizations, although many donors will resist this notion. Individual microfinance institutions are hard pressed to prove their clients would not be served by their competitors; nor are they the sole source of credit to their clients as formal options are increasingly available. Grant-funding of capacity building and organizational systems is a tougher call. Who can argue with the intent? The donor's dilemma is how to support commercial companies, owned by shareholders, without supporting unfair competition in a market where NGOs, commercial MFIs and

---

[172] Chhay Soeun, ACLEDA Bank Finance Department Manager. Author interview.

banks are all active players. Despite ideas about a large unsatisfied demand that national statistics would indicate, there are areas that are well served with credit from a variety of organizations, and those areas have become highly competitive. There are as well areas that are under-served and products on offer remain limited. Yet MFIs are expanding to serve those markets, and developing new products to reach them.

The domestic savings rate lags behind that of other Southeast-Asian countries, just as the availability of savings products lags behind the availability of credit. NGOs turned regulated financial institutions are rightfully cautious about deposit mobilization. Several have sought larger deposits as a first foray into a product offering that requires a reversal in the trust relationship between the customer and the institution. Saving is determined by the customer's confidence in the institution; lending is governed by the institution's confidence in the customer.

As ACLEDA's experience illustrates, it takes time to build that new relationship and the systems and competence to support it. Designing an attractive product line is the lesser task. Those institutions with compulsory savings products will experience the greatest challenge, as their tried and true credit products undergo significant change at the same time as organizational transformation, and financial intermediation demands more from them. Yet deposit mobilization too will come for organizations that have strong governance, solid financial performance, and the internal transparency and discipline to remedy their own constraints.

As donors look for new ways to support Cambodia's evolving financial system, perhaps they will take another look at supporting the "public good" found in the stability of the financial system itself. What is good for the financial system is good for microfinance and its customers. Support of microfinance will be effective when it is rooted in the health, transparency and stability of the financial sector and the market mechanisms that influence long-term growth.

Support for a legal system that promotes property rights and enforces them through the court system will be important for the continued evolution of Cambodia's financial sector, as will the range of financial infrastructure contemplated in the Financial Sector Blueprint. The key challenge will be how to support the growth of financial markets without undermining them.

There are nascent, but positive steps towards increasing transparency in the banking sector. Those efforts are led by the National Bank of Cambodia that is occasionally overwhelmed with the responsibility of supervising such a large and diverse group of commercial entities. Yet confidence in the banking sector is growing, and with it increasing vigilance is demanded. The evolving financial sector in Cambodia moved to become an inclusive financial sector. One that includes poor people as well as the average Cambodian, one that has begun to inspire their confidence and one that must continue to merit that confidence by creating lasting value.

The ACLEDA Legacy

At the most basic level, microfinance is about money. In its modern history microfinance has been about donor money, government money, private investors' money, and ultimately, the people's money. The debates about whether there is too much or too little of a particular kind of money continue. The uses and impact of money in microfinance attract scholars, researchers and experts from multiple disciplines. They disagree about the value of microfinance, and the purpose. But one thing is clear from Cambodia's experience. From a time "when there was no money" to today, at the core, microfinance, just like banking, is about people. It is about confidence, competence and commitment.

An organization's history creates its own possibilities for the future, its legacy lives on in the broader society. We hope for a legacy that creates lasting value and contributes both the tangible benefits sought by development assistance and the intangible benefits that reach beyond the value of a small loan. When a microfinance institution becomes just another part of the financial system, just another bank, the magic seems disappear. But that is the real illusion, because that is the true accomplishment.

The ACLEDA story is an extraordinary story. It is a story of sustainable microfinance in a post-conflict country. It is only one version of a story that is waiting to be told by many more microfinance organizations, regardless of where they work. The early ACLEDA staff grew up in a Cambodia closed to the rest of the world; half of them a diaspora scattered on foreign soil and each of them touched by a vicious regime intent on reaching Year Zero. They reinvented themselves in a world of reconstruction chaos when large donors competed to spend a largess of a western world that had too long ignored the small Southeast-Asian country. They worked at a time when Cambodia served up its own wild west, when deals were offered bluntly and refused at one's own peril. They saw offices burn to the ground, borrowers and staff swept off to jail, gun-toting troops of different factions rounding the bend in the road. They lost comrades along the way. They argued in boardrooms, and battled government inefficiencies, corruption, and a press that could be merciless or kind in the pursuit of the next feature story.

The ACLEDA story is the story of sustainable microfinance. ACLEDA's rise through the ranks of a project, NGO, MFI, specialized bank and commercial bank shows the maturation of microfinance itself. ACLEDA was relatively small and primitive in the 1993 world of microfinance, one that broke new ground each year with bond issues and listings on local stock exchanges. For most of the 1990s that world seemed far away and difficult to reach; it evolved with greater speed than they could muster. They saw their many transitions as climbing mountains; each time they reached the top, they found it better. They faced crisis after crisis in doing so, and each climb ended with a new resolve to survive, to protect, to grow, to build a financial institution that included people not unlike themselves. People who had tasted poverty, who were homeless more often than not, who remembered a past and determined never to go backward, no matter what.

ACLEDA, a small operation in a distant post-conflict country, was dwarfed by the performance of the Latin American powerhouses, and often rejected both abroad and within its own country as a small bank of insignificant consequence. If Cambodian officials criticized ACLEDA as "big talk about a small bank", their international colleagues regarded its experience as too slow to match the pace of the microfinance leaders who could be articulate, charismatic advocates for the microfinance movement. The slow pace of its human resource base was viewed with concern and alarm when systems couldn't produce information they knew was important to their growth. It would take some time and those who moved the field ahead were impatient. ACLEDA staff could not afford to ignore the reality of their own country or disregard their experience in favor of well-presented theory. But they did not reject the world around them or the thinking that crossed continental divides and vast oceans; they invited it. Each scrap of knowledge landed on minds eager to devour it. They confronted their own inadequacies and matched political will with the discipline to change. They became the true entrepreneurs in the burgeoning micro and small lending business in Cambodia; and they turned their small project into a full service bank of significance.

The challenges ACLEDA faced matched its lucky stars. Joachim Trede found "a diamond in a desert of stones". Femke Bos insists "these people of ACLEDA inspire me." The cautious optimism of Tal Nay Im propelled her vision for microfinance in Cambodia, and ACLEDA's role in the financial sector. Their technical advisors did not try to control; they tried to enable. Everyone who could put aside their own self-interests and instead see a Cambodia with a banking system that reached the people wanted to support them. Why, because they believed in the people of ACLEDA. At first they believed in their determination not to fail; later they believed in their drive to succeed. They were modestly building something in an uncertain environment; the truth be told, they didn't know whether it would work or not. They would try.

Critics wait for them to fall. They assert that one day they too will succumb to the corruption and greed that surrounds them. But maybe that is not the case. That chance is no longer linked to the development community, if it ever was. It is rooted in the corporate soul of ACLEDA Bank. In the beginning, it came from the closely held values of a small group of people and an airy concept about national ownership of the development process. They recruited others who shared their values and wanted to build. That ownership and those values are found in a new generation of ACLEDA bankers.

Microfinance has emerged from the romantic age where a small loan was thought to solve the problems of global poverty. Despite the admonition that "microfinance is not a panacea", passionate advocates did more to promote that thinking than to correct it. Donors and critics became disappointed that microfinance fell short of the great cure for poverty, a cure that was never promised by those who had a more realistic view of the complexities of poverty. Some donors may walk away disgruntled by a promise that remains unfulfilled. Most critics will never give up the good fight. But neither can ignore the millions of people below the poverty line – and those above it – who depend on banking services to survive. They too contribute to the development of their countries. It just takes a little longer than a three-year project life cycle to build a bank and a financial sector that admits poor and low-income people into the hallowed institutions generally reserved for the rich.

With the advancement of microfinance to the modern age a spurt of investment funds find their eagerness to place capital outwitted by the slow pace of microfinance institutions that reach the magical point of profitability. Too few organizations have arrived at a state where they merit such an investment. Yet the past conflicts of social purpose and profit seem to have given way to respectable alliances, where poor borrowers are treated as worthy players in the market, not as sheep that must be protected from it. New issues emerge in the field as globalization tempts philosophical debates on the ownership of capital, repatriation of profit to foreign sources, and the slow pace of creating domestic private investors who can uphold the bargain of social mission with profit motivation. No doubt these issues will play out in the future, based on the failures and success of this emerging phenomenon of banking for the people.

In the meantime, a new generation of Cambodians – customers and staff alike – joins ACLEDA Bank, a bank that does not discriminate between the poor and the rich, a bank that aspires to serve the people of Cambodia. The people come to ACLEDA Bank because of its reputation for transparency, the 'no tolerance for corruption' policies and practices, and the opportunity to build what is important to them. The new generation is too young to remember the struggles of the past. They want to be part of a better future and they will work hard for a chance to get it.

Bibliography

Cambodia: History, Politics and Economic Development

ADB (1998) Asian Development Outlook, 1999. Manila: ADB.

ADB (2000) Cambodia Country Economic Review. Manila: ADB.

ADB (2003) Cambodia: Country Strategy and Program Update 2004-2006. Manila: ADB.

ADB (2004) Annual Report. Manila: ADB.

ADB (2005) Asian Development Outlook 2005. Manila: ADB.

ADB (2005) Cambodia Country Strategy and Program 2005-2009. Manila: ADB.

Barnes S, Retiere A (2001) Peace Building from the Ground Up: A Case Study of UNDP's CARERE Programme in Cambodia 1991-2000. Phnom Penh: UNDP.

Brown F, Timberman D (eds) (1998) Cambodia and the International Community: The Quest for Peace, Development and Democracy. New York: Asia Society.

Center for Social Development (1998) National Survey on Public Attitudes Towards Corruption. Phnom Penh: Center for Social Development.

Chan S, Kato T, Long VP, So S, Tia S, Hang CN, Kao KH, Chea V (1999) Impact of the Asian Financial Crisis on the SEATEs: The Cambodian Perspective. Working Paper No. 12. Phnom Penh: CRDI.

Chandler D (2000) A History of Cambodia, 3d edn. Boulder: Westview Press.

Chim C, Srun P, So S, McAndrew J, Nguon S, Pon D, Biddulph R (1998) Learning from Rural Development Programmes in Cambodia. Working Paper No. 4. Phnom Penh: CDRI.

Council for Social Development, Kingdom of Cambodia (2002). National Poverty

Reduction Strategy (NPRS) 2003-2005. Phnom Penh: Council for Social Development, Royal Government of Cambodia.

Curtis G (1998) Cambodia Reborn? The Transition to Democracy and Development. Washington DC: Brookings Institution Press.

Dalpino C (2002) From Paris to Bonn: Lessons for Afghanistan from the Cambodian Transition. Working Paper No. 14. Washington DC: The Brookings Institution.

de Zamaroczy M, Sa S (2002) Macroeconomic Adjustment in a Highly Dollarized Economy: The Case of Cambodia. WP/02/92. Washington DC: IMF.

Ear S (1997) Cambodia: Negotiating the Peace Accords. Lausanne: Center for Asian Interdisciplinary Studies and Research.

Economics Institute of Cambodia (2004) Cambodia Economic Watch. Phnom Penh: Economics Institute of Cambodia.

Fujji T (2003) Commune-level Estimation of Poverty Measures and Its Application in Cambodia. Paper prepared for the World Food Programme. Berkley: University of California.

Godfrey M, Chan S, Kato T, Long VP, Pon D, Tep S, Tia S, So S (2000) Technical Assistance and Capacity Development in an Aid-dependent Economy: The Experience of Cambodia. Working Paper No. 15. Phnom Penh: CDRI.

Gottesman E (2003) Cambodia: After the Khmer Rouge Inside the Politics of Nation Building. New Haven and London: Yale University Press.

Heenan P Lamontagne M (eds) (2001) Southeast Asian Handbook. London: Fitzroy Dearborn Publishers.

Heininger J (1994) Peacekeeping in Transition: the United Nations in Cambodia. New York: The Twentieth Century Fund Press.

IMF (2003) Cambodia: Selected Issues and Statistical Appendix. IMF Country Report 03/59. Washington DC: IMF.

IMF (2004) Cambodia Poverty Reduction Strategy Paper Progress Report. IMF Country Report No. 04/333. Washington DC: IMF.

Kang C, Chan S. (2003) Cambodia's Annual Economic Review – 2003. Issue 3. Phnom Penh: CDRI.

Kiernan B (1996) The Pol Pot Regime: Race, Power and Genocide Under the Khmer Rouge. New Haven: Yale University Press.

Kim, S Chan S, Sarthi A. (2002) Land, Rural Livelihoods and Food Security in Cambodia. Working Paper No. 24. Phnom Penh: CDRI.

Knowles, J (1997) A Poverty Profile of Cambodia -1997. Phnom Penh: Ministry of Planning.

Ledgerwood J (1998) Rural Development in Cambodia: The View from the Village. In: Brown F, Timberman D (eds) Cambodia and the International Community: The Quest for Peace, Development and Democracy. New York: Asia Society.

Ministry of Economy and Finance (2001) Prakas No 493 PRK, on Number, Name and Boundaries of the Communes and Sangkats of the Kingdom of Cambodia, 30 April 2001. Phnom Penh: Ministry of Economy and Finance.

Ministry of Planning and the National Institute of Statistics (1999) Cambodia Socio-economic Survey: A Poverty Profile of Cambodia. Phnom Penh: National Institute of Statistics and Ministry of Planning.

Nelson KE (1996) They Killed all the Lawyers: Rebuilding the Judicial System in Cambodia. Occasional Paper No. 13. Vancouver: Centre for Asia-Pacific Initiatives.

Peou S, Samnang H, Sisowath C, Bophany U, Kum K, Sovirak S. (2004) International Assistance for Institution Building in Post-conflict Cambodia. Working Paper 26. The Hague: Clingendael.

Prescott N, Pradhan M (1997) A Poverty Profile of Cambodia. World Bank Discussion Paper No. 373. Washington DC: World Bank.

Ross RR (ed) (1987) Cambodia: A Country Study. Washington DC: Federal Research Division, Library of Congress.

Shawcross W (1979) Sideshow: Kissinger, Nixon and the Destruction of Cambodia. New York: Simon and Schuster.

Shawcross W (1984) The Quality of Mercy – Cambodia, Holocaust and Modern Conscience. New York: Simon and Schuster.

Sok H, Sarthi A (2002) Cambodia's Annual Economic Review – 2002. Issue 2. Phnom Penh: CDRI.

United Nations (1996) Cambodia – United Nations Transitional Authority in Cambodia. New York: United Nations.

UNDP (2003) Human Development Report 2003. UNDP: New York.

UNDP (2004) Cambodia: Transition Experience. Paper presented at International Policy Conference on Transition Economies, Hanoi.

Van Acker F (1999) Hitting a Stone with an Egg?: Cambodia's Rural Economy and Land Tenure in Transition. Discussion Paper No. 23. Antwerp: Centre for ASEAN Studies.

World Bank (1995) Cambodia Rehabilitation Program: Implementation and Outlook. Report No. 13965-KH. Washington DC: World Bank.

World Bank (1994) "Kingdom of Cambodia: Technical Assistance Project, Technical Annex", Report no. T-6424-KH. Washington DC: World Bank.

World Bank (1996) Cambodia from Recovery to Sustained Development. Report No. 15593-KH. Washington DC: World Bank.

World Bank (1999) Cambodia Poverty Assessment. Report No. 19858-KH. Washington DC: World Bank.

World Bank (2003) Cambodia: Enhancing Service Delivery through Improved Resource Allocation and Institutional Reform: Integrated Fiduciary Assessment and Pubic Expenditure Review. Report No. 25611-KH. Washington DC: World Bank.

World Bank (2004) Cambodia: Seizing the Global Opportunity: Investment Climate Assessment and Reform Strategy for Cambodia. Washington DC: World Bank.

World Bank, International Finance Corporation, Mekong Project Development Facility and Public-Private Infrastructure Advisory Facility (2004) Towards a Private Sector Development Strategy for Cambodia: Investment Climate Assessment: A World Bank Group Consultation Summary in 2004.

Yale University. Yale University Cambodian Genocide Program, a project of the Genocide Studies Program at the Yale Center for International and Area Studies. Available: www.yale.edu.cgp.

Finance and Microfinance

ADB (2004) Country Economic Review – Indonesia. Manila: ADB.

Binns DM, Gilbert RJ (2004) The Role of Employee Stock Ownership Plans in the Restructuring and Privatization of State-owned Financial Institutions. Paper presented to a World Bank conference on the role of state-owned financial institutions: policy and practice. Washington DC: World Bank.

Bornstein D (1997) The Price of a Dream: The Story of the Grameen Bank. Chicago: University of Chicago Press.

Brinsden J (2005) Creating a Virtuous Triangle: Government, Development Agencies and the Private Sector in Microfinance. Microfinance Matters. Issue 10. New York: UNCDF.

Campion A, White V (1999) Institutional Metamorphosis: Transformation of Microfinance NGOs into Regulated Financial Institutions. Occasional Paper No. 4. Washington DC: Microfinance Network.

Campion A, White V (2001) NGO Transformation. Bethesda: Development Alternatives, Inc.

Campion A, Dunn E, Arbuckle G. (2002) Creating a Microfinance Bank in Peru: Accion Communitaria del Perú's Transformation to Mibanco. In: Drake D, Rhyne E (eds) The Commercialization of Microfinance: Balancing Business and Development. Bloomfield: Kumarian Press.

Charitonenko S, Campion A, Fernando N (2004) Commercialization of Microfinance: Perspectives from South and Southeast Asia. Manila: ADB.

Christen RP, Rosenberg R (2000) The Rush to Regulate: Legal Frameworks for Microfinance. Occasional Paper No. 4. Washington DC: CGAP.

Christen RP, Lyman T, Rosenberg R (2003) Microfinance Consensus Guidelines: Guiding Principles on Regulation and Supervision of Microfinance. Washington DC: CGAP/World Bank.

Churchill C (1997) Managing Growth: The Organizational Architecture of Microfinance Institutions. Bethesda, MD: Development Alternatives Inc.

Clark H (2004) Commercial Microfinance: The Right Choice for Everyone? ADB Newsletter vol 5 no 3. Manila: ADB.

Fernando N (2003) Mibanco Peru: Profitable Microfinance Outreach, With Lessons for Asia. Manila: ADB.

Fernando N (2004) Micro Success Story?: Transformation of Nongovernmental Organizations into Regulated Financial Institutions. Manila: ADB.

Frankiewicz C (2001) Building Institutional Capacity: The Story of Prodem, 1987-2000. Toronto: Calmeadow.

Gibbons D, Meehan J (2000) The Microcredit Summit's Challenges: Working Towards Institutional Financial Self-Sufficiency While Maintaining a Commitment to Serving the Poorest Families. Washington DC: Microcredit Summit Secretariat.

Glosser A (1994) The Creation of BancoSol in Bolivia. In: Otero M, Rhyne E (eds) (1994) The New World of Microenterprise Finance: Building Healthy Financial Institutions for the Poor. West Hartford: Kumarian Press.

Gonzalez-Vega, C (2002) Deepening Rural Financial Markets: Macroeconomic, Policy and political dimensions. Paper presented at Paving the Way Forward for Rural Finance: An International Conference on Best Practices.

Helms B, Reille X (2004) Interest Rate Ceilings and Microfinance: The Story So Far. Occasional Paper No 9. Washington DC: CGAP.

IFC (2004) Banking for the Poor. Washington DC: IFC.

Jansson T (2003) Financing Microfinance: Exploring the Funding Side of Microfinance Institutions. Sustainable Development Department Technical Papers Series MSM-118. Washington DC: Inter-American Development Bank.

Jones PA (2002) Modernising Credit Unions: The Guatemala Credit Union Strengthening Project, 1987-1994. Manchester: Association of British Credit Unions.

Kaddaras J, Rhyne E (2004) Characteristics of Equity Investments in Microfinance: A Study of the Council of Microfinance Equity Funds. Washington DC: Accion International.

McGuire PB, Conroy JD (1998) Effects on Microfinance of the 1997-1998 Asian Financial Crisis. Brisbane: The Foundation for Development Cooperation.

McGuire PB, Conroy JD, Thapa GB (1998) Getting the Framework Right: Policy and Regulation for Microfinance in Asia. Brisbane: Foundation for Development Cooperation.

M-CRIL (2004) The M-CRIL Microfinance Review 2003. Gurgaon: Micro-Credit Ratings International Ltd.

Otero M, Rhyne E (eds) (1994) The New World of Microenterprise Finance: Building Healthy Financial Institutions for the Poor. West Hartford: Kumarian Press.

Otero M, Chu M (2002) Governance and Ownership of Microfinance Institutions. In: Drake D, Rhyne E (eds) The Commercialization of Microfinance: Balancing Business and Development. Bloomfield: Kumarian Press.

Rhyne E (2001) Mainstreaming Microfinance: How Lending to the Poor Began, Grew and Came of Age in Bolivia (Bloomfield: Kumarian Press.

Richardson DC (2000) Model Credit Unions into the Twenty First Century. In: Westley GD, Branch B (eds) Safe Money: Building Effective Credit Unions in Latin America. Washington DC: Johns Hopkins University Press.

Robinson M (2001) The Microfinance Revolution: Sustainable Finance for the Poor (Washington DC: World Bank.

Rock R (1996) Regulation and Supervision of Microfinance Institutions: Stabilizing a New Financial Market. CGAP Focus Note 4. Washington DC: CGAP.

Rosengard JK, Rai AS, Dondo A, Oketch HO (2000) Microfinance Development in Kenya: K-Rep's Transition From NGO to Diversified Holding Company and Commercial Bank, HIID Discussion Paper No. 762. Cambridge MA: Harvard Institute for International Development. Harvard University.

Rutherford S (2000) The Poor and Their Money. New Delhi: Oxford University Press.

Schreiner M, Yaron J (1999) The Subsidy Dependence Index and Recent Attempts to Adjust It. St. Louis: Microfinance Risk Management.

Steege J (1998) The Rise and Fall of Corposol: Lessons Learned from the Challenges of Managing Growth. Bethesda, Md.: Development Alternatives Inc.

Valenzuela L (2002) Getting the Recipe Right. In: Drake D, Rhyne E (eds) The Commercialization of Microfinance: Balancing Business and Development. Bloomfield: Kumarian Press.

von Pischke JD (1991) Finance at the Frontier: Debt Capacity and the Role of Credit in the Private Economy. Washington DC: World Bank.

von Stauffenberg D (2001) How Microfinance Evolves: What Bolivia Can Teach Us. Microenterprise Development Review, vol 4 no 1. Washington DC: Inter-American Development Bank.

White V, Campion A (2002) Transformation: Journey from NGO to Regulated MFI. In: Drake D, Rhyne E (eds) The Commercialization of Microfinance: Balancing Business and Development. Bloomfield: Kumarian Press.

Women's World Banking (1995) The Missing Links: Financial Systems that Work for the Majority. New York: Women's World Banking.

Finance and Microfinance in Cambodia*

ACLEDA. Annual Reports 2001-2004. Phnom Penh: ACLEDA.

ACLEDA. Audited Financial Statements 1993-2004. Phnom Penh: ACLEDA.

ADB (2000) Report'and Recommendation of the President to the Board of Directors on a Proposed Loan to the Kingdom of Cambodia for the Rural Credit and Savings Project. Manila: ADB.

Ballard B (2004) Short-term Trend or Long-term Shift?: Institutional Credit in Rural Cambodia. Cambodia Development Review, vol 8 issue 4. Phnom Penh: CDRI.

Bousso P, Daubert P, Gauthier N, Parent M, Zieglé C (1997) The Micro-economic Impact of Rural Credit in Cambodia. Paris: GRET.

Cambodian Committee for Rural Development, Technical Unit (1996) Policy of the Royal Government in the Field of Rural Credit in the Kingdom of Cambodia. Phnom Penh: CDRI. Photocopy.

Cambodian Committee for Rural Development (1995)Proposal on Policy for Rural Credit Development in the Kingdom of Cambodia. Results of the Seminar on Rural Credit 05-07 June, 1995. Phnom Penh: CCRD. Photocopy.

Chea C, Keat C (2000) Statement of Hon. Chea Chanto and Hon Keat Chhon, IMF Board of Governors, 2000 Annual Meeting, Prague, Czech Republic, September.

Chun BJ, Zhang X, Sharma A (2001) Cambodia: Financial Sector Blueprint for 2001-2010. Phnom Penh: Royal Government of Cambodia and ADB.

Clark, H (2004) Capacity Leads, Capital Follows: Donors and Investors Match Instruments to ACLEDA's State of Development. CGAP Case Study in Donor Good Practices, No. 14. Washington DC: CGAP.

Conroy J D (2003) The Challenges of Microfinancing in Southeast Asia. In: Freeman N (ed) Financing Southeast Asia's Economic Development. Singapore: Institute of Southeast Asian Studies.

Dammers C, Firebrace J, Gibbs S, Keo K, Ly S, Men S (1996) Differing Approaches to Development Assistance in Cambodia: NGOs and the European Commission. Phnom Penh: NGO Forum on Cambodia.

Flaming M, Duflos E, Latortue A, Nayar N, Roth J (2005) Country level effectiveness and accountability review: Cambodia. Washington DC: CGAP/The World Bank.

Fukui R, Llanto G (2003) Rural Finance and Micro-Finance Development in Transition Countries in South-East and East Asia. Paper prepared for the International Workshop on Rural Finance and Credit Infrastructure in China, Organization for Cooperation and Development, Paris, October13-14.

Hakemulder R (1997) Promoting Local Economic Development in a War-Affected Country: The ILO Experience in Cambodia. Geneva: International Labor Organization.

Harner S (2003) Financing SMEs in Cambodia: Why do Banks Find it so Difficult? MPDF Private Sector Discussions, Paper Number 14. Hanoi: MPDF.

Harpe S, Calvin B (1998) ACLEDA, Cambodia: Past Performance, Projected Performance and Readiness to Transform into a Regulated Financial Institution. Toronto: Calmeadow.

Horus Bank and Finance (1998) Report on Institutionalization of Microfinancing Institutions in Cambodia: General Conclusions. Phnom Penh.

ILO (1994) Small Enterprise and Informal Sector Promotion Report. Geneva: ILO.

ILO (2000) Report on Micro and Small Enterprise Development for Poverty Alleviation in Cambodia. Bangkok: ILO.

IMF (1998) Cambodia: Recent Economic Developments. Staff Country Report No. 98/54. Washington DC: IMF.

IMF (2000) Staff Country Report 00/127. Washington DC: IMF.

IMF (2000) Cambodia: 2000 Article IV Consultation and First Review under the Poverty Reduction and Growth Facility – Staff Report. Washington DC: IMF.

IMF (2003) Cambodia: Selected Issues and Statistical Appendix. IMF Country Report no 03/59 Washington DC: IMF.

IMF (2004) Cambodia: Statistical Appendix. IMF Country Report No. 04/330. Washington DC: IMF.

IMF (2004) Cambodia: Selected Issues October 2004 IMF Country Report No. 04/331. Washington DC: IMF.

In C (2002) From NGO/Project to Microfinance Institution. The Experience of ACLEDA Bank. Paper presented as part of the FAO-APRACA Regional Workshop From NGO/Project to MFI, Bangkok, Thailand, February 20-22, 2002.

In C (2003) Rural Financial Institutions: Start-Ups The Case Study of ACLEDA Bank. Paper presented at Paving the Way Forward for Rural Finance, An International Conference on Best Practices, Washington, D.C. June 2-4.

In C (2004) Speech on the Occasion of the Grand Opening and Licensing of ACLEDA Bank Plc. on March 1, 2004.

Kang C (2002) The Development of Microfinance in Cambodia. Cambodia Development Review. July-September Phnom Penh: CDRI.

Keat C (2001) Speech of Hon. Keat Chhon, Governor, at the 34th Annual Meeting of the Board of Governors of the Asian Development Bank. May 9.

Kooi P (2001) "Raising Capital through Equity Investments in MFIs: Lessons from ACLEDA, Cambodia". Paper presented at the UNCDF/SUM and UNDP Africa Global Meeting on Young and Promising Microfinance Institutions, May 30 to June 1, 2001, New York.

Lucock D (1997) Project Evaluation Study of Alleviation of Poverty through ACLEDA's Financial Services. Phnom Penh: UNDP.

National Bank of Cambodia (1999) The Law on Banking and Financial Institutions. Phnom Penh: National Bank of Cambodia.

National Bank of Cambodia (2002) Rural Credit in Cambodia. Phnom Penh: NBC.

Okonjo-Iweala N, Kwakwa V, Beckwith A, Ahmed Z (1999) "Impact of Asia's Financial Crisis on Cambodia and the Lao PDR". Finance & Development. Washington DC: World Bank.

Postlewaite S (2001) Banking on Poor Borrowers. Businessweek 2001/01.

Prins H (1996) Rural Credit Review: Cambodia. Manila: Asian Development Bank.

Prins H (1997) ACLEDA: Transformation Study. Phnom Penh.

Royal Government of Cambodia (1997) Prakas No. B 8-97-129 PK, dated November 25.

Royal Government of Cambodia (1998) Sub-Degree No. 01 A.N.K dated January 21.

Royal Government of Cambodia (2000) Prakas No. B 7-00-06 dated 11 January. On the Licensing of Micro-Finance Institutions.

Royal Government of Cambodia (2001) Hun Sen Samdech, Prime Minister, Closing Address to the Forum for Dissemination of the Governance Action Plan and the Public Administration Reform. Cambodia New Vision, Issue 47, December 2001. Phnom Penh: CNV.

Royal Government of Cambodia (2002) Prakas No. 7.02-49 dated 25 February. On Registration and Licensing of Microfinance Institutions.

Son KT (2002) The Effects of Trade Liberalisation on Rural Financial Institutions. Paper presented in APRACA, Bangkok, Thailand, May 20-24.

Torres, O (2004) Rural Finance and the Microfinance Sector in Cambodia. Paper prepared for the Rural Sector Strategy Note of the World Bank. Washington DC: World Bank.

Unteroberdoerster O (2004) Banking Reform in the Lower Mekong Countries. IMF Policy Discussion Paper 04/5. Washington DC: World Bank.

Webster L, Tucker W (1996) ACLEDA: An Appraisal for CGAP. Washington, D.C.: The World Bank, Private Sector Department.

Organizational Change and Development

Collins J (2001) Good to Great: Why Some Companies Make the Leap…and Others Don't. New York: HarperCollins.

Collins J, Porras JI (2002) Built to Last: Successful Habits of Visionary Companies. New York: HarperCollins.

Drucker, PF (1964) Managing for Results. New York: Harper & Row.

Myers R (2003) Chairman + CEO: Two jobs, two people. Corporate Board Member, March/April.

Prahalad CK (2004) The Fortune at the Bottom of the Pyramid: Eradicating Poverty Through Profits. Upper Saddle River: Wharton School Publishing.

Technical Note

Unless otherwise indicated in the text or accompanying table note, the ratios and formulae used to compute them follow the definitions below. General guidance on definitions and terms is found in the Microfinance Consensus Guidelines: Definitions of Selected Financial Terms, Ratios, and Adjustments for Microfinance. 3rd ed. (Washington, D.C.: CGAP/The World Bank Group, September 2003). The document can be downloaded from the websites of CGAP and the SEEP Network: CGAP www.cgap.org or SEEP www.seepnetwork.org. Adjustments follow methods used by the Microbanking Bulletin, expect where noted below. Guidance on adjustments can be found at www.mixmarket.org.

Common Ratios, Terms and Methods of Calculation Used in this Book

Adjusted Return on Average Assets (AROA). The calculation of the AROA uses the adjusted net operating profit after taxes in the numerator and the average assets for the period in the denominator. Income from grants is excluded from the calculation of operating profit. Adjusted expenses included in the adjusted net operating profit are the following: adjusted expense for the effects of inflation on equity; adjusted expenses for the subsidized cost of capital; adjusted expenses for other subsidies, such as in kind donations, and costs borne by others.

Adjusted Return on Average Equity (AROE). The calculation of the AROE uses the net operating profit after taxes in the numerator and the average equity for the period in the denominator. The adjusted return on average equity does not include subordinated debt as equity. Income from grants is excluded from the calculation of operating profit. Adjusted expenses include the same as those listed above in AROAA.

Adjustment for Inflation. The inflation adjustment uses the following method: net fixed assets are subtracted from equity and the result is multiplied by the inflation rate for the period. This amount is treated as an adjusted expense for the calculation of adjusted return on equity, adjusted return on assets and financial self-sufficiency ratios. Net fixed assets are revalued using the same inflation rate for the period. This amount is treated as an income adjustment for the relevant period. Inflation data are obtained taken from line 64x of the International Financial Statistics, International Monetary Fund, various years. During the years 1993-1994, the IMF line 64x does not report inflation rates for Cambodia. Inflation data for these years are obtained from World Bank, Cambodia: From Recovery to Sustained Development (Washington, D.C.: World Bank, 1996), 7. For 2004, the inflation rate is taken for the National Institute of Statistics website that monitors the Consumer Price Index on a monthly basis. The figure used is one that measures the increase in inflation by November 2004 over the prior 12-month period.

Adjustment for subsidized cost of capital. The subsidy adjustment for the cost of capital for the years (1995-2003) is calculated using International Monetary Fund, *International Financial Statistics,* line 60L, deposit rate. All funding liabilities (expect for contingent liabilities which are treated as donated equity subject to the inflation adjustment) are multiplied by the amount in IMF, line 60L as the relevant shadow price for the period. The amount is treated as an adjusted expense and figures in the calculation of Adjusted Return on Average Assets, the Adjusted Return on Average Equity, and the percentage of Financial Self-Sufficiency for the period. Prior to 1995, no deposit rate is listed for Cambodia on line 60L. The adjustment for subsidized loans during this early period is priced at the inflation rate. Subsidized loans during this period figure as a miniscule amount on the balance sheet.

Adjustment for technical assistance subsidy. No attempt is made to include the costs of technical assistance in the subsidy adjustment during 1993-1999. The main reason is the practical one of finding the accurate amounts in the financial reports of many different organizations from over ten years ago. In addition, from 1993 to the present ACLEDA did not rely on international technical managers to manage the operation. Technical advisors played an advisory role. The costs of technical assistance are not included in the subsidy adjustment from 2000 onwards. The amounts paid for technical assistance are included as part of the normal expenses of the ACLEDA Bank in its audited income statements, and no adjustment is required.

Averaging. The method used is the simple year-end balance method of averaging. Averages for the year are calculated by adding the amount at the beginning of the year and the amount at the end of year, then dividing the total by two.

Debt/Equity Ratio. In this document the debt/equity ratio is used to view leverage of commercial funds. The numerator includes deposits mobilized from the public, commercial borrowings and subordinate debt that carries commercial terms of interest. The denominator includes equity, such as shares, retained earnings, and any grant funding in the operation at the time.

Donated equity. Accumulated donations as shown through progressive balance sheets from audited financial statements. The accumulated donated equity includes all donations, regardless of their use. During the initial period, contingent liabilities figured on the balance sheet. These amounts are treated as donated equity, since they were subsequently donated to ACLEDA as originally intended.

Financial Self-Sufficiency (FSS). The ratio used throughout this document is adjusted operating revenue / (financial expense plus loan loss provision expense plus operating expense plus expense adjustments for inflation and subsidies).

Operating expense ratio. There are two operating expense ratios that are relevant during the time period of the ACLEDA Story. The first period (1993-2000) when ACLEDA managed a credit operation, and the later period (2000-2004) when it operates as a bank that offered a range of products, including credit. In the earlier stage the operating expense ratio used is one that includes administrative and personnel expenses in the numerator, and the average gross loan portfolio in the denominator. As a commercial bank this ratio becomes less meaningful. The operating expense ratio used from 2000 on includes all administrative and personnel expenses in the numerator and average total assets in the denominator. For the sake of consistency, and viewing meaningful change over time, the ratio using average total assets in the denominator is used when viewing the entire 12-year history.

Operational Self-Sufficiency (OSS). The ratio used throughout this document, unless otherwise stated in a note is operating revenue / (Financial expense plus loan loss provision expense plus operating expense).

Portfolio at risk (PAR). Portfolio at risk is the value of all loans outstanding that have one or more installments of principal past due. The numerator includes the entire unpaid principal balance, including both past-due and future installments. It does not include accrued interest. The denominator includes the total amount of the gross portfolio as of the same date.

PAR > 30 days is the value of all loans outstanding that have one or more installments of principal past due more than 30 days. The formula used is the same as the above.

Portfolio Yield. Interest, fees and penalties earned on the portfolio for the period, divided by the average portfolio for the period.

Return on Assets (ROA). The calculation of return on assets uses the net operating profit after taxes in the numerator and the average assets for the period in the denominator. Income from grants is excluded from the calculation of operating profit.

Return on Equity (ROE). The calculation of the return on equity uses the net operating profit after taxes in the numerator and the average equity for the period in the denominator. Income from grants is excluded from the calculation of operating profit. Subordinate debt is not included in the calculation of average equity.

Staff attrition rates. Staff attrition rates are calculated by determining the average number of staff during the year using a simple averaging method of the number of staff at the beginning of the year plus the number of staff at the end of the year divided by two. Attrition rates are calculated by using the number of staff who left during the year and dividing by the average number of staff during the year using the method described above.

Subsidy Dependence Index (SDI). The SDI measures the amount of subsidy in an operation. Negative amounts indicate the operation is profitable. Positive numbers indicate that the operation would need to adjust its interest rate on lending upwards to cover the subsidy. The SDI fluctuates with the profitability of the institution and is a strong tool for measuring the subsidy in financial institutions whose main source of income is from lending. It does not consider price adjustments or increasing volume of off-balance sheet income streams (for example, transfers, payroll services) except as these income streams figure in net profit. The method of calculation follows guidance in Mark Schreiner and Jacob Yaron, The Subsidy Dependence Index and Recent Attempts to Adjust It (St Louis, Mo.: Microfinance Risk Management, February 1999), 37-41. The opportunity cost on the use of public funds is priced at 10%, about 1.5-5 percentages points higher than the deposit rate and the cost of commercial borrowing from the market during 2001-2003. As such it is a conservative rendering of the SDI. For the period (1998-2003) the SDI for ACLEDA is calculated in the following table.

	1998	1999	2000	2001	2002	2003 ·
SDI	0.063	-0.027	-0.101	-0.009	0.082	-0.074

Write-off Rate. The numerator includes the amount of all loans that have been written off during the period. The denominator is the amount of the average portfolio for the period, using the simple annual averaging method. The write-off rate does not include the amount of previously written off amounts that were collected during the period.

Write-off Recovery Rate for the Year. The denominator includes the amount of principal that was written off during the year. The numerator includes the amount of previously written off principal that was collected during the year. A rate over 100% indicates that previous years' bad debt is recovered during the year with a write-off recovery rate above 100%.

Index

KfW Bankengruppe. Brands for the Future

KfW Bankengruppe (KfW banking group) gives impetus to economic, political and social development worldwide. As bankers we strive to work efficiently every day. As promoters we stand for the meaning and sustainability of our actions. The proceeds from our work flow back into our promotional activities and help to secure our promotional potential in the long term. As a creative bank we not only encourage innovations, but we ourselves also develop new financing instruments for our customers and partners. Our competence and experience are combined into five strong brand names.

KfW Förderbank (KfW promotional bank): It is the right address for all measures in the product areas construction, infrastructure, education, social services and the environment. Through low-interest loans we help many citizens realize their dream of owning their own home, just as we promote interest in environmentally friendly modernization measures. As KfW Förderbank we also provide support to companies investing in environmental and climate protection, municipal infrastructure measures as well as training and advanced training.

KfW Mittelstandsbank (KfW SME bank): The name tells all. Here we have combined all of our promotional activities for business founders and small and medium-sized enterprises. These include, on the one hand, classic long-term loans and, on the other, innovative programmes aiming to strengthen the companies' equity base. Both are offered to our customers through their regular bank. Target-oriented advice is naturally also part of our business.

KfW IPEX-Bank: Our export and project finance has become the KfW IPEX Bank, which does business under the umbrella of KfW Bankengruppe. It is customer-oriented and competitive, operating at standard market conditions. For companies with international operations it is a reliable partner for the long term who can offer them customized financing. The financing solutions that the KfW IPEX Bank offers to its customers include structured finance, project finance, corporate loans and traditional export finance. The success of KfW IPEX Bank is due above all to many years of experience all over the world in the most important markets and industry sectors.

KfW Entwicklungsbank (KfW development bank): On behalf of the German Federal Government it finances investments and advisory services in developing countries. It typically works together with governmental institutions in the corresponding countries. Its aim is to build up and expand a social and economic infrastructure and to create efficient financial institutions while protecting resources and ensuring a healthy environment.

DEG: As a partner of the private sector DEG supports companies wanting to invest in developing and reforming countries. It provides financing for profitable, environmentally friendly and developmentally effective projects in all economic sectors. In this way it sets the foundation for sustainable economic growth – and better quality of life for the people in these countries.

KfW Bankengruppe has also become a strategic partner of the economy and politics. As an advisor to the Federal Republic we offer our expertise in the privatization of federally owned companies. On behalf of the government we also handle business for the Federal Agency for Special Tasks associated with Unification (Bundesanstalt für vereinigungsbedingte Sonderaufgaben, BvS) and the Compensatory Fund of Securities Trading Companies (Entschädigungseinrichtung der Wertpapierhandelsunternehmen).